RICHARD HOLMES is one of Britain's most successful historians and television presenters. He has written and presented five BBC television series, including *Battlefields* (2001) and *The Western Front* (1999). His many other books include *Firing Line* and the best-selling *Redcoat*. He is also general editor of the definitive *Oxford Companion to Military History*. He has taught military history for many years, and is now Professor of Military and Security Studies at Cranfield University and the Royal Military College of Science.

WELLINGTON

THE IRON DUKE

RICHARD HOLMES

HarperCollins*Publishers*

HarperCollins*Publishers*
77–85 Fulham Palace Road,
Hammersmith, London w6 8jb

www.**fire**and**water**.com

This paperback edition 2003
5 7 9 8 6

First published in Great Britain by
HarperCollins*Publishers* 2003

ISBN 0 00 713750 8

Maps by John Gilkes

Set in PostScript Linotype Minion
with Modern display by
Rowland Phototypesetting Ltd,
Bury St Edmunds, Suffolk

Printed and bound in Great Britain by
Clays Ltd, St Ives plc

CONTENTS

LIST OF ILLUSTRATIONS

Tipoo Soldier Loading his Rocket, 18th century drawing by Robert Home. Courtesy of the V&A Picture Library, London.

The Battle of Assaye, 23rd September 1803, coloured aquatint by J.C. Stadler after W. Heath, 1815. Courtesy of the National Army Museum, London.

The Battle of Salamanca, coloured aquatint by G. Lewis and J.A. Atkinson, 1813. Courtesy of the National Army Museum, London.

Study for a Portrait of the Duke of Wellington by Francisco de Goya, 1812. Courtesy of The Trustees of The British Museum.

The Capture of Madrid, 12th August 1812: Wellington Receiving the Keys of the City, coloured aquatint by T. Fielding after R. Weston, 1819. Courtesy of the National Army Museum, London.

Arthur Wellesley, 1st Duke of Wellington, oil on canvas by Sir Thomas Lawrence, 1824. Courtesy of the Governors of Wellington College.

The Battle of Waterloo, oil on canvas by Sir William Allen, 1843. Courtesy of Apsley House, The Wellington Museum, London/ V&A Picture Library.

The Duke of Wellington at Waterloo, oil on canvas by Robert Hillingford. Courtesy of a Private Collection/ Bridgeman Art Library.

Defence of the Chateau of Hougoumont by the flank company, Coldstream Guards, Waterloo, 1815, watercolour by Denis Dighton. Courtesy of the National Army Museum, London.

The Battle of Waterloo: The Charge of the Second Brigade of Cavalry, oil on canvas by Denis Dighton © 2002, Her Majesty Queen Elizabeth II. Courtesy of The Royal Collection.

The Waterloo Banquet, oil on canvas by William Salter. Courtesy of Apsley House, The Wellington Museum, London/ V&A Picture Library.

The House of Commons, 1833, oil on canvas by Sir George Hayter. Courtesy of the National Portrait Gallery, London.

The Master of the Ordnance Exercising his Hobby, caricatured by Isaac Cruikshank, 1819. Courtesy of The Trustees of The British Museum.

Punishment Drill, caricatured by William Heath, 1830. Courtesy of the National Army Museum, London.

The Duke of Wellington as an Old Man on the Battlefield of Waterloo, oil on canvas after Benjamin Robert Haydon. Courtesy of the National Army Museum, London.

The Duke of Wellington's dressing case with silver and ivory fittings. Courtesy of Apsley House, The Wellington Museum/ Bridgeman Art Library.

Dessert plate from the *Saxon Service*, showing a view of Apsley House. Courtesy of Apsley House, The Wellington Museum/ Bridgeman Art Library.

Dessert plate from the *Prussian Service*, showing a view of Quatre Bras. Courtesy of Apsley House, The Wellington Museum/ Bridgeman Art Library.

Three Field Marshal's batons from the Duke of Wellington's Collection. Courtesy of Apsley House, The Wellington Museum/ Bridgeman Art Library.

The Funeral of the Duke of Wellington: the Funeral Car Passing the Archway at Apsley House, November 18th 1852, lithograph after a painting by Louis Haghe. Courtesy of the Governors of Wellington College.

The interior of St Paul's Cathedral during the funeral. Courtesy of the Governors of Wellington College.

BLACK AND WHITE PLATES

The Duke of York at Valenciennes, 23rd May 1793, coloured etched aquatint by T. Sutherland after W. Heath, 1815. Courtesy of the National Army Museum, London.

South East View of Fort St George, Madras, coloured engraving by Thomas and William Daniell, 1797. Courtesy of the British Library.

Catherine Dorothea Sarah ('Kitty') Pakenham, Viscountess Wellington, drawing by John Slater, 1811 © The Duke of Wellington. Reproduced courtesy of Stratfield Saye House.

Arthur Wellesley, 1st Duke of Wellington, oil on canvas by Robert Home, 1804. Courtesy of the National Portrait Gallery, London.

The Embarkation of General Junot after the Convention of Cintra, engraving by Bartolozzi after Henri L'Eveque, 1813. Courtesy of the National Army Museum, London.

Battle of Talavera, 28th July 1809, coloured etched aquatint by T. Sutherland after W. Heath, 1815. Courtesy of the National Army Museum, London.

The Landing of the British Army at Mondego Bay, 1808, watercolour by Henri L'Eveque, 1813. Courtesy of the National Army Museum, London.

Torres Vedras from the North West, coloured aquatint by T. Clark after the Rev. Bradford, 1809. Courtesy of the National Army Museum, London.

The Devil's Own: 88th Foot at the Siege of Badajoz, 1812, wash drawing by R. Caton Woodville, 1908. Courtesy of the National Army Museum, London.

Marshal Massena, lithograph by Depelch after N.E. Maurin, 1832. Courtesy of Photo AKG London.

Marshal Marmont, lithograph by Depelch after N.E. Maurin, 1832. Courtesy of Photo AKG London.

The Peterloo Massacre, 16th August 1819, by George Cruikshank. Courtesy of the Mary Evans Picture Library.

Napoleon Bonaparte, oil on canvas by Robert LeFevre, 1812. Courtesy of Apsley House, The Wellington Museum/ V&A Picture Gallery.

Harriette Wilson, unattributed colour print. Courtesy of the Mary Evans Picture Library.

A British Battering Ram Preparing the Way for a Popish Bull, cartoon by 'HH', 1827. Courtesy of the Mary Evans Picture Library.

Political Unions Gather at New-Hall Hill, Birmingham, to Press for the Reform Bill, May 1832, engraving by Garner after Green. Courtesy of the Mary Evans Picture Library.

Daguerrotype portrait of Wellington taken in 1844 © The Duke of Wellington. Reproduced courtesy of Stratfield Saye House.

LIST OF MAPS

INTRODUCTION

I was the sort of boy who had heroes, and long before I ever dreamt of becoming a military historian, the Duke of Wellington was firmly enshrined in my personal pantheon. He seemed to have every virtue: he never lost a major battle, made war on soldiers not civilians, understood grubby logistics just as well as the rather more dashing tactics, and set the seal on his military career by defeating Napoleon, the towering genius of his age. And as someone often forcefully reminded of the couplet;

> Duty, duty, must be done
> The rule applies to everyone

I admired the duke's iron sense of duty. 'Nobody else will do it,' he complained in his declining years. 'The Duke of Wellington *must*.'[1] He was a beau, but a restrained one. When my own idea of understated elegance consisted of clean jeans and a black cashmere roll-neck, I applauded the duke's eschewing scarlet and gold braid in favour of a trim blue frock coat and the eponymous boots. He was brave, showing physical courage on a dozen battlefields, and moral courage throughout a long political career. Like many young men, I saw bravery as the ultimate virtue. There was also an attraction in his manly vices. What adolescent would not be impressed by a man described by one of Napoleon's mistresses as a good deal more vigorous than the emperor himself?

Lastly, he was master of the crisp aphorism; something I often sought but rarely found. He told the politician and diarist John Wilson Croker that: 'All the business of war, and indeed all the business of life, is to endeavour to find out what you don't know by what you do; that's what I called "guessing what was on the other side of the hill".'[2] When a gentleman mistook him for George Jones the painter (who did indeed resemble the duke), and accosted him in the street with 'Mr Jones, I believe?' he responded: 'If you believe that, you'll believe anything.'[3] The young Queen Victoria was upset to discover that sparrows were ruining the exhibits in the Great Exhibition of 1851, but could not be shot because the great building was made of glass. 'Try sparrow-hawks, Ma'am,' suggested Wellington. And when a publisher demanded payment to avoid Wellington being mentioned in the memoirs of a former mistress, he riposted: 'Publish and be damned.'[4] Even though he sometimes reviled his men as 'the scum of the earth', his essential compassion burst out when he admitted after Waterloo that: 'Nothing except a battle lost can be half so melancholy as a battle won.'

But as I grew older and looked harder at the evidence, there were an awful lot of cracks in the ducal portrait. Wellington was not invincible. He was roundly beaten in a scrambling night attack at Sultanpettah Tope outside the Mysore fortress of Seringapatam in 1799 – it left such a lasting impression on him that, forty years later, he could still draw a sketch-map of the action. Critics suggested that he might have been court-martialled had his brother not been governor-general of India at the time, and this was not the last occasion when his well-placed political connections proved useful. In 1812 he botched the siege of Burgos – 'the worst scrape that ever I was in' – and on the retreat he railed against 'the habitual inattention of the Officers of the regiments to their duty', leaving many of them with lasting resentment of his ingratitude.[5] Indeed, Lieutenant William Grattan of the 88th

Regiment (Connaught Rangers) complained that 'the never-to-be forgotten service of that wonderful army' was treated 'in a scandalous manner' by Wellington.[6] Ensign John Mills of the Coldstream Guards thought that his dispatches were dishonest:

> I have learnt one thing since I came to this country, and that is to know how easily England is duped; how completely ignorant she is of the truth of what is going on here . . . At Fuentes the French completely turned our right; Lord Wellington in his dispatch slightly notices it, and would lead you to think that the troops on the right were withdrawn rather than, as was the case, driven in; and then they give him what he himself never dreamt of claiming, a victory.[7]

Wellington's reprimands were scathing and not always just. In 1811, Lieutenant Colonel Bevan of the 4th Regiment was so distressed by being unfairly blamed by the duke for the escape of the French garrison of Almeida that he shot himself. He was also something of a snob, preferring talent with a title to talent without. He often privately expressed contempt for his allies, and the German historian Peter Hofschröer has established at least a *prima facie* case against him for dealing dishonestly with the Prussians at Waterloo. A strong thread of harshness ran through his character: Paddy Griffith observed that he 'could be a ferocious commander even by the standards of a ferocious profession in a ferocious age'. In 1813 he told a subordinate at the siege of Pamplona that 'you may shoot the governor and his officers, and decimate the rank and file', and he regretted not shooting the garrison of Ciudad Rodrigo when he stormed the place in 1812 (technically permissible within the laws of war as they then stood), because killing one garrison would have discouraged others.[8] He was steadfastly opposed to the abolition of flogging in the army, and consistently argued against commissioning officers from the ranks. While his political career had its moments of triumph, he never fully grasped the realities of his age, and by setting his face firmly against parliamentary reform, he was condemned to defend a position that was ultimately untenable.

So, despite the tendency of some historians to place Wellington 'on a pedestal so high that his human qualities and failings have been all but lost to view', it is clear that the picture is infinitely more complex.[9] I approached this book and the BBC television series it accompanies determined to rub away as much of the varnish as I could; to try to get as close to the real Wellington as he (and some of his biographers) would let me. I went back to sources I had not used for years – Lieutenant Colonel John Gurwood's *Dispatches of Field Marshal the Duke of Wellington*, a volume with almost a thousand tightly-written pages, sits in beautifully bound splendour on my desk – and I visited as many Wellingtonian battlefields as I could. Some, like the overcrowded Waterloo and the wide-open Salamanca, I already knew. But there were others I did not, and amongst them I found Assaye, scene of Wellington's victory over the Marathas in 1803, the most striking. Indeed, travelling by road in India at the tail of the monsoon told me just as much about the man as *The Maratha War Papers of Arthur Wellesley*. Conditions were so bad that our smart four-wheel drive vehicles were no use, and we took to a hastily borrowed tractor and trailer, all helping to push when it became stuck in the mud. If the climate on the Indian subcontinent struck few chords with Spain, parts of the terrain were strikingly similar: a commander who could cope with the Western Ghats would be well prepared for Extremadura.

Wellington complained that 'I have been much exposed to

authors', and the process continued after his death to the point where he is one of the most written-about figures in military history, although here his adversary Napoleon beats him by sheer weight of print. Elizabeth Longford's magisterial two-volume study remains pre-eminent, and Christopher Hibbert's *Wellington: A Personal History* is a jewel of a book, and undoubtedly the best starting-point for the general reader. Gordon Corrigan's *Wellington: A Military Life* is a soldierly account of the military side of the duke's life. The painstaking studies of Jac Weller still remain essential baggage for visitors to Wellington's battlefields, and the army he commanded is brilliantly described by Michael Glover in *Wellington's Army* and Philip Haythornthwaite in *The Armies of Wellington*. Andrew Roberts was not the first author to compare Wellington and his greatest adversary but his *Napoleon and Wellington* brought a wealth of fresh interpretation to what might have been a familiar topic. Both men were outsiders, born on islands; both lost their father at an early age, spoke French as their second language, had irregular (and strangely intertwined) private lives, and changed their surnames. Philip Guedalla was a fashionable historian in the 1930s but has long since fallen from favour, though his *The Two Marshals* set me off on a love affair with French military history from which I have never fully recovered. On re-reading his *The Duke* I was struck by its sheer elegance: my own generation has produced many historians who are defter with their footnotes, but few who write as well.

Guedalla ends his book where I ended my filming, in St Paul's Cathedral, where Wellington lies buried. At his funeral a herald read out a long and sonorous list of his titles:

Duke of Wellington, Marquis of Wellington, Marquis of Douro, Earl of Wellington in Somerset, Viscount

Wellington of Talavera, Baron Douro of Wellesley, Prince of Waterloo in the Netherlands, Duke of Ciudad Rodrigo in Spain, Duke of Brunoy in France, Duke of Vitoria, Marques of Torres Vedras, Count of Vimiero in Portugal, a Grandee of the First Class in Spain, a Privy Councillor, Commander-in-Chief of the British Army, Colonel of the Grenadier Guards ... the Lord High Constable of England, the Constable of the Tower, Warden of the Cinque Ports, Chancellor of the Cinque Ports, Admiral of the Cinque Ports, Lord-Lieutenant of Hampshire, Lord-Lieutenant of the Tower Hamlets, Ranger of St James's Park, Ranger of Hyde Park, Chancellor of the University of Oxford ...[10]

It was a far cry from his birth in Ireland, younger son of a musical Irish peer, and a shy and dreamy boyhood in which the violin figured more prominently than the musket. While Wellington's story may not be precisely one of rags to riches, it is certainly one of obscurity to fame, and of a confident maturity confounding the scanty hopes of youth. As I stood by his monument in St Paul's, so large that the statue on top almost grazes the ceiling, I was again struck by the sheer scale of the man. Whatever we may think of him, he did bestride the Britain of his age like the proverbial colossus. At the end of almost a year of filming and writing it was, I think, this feeling of size and strength that stayed with me. Almost despite myself, I realised that my youthful admiration had surged back, as strong as ever, to override all those reservations. Wellington may not always have been good: but he was unquestionably great. As I walked back towards the great west doors of the cathedral, with filming completed and another little fellowship ended, I could not escape his giant shadow. It hangs over me still.

ONE

A SOLITARY
LIFE

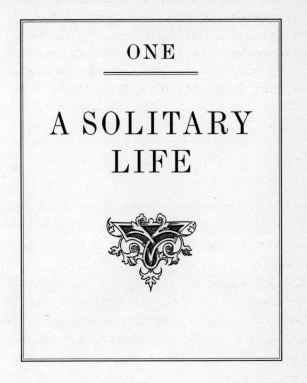

WELLINGTON WAS a child of eighteenth-century Ireland, deeply marked by the time and place of his birth. Throughout his long life there was the lonely quality of the outsider about him, and this isolation has clear origins in his childhood as a member of a besieged Protestant minority in a Catholic land. He would have resented George Bernard Shaw's assertion that he was 'an intensely Irish Irishman'. Indeed, he was to deny his Irishness by (so it was said) observing that not everyone born in a stable was a horse. The growing sense of insecurity felt by the Protestant ascendancy as nationalist pressure increased at the end of the eighteenth century helped imbue him with a sense of impending catastrophe, and a feeling that if the government's grip faltered, the result would be torched mansions and butchered gentry. But his personal contact with Catholicism deprived the religion of the ferocity it possessed for Englishmen bought up on the mythology of the fires of Smithfield in Mary Tudor's day and the risk of forcible conversion by the Jacobites and their Catholic allies. Wellington was innately conservative in most of his political opinions, but his own upbringing in Ireland and his experience of fighting alongside Catholic allies in the Peninsula encouraged him to fight a long, hard battle to remove the penal legislation which bore down so heavily upon Catholics, and the achievement of Catholic emancipation in 1829 was to be not least amongst his accomplishments.

In Wellington's approach to both military discipline and parliamentary reform we see his deep-seated fear of the mob, a harking back to an age when the social pyramid seemed firm and the civil power had armed force at its back. He was to maintain that he learnt nothing new about war after his return from India in 1806, and the library that he took to the Indian subcontinent was full of works reflecting the eighteenth century at its most formal. Social, economic and political change between Wellington's birth and death were profound. The population of Great Britain rose from approximately 13 million in 1780 to over 27 million in 1851, and its distribution altered, with a marked shift from the countryside to the towns. Revolutionary changes in agriculture enabled this burgeoning urban population to be fed, while industrial developments, beginning with the transformation of the textile industry, were to turn the Britain in which Wellington died into what was, without hyperbole, 'the workshop of the world'. There have been few other periods of history when a long life has bestridden so much change.

'Every conquest,' wrote Philip Guedalla, 'leaves a caste behind it, since conquerors are apt to perpetuate their victory in superior social pretensions.'[1] In Ireland the process was characteristically complex. In the thirteenth century the Normans overran Ireland, and intermarried with daughters of Gaelic princes so that many Norman families were absorbed by the land they had conquered. For instance, the de Burghs became the Burkes of Connacht, 'almost indistinguishable in the eyes of the government from their Gaelic neighbours'.[2] By the fifteenth century, English writ ran in

Dublin and the Pale around it: large towns were English in sympathy, but the countryside was solidly Gaelic. The Tudors set about the reconquest of Ireland, though they were not able to complete it until 1603. From 1609 there was immigration by Protestants from England and Scotland, and in 1641 a rebellion against the settlers led to a war which culminated in Oliver Cromwell's invasion in 1649. Although his 'massacres' at Drogheda and Wexford were arguably not a breach of the laws of war, they left an enduring legacy of bitterness.

When Charles II was restored to the throne in 1660, most Catholic landowners were better off than they had been under Cromwell, but were still grievously disappointed. Charles died in 1685 and his brother James II swung towards the Catholics. He made the Earl of Tyrconnell viceroy and appointed growing numbers of Catholics to key offices. But the Glorious Revolution of 1688 dashed Catholic hopes: William III invaded Ireland and beat James on the River Boyne. The Treaty of Limerick ended the war in 1691, and although its terms seemed not ungenerous to the Catholics, the triumphant Protestants immediately set about strengthening their ascendancy with a series of anti-Catholic laws. Catholics could not vote, enter parliament or the legal profession, hold commissions in the army or navy, or even own a horse worth more than £5. Restriction of land ownership ensured that by 1778 only about 5 per cent of land was in Catholic hands. The Catholic peasantry, however, did not owe their misery primarily to the penal laws but to the impact of a growing population on land that was often poor, and where famine was rarely far away.

Things were very different for members of the ascendancy. It was a social elite, professional as well as landed, defined primarily by its Anglicanism, for its descent could be Norman, Old English, Cromwellian or even Gaelic.[3] A later nationalist writer described an Ireland that the ascendancy scarcely touched, an Ireland that was 'dark, scorned and secretly romantic'.[4] There was little real contact between this hidden Ireland and the sparkling world of parties in Sackville Street, duelling behind Lucas's coffee house near Dublin Castle (the seat of the government), tea at the Kildare Street Club, and life in the Palladian mansions that sprang up across the countryside, where they stood like Protestant islands in a Catholic sea. The agricultural writer Arthur Young visited Ireland in the late 1770s and wrote of how: 'Speaking a language that is despised, professing a religion that is abhorred, and being disarmed, the poor find themselves in many cases slaves even in the bosom of written liberty.'[5] It is small wonder that some commentators drew parallels between rural Ireland and the cottonfields of the Carolinas.

One of the estates visited by Arthur Young was Dangan Castle in County Meath, close to the little town of Trim and a long day's journey by coach from Dublin. He observed that part of the estate had been turned into an ornamental lake with its own islands, pleasing enough in its effect, but not exactly the work of an improving landlord keen on his barley and turnips. The owner was Garrett Wesley, Earl of Mornington, professor of music at Trinity College Dublin and composer of such enchanting pieces as 'Here in Cool Grot', 'Gently Hear me, Charming Maid', and 'Come Fairest Nymph'. His father had been born a Colley of Castle Carbury, a member of a family that originated in the English Midlands and had lived in Ireland for three hundred years without a single Irish name appearing on its pedigree. He had taken the name and, more to the point, inherited the fortune of his cousin, Garrett Wesley of Dangan. The new Mr Wesley removed to the family seat at Dangan and sat in the Irish parliament for the family borough of Trim. A grateful government elevated him to the Irish

House of Lords, and his son Garrett continued the family's ascent by being created an earl in 1760, for reasons which, as Elizabeth Longford gently observes, are not immediately obvious.

The previous year Garrett Wesley had married Anne Hill, eldest daughter of Arthur Hill (later Lord Dungannon), and she duly presented him with a son and heir, Richard Colley Wesley, in 1760; another son, William, in 1763; a daughter, Anne, in 1768; and a third surviving son, Arthur, in 1769. Two younger sons followed, Gerald Valerian in 1770 and Henry in 1773. Arthur Wesley always celebrated his birthday on 1 May, although biographers variously maintain that he was born on 6 March or 3, 29 or 30 April. There is a similar dispute about the place of his birth, with Dangan Castle, Trim, a coach on the Dublin road, and even a packet-boat at sea amongst the many places vying for the honour. His proud parents, however, announced that the birth had taken place in their Dublin house, 6 Merrion Street, where Lady Mornington's bedroom looked out across a little garden to the charming symmetry of Merrion Square in the comfortable heart of ascendancy Dublin.

Arthur spent his early years in Dublin and at Dangan. Dangan Castle itself is now a shell, with its long, elegant two-storey façade looking out over the green landscape. The ruins behind show that the Georgian house was built on the remnants of something solid and medieval, constructed in an age when security mattered more than appearance.

Arthur was sent to the little diocesan school at Trim, in the shadow of the ruined tower of St Mary's abbey and just across the Boyne from the great square Norman keep which stands as a stark symbol of the invaders' power. The family then moved to London, something in the nature of a retreat, because the earl's finances, weakened by the musical indulgences of Dublin and

Dangan, were in decline so that 'we are not able to appear in any degree as we ought'. While the brilliant Richard shot from Harrow to Eton and then on to Christ Church Oxford, gaining golden opinions as he did so, Arthur was sent to Brown's seminary in the King's Road, where, as he admitted, he was 'a shy, idle lad'. He went on to Eton in 1781, but as he told an early biographer, G. R. Gleig, who served under him as a subaltern in the Peninsula and went on to become a clergyman:

> Besides achieving no success as a scholar, he contracted few special intimacies among his contemporaries ... His was indeed a solitary life; a life of solitude in a crowd; for he walked generally alone; often bathed alone; and seldom took part in either the cricket matches or boat-races which were then, as they are now, in great vogue among Etonians.[6]

He was a shy young Irishman in England, still an outsider, with parents who were 'frivolous and careless personages' and to whom he does not seem to have been particularly close. He could fight if he had to: at Eton he beat Bobus Smith, brother of the wit Sidney Smith, and while staying with his grandmother, Lady Dungannon, in North Wales, was soundly thrashed by a young blacksmith named Hughes, who was proud to relate how he had beaten the man who beat Napoleon, saying that 'Master Wesley bore him not a pin's worth of ill-will.'[7]

When Lord Mornington died in May 1781, it became clear that the family finances were worse than anyone had suspected. Richard, the new Lord Mornington, left Oxford without taking his degree, and Arthur was taken away from Eton so that what money remained could be spent on Gerald and Henry, who seemed to offer a better return on the investment. Lady Mornington withdrew to Brussels in 1784 and lodged with a lawyer, Louis Goubert. After some brief tutoring in Brighton, Arthur followed her and studied under their landlord in the company of John Armytage, second son of a rich Yorkshire baronet and family friend. Armytage wrote that young Wesley was 'extremely fond of music, and played well upon the fiddle, but he never gave any indication of any other species of talent. As far as my memory serves, there was no intention then of sending him into the army; his own wishes, if he had any, were in favour of a civilian's life.'[8] But he was fast running out of civilian options. The family's Irish estates were deeply mortgaged, and lack of money meant that he could not have been maintained at university even if he had had the aptitude to survive there. The witty and ambitious Richard was clearly the hope of the family: Arthur thought him 'the most wonderful person in the whole world'. He was prepared to use the family's patronage, stemming from his own seat in the Lords and control of a seat in the Commons, to gain Arthur a free commission in the army, and had already written to ask the lord lieutenant of Ireland (effectively its viceroy) on behalf of the shy sixteen year old. Lady Mornington declared: 'I vow to God I don't know what I shall do with my awkward son Arthur. He is food for powder and nothing more.'[9]

Young Wesley was destined for an army that was close to the nadir of its fortunes. The regular army, established in 1661, exhibited a familiar pattern of growing to face the challenges of major wars and shrinking rapidly afterwards, with surplus soldiers being discharged to the civilian life from which they had often been anxious to escape in the first place, and officers being sent home on half-pay. Although it had emerged victorious from the Seven Years War (1756–63), it had been beaten in the American War of Independence. Frustratingly, it had won most of the battles but had somehow lost the war, with humiliating surrenders at Saratoga in 1777 and Yorktown in 1781. Matters were not improved by the fact that a growing number of Englishmen sympathised with the colonists. When Major General Sir William Howe, MP for Nottingham, was sent out to North America in 1775, an aggrieved constituent told him: 'I don't wish you to fall, as many do, but I cannot say I wish success to the undertaking.'[10]

The low regard in which the army was held stemmed partly from the fact that, in the absence of a police force, it was frequently called upon to preserve order in a harsh and brutal society. We connect to the Georgian age through its surviving artefacts, and it is easy to forget that, just as a classical front with its long windows and smart portico had often been stuck onto an altogether less elegant building (Dangan Castle is a good example), so old, ugly undercurrents rippled on through the eighteenth century and often into the nineteenth. Executions were held in public throughout Wellington's lifetime. Traitors were hanged, drawn and quartered: partly strangled, then cut down alive to be castrated and disembowelled before their entrails were burnt and their bodies cut into four. There was, however, growing resistance to such savagery. After the Jacobite rebellion of 1715, victims of this ghastly punishment were revived after hanging to be 'bowelled alive and seeing', but after the 1745 rebellion they were hanged till they were dead, or knifed by the executioner before the butchery began. Those involved in the Cato Street Conspiracy of 1820, who had planned the murder the cabinet, of which Wellington was a member, were merely beheaded after death, and the mood of the crowd grew ugly as the executioner sawed away at spines and sinews.

Even straightforward hanging did not guarantee a quick death, and the victim's friends would often rush forward to pull on his legs and hasten death. Bodies were usually sent to the surgeon's hall for dissection, although they might be gibbeted in some appropriate place as a warning to others: the body of Maria Phipoe, a murderess hanged in 1797, was displayed outside the Old Bailey. There was an odd democracy to the business. In 1760 Earl Ferrers, convicted of murder by the House of Lords, was duly hanged and then dissected, but he went to Tyburn in a landau drawn by six horses rather than the common cart, and died so well that the mob, fickle as ever, showed more sympathy than anger.[11]

Many popular 'sports' were dangerous and brutal. Bull- and bear-baiting were popular, and noblemen jostled with kitchen-porters in drunken, sweaty cockpits where fighting cocks, their natural talons reinforced with spurs wrought in the best of Georgian taste, fought to the death. A French visitor, César de Saussure, observed that the populace enjoyed 'throwing dead dogs and cats and mud at passers-by' as well as playing football, in the process of which 'they will break panes of glass and smash the windows of coaches and also knock you down without the smallest compunction . . .'[12]

As the eighteenth century wore on, there was a growing number of violent reactions to economic fluctuations: a depression in the textile industry triggered rioting in Spitalfields in 1719, and there were very serious food riots in Somerset and Wiltshire in 1766–67. But as the country faced a sequence of economic recessions with the transition from war to peace at the end of the Seven Years War and the War of American Independence, rioting became more serious and the ruling elite increasingly saw it as a threat to its hold on power.

The climax came in 1780 when the unsteady anti-Catholic Lord George Gordon gained widespread support, much of it from the 'middling sort' of men who coincidentally also favoured political reform, in his demand for the repeal of an act of 1778 which had removed some of the restraints on Catholics. When parliament rejected his petition, there was an outbreak of violent disorder. It began with attacks on Catholic chapels attached to foreign embassies (the only ones legally allowed), and then, more seriously, went on to take in all the law's visible manifestations like the houses of prominent judges and magistrates and Newgate prison itself. This was evidently an assault on the establishment, and the government brought over 11,000 regular soldiers into the capital. Almost 300 rioters were shot, another 25 were hanged. Not only was the government badly rattled by the sheer scale of the violence, but many middle-class radicals who had supported Gordon (himself cleared of high treason), were so frightened by the spectre of the mob that they shied away from reform thereafter.

Both the regular army and the less reliable militia played a leading role in the preservation of order, and in doing so found themselves execrated by the populace and at risk of prosecution for murder if they killed anybody. In 1736 Captain John Porteous of the Edinburgh Town Guard ordered his men to fire on a crowd that indulged in stone-throwing at an execution, killing five or six. He was condemned to death for murder, and although he received a royal pardon, the mob burst into his prison, dragged him out, and lynched him. As the English constitutional lawyer Dicey put it:

> The position of a soldier may be, both in theory and in practice, a difficult one. He may, as it has been well said, be liable to be shot by a Court-Martial if he disobeys an order, and to be hanged by a judge and jury if he obeys it.[13]

There was an added shade of complexity. Jurors were, by definition, men of property, and while the military could shoot rioting weavers or colliers without much risk, matters were different if their victims were middle-class men with whom a jury might sympathise. In 1768 a magistrate ordered troops to fire on a crowd supporting the reformer John Wilkes: six were killed and fifteen wounded. The magistrate was tried for murder but acquitted by the judge before a jury (far more likely to take a hostile line) was empanelled, and it followed that the troops themselves could then not be convicted. The Gordon riots, however, aroused no middle-class sympathy. Troops were eventually given carte blanche, and duly dealt with the mob by volley-firing more suitable for a conventional field of battle.

Whatever the importance of its forays to bolster the civil power, the army was designed for use on battlefields and was shaped by the flintlock musket, the weapon carried by the bulk of the armies of the age. And while there were changes in the theory and practice of war during Wellington's lifetime – for instance the development of the *corps d'armée* system by Napoleon, and the increasing use of light troops, like the 95th Rifles who earned such lustre in the Peninsula – there was more continuity than change.

It was the age of the flintlock. In the early eighteenth century the flintlock musket, its charge ignited by the sparks flashing out when flint struck steel, at last replaced the matchlock, which had relied on a length of smouldering cord. To load his musket the soldier tore open a paper cartridge with his teeth – a blackened mouth and brick-dry throat were amongst the lesser hazards of battle – and dribbled some powder into the priming pan of his musket, shutting the pan off by snapping a hinged striking-plate, the steel, across it. He then tipped the remainder of the powder down the weapon's muzzle, following it with the round lead musket ball and then the empty cartridge, ramming it all firmly home. To fire, he first drew back the cock, which held a flint gripped firmly in its steel jaws. When he pressed the trigger the flint snapped forward to strike the steel, which swung forward, uncovering the pan. Sparks ignited the priming powder, which flashed through the touch-hole to ignite the main charge.

Misfires were common. Flints had a life of twenty or thirty shots and gave little warning of imminent failure: they simply failed to spark and had to be replaced. Sometimes flint and priming-powder both did their job, but resulted only in a 'flash in the pan' which did not ignite the charge. And even when the weapon did fire, it was shockingly inaccurate. In 1814 Colonel George Hanger suggested that although a musket might hit a man at 80 or even 100 yards, a man would be very unlucky indeed to be hit at 150 yards by the man who aimed at him. And that, of course, was the catch, for most infantry soldiers aimed not at individuals but at the mass of the enemy's line. A Prussian experiment on a canvas target 100 feet long and 6 feet high demonstrated that there were only 23 per cent hits at 225 yards, 40 per cent at 150 yards and 60 per cent at 75 yards. In 1779 a battalion of Norfolk militia, many of its members no doubt more handy with the plough than the musket, hit a similar target with 20 per cent of its shots at 70 yards. These experiments were exactly that, and with an enemy returning fire, results in battle were likely to be far worse. With such a weapon, the volume of fire counted for more than its accuracy, and recruits were drilled repeatedly until the sequence of loading had become second nature and they could fire three or even four shots a minute. Drill was also important in enabling them to move forward in columns, the usual formation for covering the ground, and then to deploy into line so that the maximum number of muskets be brought to bear.

It was axiomatic that good infantry, drawn up in suitable formation (squares or oblongs were ideal) on favourable ground, should be able to resist the attack of cavalry. Although the cavalry of the age still sought to charge whenever possible, it often rendered more useful service by dealing in the small change of war. Cavalry in general, and especially light cavalry, provided a framework of pickets which screened armies in camp or on the march. Although Wellington figured briefly in the Army List as a light dragoon, he was never a real cavalry officer, and rarely showed the arm much sympathy, complaining that its officers had a trick of 'galloping at everything'. Recent research has shown that he was as unfair in this as in some of his other sweeping judgements, and the achievements of the cavalry which served him were by no means derisory.[14]

Artillery had already begun its long rise that was to end in it dominating the battlefield a generation after Wellington's death. Cannon were categorised by the weight of the iron roundshot they fired, with handy 6-pdrs to heavy 12-pdrs forming the mainstay of field artillery and more cumbersome pieces, like 24-pdrs and 32-pdrs, taking pride of place when it came to battering the walls of fortresses. The roundshot, pitched to hit the ground just in front of its target and then to ricochet through the enemy's formation smashing limbs and striking off heads at every bound, was the most common projectile, with an effective range of about 800 yards and a maximum range of perhaps twice that. At close range gunners switched to canister, a circular tin containing a number of lead or iron balls. The tin burst open when it left the muzzle, turning the cannon into a giant shotgun. Almost half the balls from a British 6-pdr would hit a large target at 400 yards, making canister a lethal weapon. One of my abiding memories of the battlefield of Assaye is the sheer prevalance of canister shot, from small shot the size of a thumb-nail to big shot the size of a golf-ball. The path of the Maratha gun-line could almost be traced by the battalions of urchins pressing canister upon the unwary visitor.

A third artillery projectile, spherical case – known in the British service as shrapnel after its inventor, Lieutenant Henry Shrapnel of the Royal Artillery – consisted of an iron sphere filled with powder and musket-balls. The shell was ignited by a fuse composed of tightly-packed powder in an ash or beech plug; bursting range was regulated by cutting the end off the fuse.

Cannon, like infantry muskets, were muzzle-loading throughout Wellington's service. They were horse-drawn, with field guns requiring teams of six or eight horses. In most artillery units the gunners marched behind their pieces, but in horse artillery, designed to keep pace with, and cross the same country as cavalry, all gunners rode. Finally, the rocket made a brief and inglorious appearance in the British army during the Napoleonic Wars, but it was not deemed a success, and Wellington in particular had poor regard for it. When told that sending a rocket troop away would break its commander's heart, he snapped: 'Damn his heart: let my orders be obeyed.'

The Georgian army was a mirror of the state it served. It was heterogeneous, decentralised and riddled with patronage and per-quisite. The commander-in-chief at Horse Guards in Whitehall presided over the household troops (horse and foot guards), and the infantry and cavalry of the line. He was, however, subject to political control, itself unevenly applied by the two cabinet minis-ters with primary responsibility for military matters – the secretary of state for war and the colonies, and the secretary at war. The monarch also took an interest in military affairs, regarding the household troops as a personal preserve, and often becoming involved in that most fecund of royal pursuits, the design of uniform. Artillery and engineers were the creatures of the master-general of the ordnance, usually a peer with a seat in the cabinet, and proved the point by wearing blue uniforms rather than the red which characterised most of the rest of the army. Wellington served on both sides of the fence, both as commander-in-chief and as master-general of the ordnance, an unusual distinction.

The heavy hand of the Treasury lay on the whole machine, for it controlled the commissariat which was responsible for supplying the army with most of what it required in peace and war, although its representatives were regarded as civilian officials rather than military officers. Yet even here there was little consistency, for some items (soldiers' water bottles, for instance), were supplied by the board of ordnance and stamped with its initials, BO, and others, like uniforms and some accoutrements, were supplied to regiments by their colonels. The latter were actually not colonels at all, but generals given the appointment as a reward or as the equivalent of a pension. Wellington became colonel of the 33rd Regiment in 1806, and remained colonel of a regiment until he died. They purchased their regiment's requisites, using a government grant which they often managed to under spend by economising on the quality of cloth from which uniforms were made or the frequency with which items were replaced.

Artillery and engineer officers were commissioned after attending the Royal Military Academy at Woolwich, and were thereafter promoted by inexorable seniority. In the infantry and cavalry, however, colonels were intimately concerned in the selection and promotion of the officers in their regiments. About two-thirds of commissions in these arms were purchased, although during major wars it was difficult to find sufficient young men whose relatives were prepared to buy the fortunate youth an accelerated chance of an early death: in 1810 only one fifth of all commissions were bought. An individual wishing to buy a commission had to pay the government the regulation price, adding a non-regulation bonus to the officer he was replacing, using the colonel's representative, the regimental agent, as his intermediary. Regulations on promotion grew increasingly tight during Wellington's lifetime, and the Duke of York, commander-in-chief 1798–1808 and 1811–1827, forbade commissioning youths under the age of sixteen. He also established time limits that prevented an officer becoming a captain with less than two year's service and a major with less than six, increasing these limits to three and nine years in 1806.

Up to the rank of lieutenant colonel, promotion was regimental. A normal peacetime vacancy for a captain, arising because an officer had decided to retire on half-pay, would be offered to the senior lieutenant. If he could afford it, all well and good: if not, the offer was made to the next senior, and so on. The promotion of a lieutenant opened an opportunity for the promotion of an ensign, which was filled in the same way. An astute young man with money behind him could slip from regiment to regiment as opportunities arose, obtaining seniority in an unfashionable regiment and transferring back, in his new rank, to his old regiment, provided its colonel was kept sweet. When officers were killed in action or died of wounds, however, the vacancy was filled by seniority alone: it was small wonder that the ambitious but impecunious drank to 'a bloody war or a sickly season'.

In practice, more commissions were granted without purchase than ought to have been the case, and an applicant's ability to bring influence to bear was crucial. Control of a family parliamentary seat, support for the ministry in Commons or Lords, past favours or future promises all helped secure an epaulette. Sometimes a young man could make his way by courage alone. Gentleman volunteers attached themselves to a regiment, messing with its officers but serving as private soldiers, hoping to distinguish themselves and gain a free commission.

Promotion beyond lieutenant colonel was by seniority within the army as a whole. An officer who made lieutenant colonel was bound to die a general if he lived long enough, but there was no guarantee that he would be employed as a general even if he gained the rank. There were always more generals than there were jobs, and officers steadily notched their way up from major general to lieutenant general and so to general, even if they never actually served in any of these ranks. Promotion for a man with neither contacts nor particular talent was a mixed blessing: he might find himself a major general, living at home on his half-pay as lieutenant colonel, waiting for a call which never came.

Arthur Wesley had his own call to arms in 1786, when he was sent to the Royal Academy of Equitation in the French town of Angers. The school's register describes him as 'Mr Wesley, *gentilhomme Irlandais, fils de Mylaidi Mornington*.' With his friends Mr Walsh and Mr Wingfield, sons of Lords Walsh and Powerscourt, the '*groupe des lords*', Wesley was entertained by local noble families, and made a good impression on M. de Pignerolle, the academy's director, who described him as 'an Irish lad of great promise'. Yet he was still noticeably frail and was often not well enough to ride, but spent happy hours on the sofa, playing with his terrier Vick. He was never really fond of dogs, but made an exception for terriers. When in India he had a white terrier called Jack which, badly frightened when a salute was fired, made its own way over a hundred miles home.

Angers taught him three things. He became a good horseman, albeit, despite the Academy's motto of 'Grace and Valour', more practical than he was elegant. His French was in much the same style, because although his vocabulary and grammar were good enough, he tended to take the language by frontal assault: somebody later remarked that he spoke French as he fought them, *bravement*. His French stood him in good stead in a Europe where French was the language of diplomacy and the arts, and his comparative fluency eluded all too many of his countrymen. In 1814 his senior aide-de-camp, Colin Campbell, was disputing possession of an umbrella with the mayor of Bordeaux after a civic reception. Campbell tugged, bowed, and declared '*c'est moine*'.[15] Lastly, in these formative years, Wesley was influenced by gentlemen like M. de Pignerolle; old-style royalists who owed proud allegiance to a notion of absolute monarchy whose days were already numbered. Elizabeth Longford recounts a telling anecdote. In 1840, at a dinner in Apsley House, his London home, the duke gazed at portraits of Louis XVIII and Charles X in all their finery, and said to Lord Mahon: 'How much better, after all, these two look with their *fleurs de lys* and *Saint-Esprits*, than the two corporals behind or the fancy dress in between.' The corporals were Tsar Alexander I of Russia and King Frederick William III of Prussia in uniform, and the fancy dress was George IV in full Highland fig.[16]

When Wesley returned to England in late 1786 his mother was astonished at the improvement in 'my ugly boy Arthur'. But he had to be found a job, and the family was still short of money. His brother Mornington immediately wrote to the Duke of Rutland, lord-lieutenant of Ireland.

> Let me remind you of a younger brother of mine, whom you were so kind as to take into your consideration for a commission in the army. He is here at this moment, and perfectly idle. It is a matter of indifference to me what commission he gets, provided he gets it soon.[17]

Mornington was already a rising man, with a seat in the Westminster parliament and brother William sitting for the family seat of Trim in the Irish Commons: it was in Rutland's interest to indulge him. A commission in the cavalry or foot guards might have been more than the market would bear, as Mornington must have known. But a junior regiment in India was another matter altogether, and on 7 March 1787, shortly before his eighteenth birthday, Arthur Wesley was gazetted ensign in the 73rd Highland Regiment of Foot. Mornington continued to pluck the harp-strings of patronage: in October that year he induced the new lord-lieutenant, Lord Buckingham, to appoint Arthur one of his aides-de-camp on ten shillings a day (almost twice his daily pay as an ensign), and on Christmas day 1787, he became a lieutenant in the 76th Regiment. An attempt by the secretary at war to econ-omise by putting all aides-de-camp on half-pay caused some flut-tering, but the scheme was soon dropped. Arthur now transferred to the 41st Regiment, as the 76th had been designated for service in the unhealthy East Indies. He set off for Ireland in January 1788, and on his way visited those 'inseparable friends', the Ladies of Llangollen, who had been told by his excited mother that:

> There are so many little things to settle for *Arthur* who is just got into the army and is to go to Ireland in the capacity of Aid De Camp to Lord Buckingham, and must be set out a little for that, in short I *must* do *everything* for him and when you see him you will think him worthy of it, as he really is a very charming young man, never did I see such a change for the better in anybody. He is wonderfully lucky, in six months he has got two steps in the army and appointed Aid De Camp to Lord Bucking-ham which is ten shillings a day.[18]

Lady Dungannon accompanied him to see the ladies, one of whom reported on him as: 'A charming young man. Handsome, fashioned tall, and elegant.'

What charmed rural Wales did not appear to such advantage in more cosmopolitan Dublin, and Lady Buckingham called Arthur and his fellow aides, 'the awkward squad'. Arthur ordered supper for the vicereine and her ladies, picked up flowers knocked over by a bearish nobleman, was dubbed 'a mischievous boy' by an irritated picnic guest, and was abandoned by a beauty at a ball when his small-talk ran dry. He had gambled at Angers, and bet more deeply in Dublin, winning 150 guineas, close to a year's pay, from 'Buck' Whaley by walking from Cornelscourt to Leeson Street in under an hour. He lodged on Lower Ormond Quay, and his landlord, a boot-maker, lent him money when some of his other bets did not turn out as well. In later life he told George Gleig that debt: 'Makes a slave of a man. I have often known what it was to be in want of money, but I never got helplessly into debt.'[19] Gleig deferentially assumed that his hero did not get into debt at all, but it is truer to say that in borrowing, as in war, he never over-extended himself completely (though there were tense moments), and an aide-de-camp's credit was good in the bright Dublin summer of 1789. Yet news of the French Revolution cast a shadow over the gaiety. 'A'n't you sorry for poor dear France,' wrote his sister Anne, now expediently married to a peer's son. 'I shall never see Paris again.'[20]

Wesley was still not firmly set on his career. Although he spoke of trying to take his new profession seriously, much later in life he rebutted John Wilson Croker's assertion that it was at the very beginning of his career that he 'had a private soldier & all his accoutrements & traps separately weighed, to give you some insight into what the *man* had to do & his power of doing it'.[21] He transferred to the 12th Light Dragoons, still as a lieutenant, in June 1789, but far from devoting himself to the intricacies of his new arm, he dipped a reluctant toe into politics. Brother William had been found a seat in Westminster, and Arthur was destined for Trim, the family borough in Ireland. It was not an easy time to venture into Irish politics, for the tide of nationalism was sweeping across the country. The American War and its Declaration of Independence in 1776 had repercussions for Ireland. There were clear similarities between the position of Ireland and England's colonies in North America, and when France and Spain entered the war against Britain, Ireland, denuded of regular troops, was a likely target for a hostile expedition. Many Irishmen, from the Protestant minority for the most part, joined volunteer military units, and were soon complaining about the commercial restrictions imposed on Ireland and questioning the right of the Westminster parliament to legislate for it.

In Henry Grattan the nationalist movement had an eloquent parliamentary leader, and shortly before the general election of 1789, Wesley was sent to Trim on his first political errand. The little town's burgesses were in danger of making Grattan a freeman, something Dublin Castle was anxious to avoid. Wesley made his first political speech to an audience of eighty burgesses, reporting that he:

> got up and said that the only reasons why Mr Grattan should get the freedom of the corporation was his respectability, that really if we were to admit every man because one of two people said he was respectable, the whole community would belong to the corporation, that *he* could never be of any use to us and would never attend, and that I would certainly object, however great my respect for him.[22]

During a break before the vote, Wesley moved about the room rallying his supporters: 'I told my friends that it was a question of party and they must stick by me.' Wesley duly carried the day. He then showed great discretion by declining to yield to 'requests of all kinds'. An elderly voter asked what he proposed to do about £70 owed by Lord Mornington: 'I would have nothing to do with it,' replied Wesley, 'as in the case of a General Election such a transaction would entirely vitiate my return.'

When the election came on 30 April 1790, Wesley was duly elected, and although opponents briefly disputed his return when the house met in July, they failed to proceed with their petition. He found himself sitting in a parliament in which at least two-thirds of the members owed their election to the proprietors of less than a hundred boroughs. A third of members enjoyed salaries or pensions from the government, absorbing an eighth of Irish revenue. A young Protestant barrister, Theobald Wolfe Tone, leader of the United Irishmen, already in 1790 more militant than Grattan, tellingly described the government's well-fed but silent majority as 'the common prostitutes of the Treasury Bench'.[23] The harp of patronage played on, and in addition to his political role, Wesley became a captain in the 58th Regiment in 1791, slipping sideways into the 18th Light Dragoons the following year.

Yet there was still no clear career ahead of him. He dutifully voted for the government, scuttled about on Castle business, and acted for his brother Mornington in disputes over the mortgaged estate at Dangan. And there were more discreet family tasks. Mornington was living with a French courtesan, Gabrielle Hyacinthe Rolland, who bore him several children, but he had also managed to father a son in Ireland, and Arthur was entrusted with the maintenance of his brother's 'friend' and the education of her son. Lord Westmoreland had replaced Lord Buckingham as viceroy in 1789 and economy did not figure among the 'few good points' this nobleman was acknowledged to possess. A captain's pay did not go far and as aide-de-camp to Westmoreland, Arthur found himself drawing on the family agent for loans, and looking for a way of establishing his finances on a firmer footing: marriage seemed the answer.

There was already more to the relationship between Arthur Wesley and Kitty Pakenham than a young man's quest for an heiress. The Pakenhams lived at Pakenham Hall, Castlepollard, in County Westmeath, a day's ride from Dangan. Kitty and Arthur had probably met in Dublin in 1789 or 1790, for her charm and good looks made her a great favourite at the Castle, and Arthur became a frequent visitor to the Rutland Square house of her father, Lord Longford, a naval captain and keen agricultural improver. We cannot be sure what Longford would have made of a match between the couple, who were evidently very fond of one another, because he died in 1792 and was succeeded by his son Tom, who was himself to step up from baron to earl on his grandmother's death in 1794. Perhaps it was Tom's 'incipient ideas of grandeur' that persuaded Arthur to project himself in the best possible light. He borrowed enough money from Richard to buy a majority in the 33rd Regiment in April 1793. He even began to speak in parliament, seconding the address from the throne, deploring the imprisonment of Louis XVI and the French invasion of the Netherlands, and congratulating the government on its liberal attitude to Catholics.

If he hoped that all this was likely to impress Kitty's brother, he was sorely mistaken. For if the Wesleys had lost most of their money, with nothing but mortgaged estates to show for it, the Pakenhams were comfortably off, and Kitty's brother Ned had his majority bought for him when he was only seventeen. It cannot have been easy for Arthur to ask Tom, actually a little younger than he was, for Kitty's hand in marriage. He was turned down flat. Arthur Wesley was a young man with very poor prospects, and Kitty could do far better.

I believe that the fatal interview took place in the library at Pakenham Hall, now known as Tullynally Castle, and still in the hands of the hospitable Pakenhams. The house is set in a landscaped park with a lake close by and views to distant hills, with treasures scattered casually about the place. A row of swords, hanging unlabelled from coat-hooks, includes slender small-swords, an essential part of a gentleman's everyday dress until the end of the eighteenth century; a mighty meatcleaver of a light cavalry officer's sword; a heavy, neo-classical (and quite useless) ceremonial sword of the Order of St Patrick; and an Edwardian sword that must have belonged to Brigadier General Lord Longford, killed commanding a Yeomanry brigade in an impossible attack at Gallipoli in August 1915.

Reading General Sir George Napier's autobiography in the library at Tullynally Castle, I was struck, yet again, by the Irish contribution to the army of Wellington's age. The Napier brothers, Charles, George and William, all served in the Peninsula and duly became generals. Such was their courage that they were repeatedly wounded, and in 1812 Wellington began a letter to their mother, Lady Sarah, telling her that George had lost his arm, with the words: 'Having such sons, I am aware that you expect to hear of those misfortunes which I have more than once had to communicate to you.'[24] The problem of balancing conscience and duty in the politics of the period is underlined by the fact that Sarah's nephew, Lord Edward Fitzgerald, who had served as an infantry captain in America, became a leader of the United Irishmen and was mortally wounded resisting arrest on the eve of the Great Rising of 1798.

Ireland's contribution to the British army cannot be judged

simply by the officers it provided, whether from noble families like the Napiers or Pakenhams, or the sons of lesser squireens – men like Ensign Dyas of the 51st Regiment, 'an Irishman whose only fortune was his sword', whose exploits were a byword for sheer courage.[25] The Ireland of turf-roofed cabins outside the park gates provided the army with a high proportion of its rank and file: 42 per cent of the Royal Artillery towards the end of the eighteenth century, and precisely the same proportion of the whole army by 1830. Although Irish soldiers were concentrated most heavily in ostensibly Irish regiments like the Connaught Rangers, there was scarcely a regiment without them: the 57th (West Middlesex) Regiment was 34 per cent Irish in 1809, and even the 92nd Regiment (Gordon Highlanders) was 6 per cent Irish in 1813.

Lord Longford's rejection of his suit for Kitty was devastating, and a turning-point for Wesley. His violins, he noted bitterly, 'took up too much of his time and thoughts': he burnt them with his own hands soon afterwards, and never played again. He did his best, however, to tease a few more notes from the harp of patronage. Infantry battalions had two flank companies apiece, one of grenadiers and the other of light infantry, and he heard that some of these were to be brigaded together and sent abroad. He begged Mornington to intercede with the prime minister, and to

> ask Mr Pitt to desire Lord Westmoreland to send me as Major to one of the flank corps. If they are to go abroad, they will be obliged to take officers from the line, and they may as well take me as anybody else ... I think it is both dangerous and improper to remove any part of the army from this country at present, but if any part of it is to be moved, I should like to go with it, and have no chance of seeing service except with the flank corps,

as the regiment I have got into as Major is the last for service.[26]

His appeal was unsuccessful, which was as well, for the flank companies from Ireland went off to die of yellow fever in Martinique. Mornington lent him more money, and with it he purchased a lieutenant colonelcy in the 33rd that September. He went off to command his regiment, immersing himself in the minutiae of its accounts and preparing standing orders that became a model of their kind.

An expedition to the coast of Normandy under Lord Moira was mooted, and the 33rd seemed likely to take part. Wesley resigned his parliamentary seat, found an affluent linen-draper who was prepared to deal with his Dublin debts, but then heard that his regiment was not to go after all. Then came good news: Lord Moira's force would indeed include the 33rd, and would be sent to reinforce the Duke of York's little army in Flanders. It was accompanied, as good news so often is, by bad. Lord Longford wrote to say that he was firmly resolved that a match with Kitty was impossible. Wesley, however, could not accept the decision as final for, as it was based on 'prudential motives', a change in his own circumstances might yet win him Kitty. He wrote and told her that if her brother ever relented, 'my mind will still remain the same'.[27]

Wesley sailed from Cork in early June 1794 and arrived at Ostend on the 25th to join a campaign which had started with a flicker of promise but was already turning sour. The British government, trying hard to repair the damage done to its army by peacetime parsimony, had enlisted men as quickly as it could for the war against revolutionary France. The historian Sir John Fortescue reckoned that at least 30,000 men were enlisted into the regular army between November 1793 and March 1794.[28]

Amongst them was a corps of waggoners, the army's first military transport unit, known from the colour of its uniform and the supposed origin of its members as 'The Newgate Blues'. 'A greater set of scoundrels never disgraced an army,' complained an officer on the Duke of York's staff.

The consequences of this rapid expansion were little short of disastrous. There were too few muskets: the 31st Regiment was composed chiefly of recruits, 240 of whom were unarmed. Many soldiers had not been issued with proper uniforms, but went to war in their 'slop-clothing', the barrack dress of linen jacket and trousers they received when they arrived at their depots. A high proportion of officers and men were poorly trained. Private William Surtees of the 56th Regiment was delighted to be posted to his battalion's light company 'as I considered it . . . an honour to be made a light-bob', but was given no specialist training, and when he met properly trained French light infantry, he discovered that they 'had greatly the advantage over us in point of shooting . . .'[29] Fortescue complained that too many officers had attained their rank through exactly that mixture of patronage and purchase that had enabled Wesley to command a battalion at the age of 24 without any formal training:

> The commanders of the new army, who had been juggled into seniority by the Government and the army-brokers, were not fit to command a company, much less a brigade. Some of them were boys of twenty-one who knew nothing of their simplest duties. Though they went cheerfully into action, they looked upon the whole campaign as an elaborate picnic . . . Thrust into the army to satisfy the claims of dependants, constituents, importunate creditors, and discarded concubines, many of these young men were at once a disgrace and an encumbrance to the force.[30]

The Duke of York's Anglo-Hanoverian force was fighting along-side an Austrian army under the Prince of Coburg, and the future major general, John Gaspard Le Marchant (his birth in the Channel Islands accounting for his Gallic name), reckoned that the Austrians were 'as superior to us as we are to the train-bands in the city'.[31] The allies took Valenciennes in 1793 but then spent a terrible winter, worsened for the British by the government's diversion of resources to the West Indies and the Mediterranean. By the time Wesley arrived, the French had launched a counter-offensive. Wesley, temporarily commanding a brigade containing the 8th and 44th in addition to his own regiment, was left to check the French at Ostend while Moira took the rest of the force on to join the Duke of York. With Moira safely away, Wesley deftly re-embarked his brigade and had it moved by sea to Antwerp, whence he joined the Duke of York before the rest of Moira's force marched in. The episode demonstrated to him the enormous advantage conferred by seapower, especially when confronting an enemy who seemed supreme on land.

In mid-September 1794 Wesley had his baptism of fire just east of Breda. On the 14th, the French attacked the Duke of York's advanced post at Boxtel on the River Dommel, and captured it and two battalions of German troops. The duke sent Major General Sir Ralph Abercromby with ten battalions of infantry and ten squadrons of cavalry to recover the place next day, but Abercromby almost collided with the main French force, slipping past eastwards, and was lucky to escape with the loss of ninety men, most of them prisoners. The 33rd helped check the attack, waiting quietly in line until their young colonel gave the order to fire on an approaching column. He had already learnt a valuable lesson about sea-power, and now he learnt another, about the merits of steady lines facing exuberant columns. Both were to prove invaluable.

Abercromby, whose bushy eyebrows gave him the air of a bene-
volent lion, called on Wesley a few days later to convey 'the Duke
of York's thanks and his to the Thirty-third for their good conduct
on the 15th'.[32] The army retreated in terrible weather, and Wesley,
commanding a brigade once more, found himself defending the
line of the River Waal, whence he wrote to Mornington to say
that he doubted if even the French army could keep the field in
such conditions, and if the army went into winter quarters, he
would be back in Ireland to deal with some problems on the
family's much-reduced estates. But winter quarters were a reflection of a more measured age, and the French kept up the pressure.
'We turn out once, sometimes twice every night; the officers and
men are harassed to death . . .' wrote Wesley. 'I have not had the
clothes off my back for a long time, and generally spend the greater
part of the night upon the bank of the river.'[33] It was small wonder
that he was plagued by a return of an old illness, an 'aguish
complaint from fatigue, damp etc' which his doctor treated with
pills containing 'three grains of Calomel combined with three
grains of the Cathartic Extract'. He was on the Waal from October
1794 to January 1795, and was only once visited by a general from
headquarters. And when he rode over to headquarters, thirty miles
away, he found it 'a scene of jollifications'. A dispatch arrived
while the port was circulating, and was airily waved away by a
general who declared that it would keep till tomorrow. Wesley
concluded that it was the leaders who were at fault, not their
wretched and half-starved men. 'Many of the regiments were
excellent,' he recalled, but:

> no one knew anything of the management of an army
> . . . We had letters from England, and I declare that those
> letters told us more of what was passing at headquarters
> than we learned from the headquarters themselves . . .

The real reason why I succeeded in my own campaigns is because I was always on the spot – I saw everything, and did everything myself.[34]

The army fell back to Bremen, whence it was to be evacuated by the navy, in appalling circumstances.

Far as the eye could reach over the whitened plain were scattered gun-limbers, wagons full of baggage, of stores, of sick men, sutlers' carts and private carriages. Beside them lay the horses, dead; around them scores and hundreds of soldiers, dead; here a straggler who had staggered onto the bivouac and dropped to sleep in the arms of the frost; there a group of British and Germans around an empty rum-cask; here forty English Guardsmen huddled together around a plundered wagon; there a pack-horse with a woman lying alongside it, and a baby, swathed in rags, peeping out of the pack, with its mother's milk turned to ice upon its lips – one and all stark, frozen, dead.[35]

Wesley sailed for England in March 1795, with his regiment close behind. The campaign marked the nadir of British fortunes. It embodied the characteristics often seen in the British army at the beginning of long conflicts: all the strains caused by rapid expansion, and commanders who failed to appreciate that the nature of war had changed. That dreadful winter in Holland taught Wesley much about war. It may not have told him what to do, but, as he observed later, he had 'learnt what not to do, and that is always something'.

It was less than clear what the returning hero should do with himself, for pay as lieutenant colonel and aide-de-camp brought in only £500 a year and creditors abounded. Leaving his regiment encamped in Essex, he set off for Dublin in search of money and preferment. Trim dutifully returned him as its MP once more, and he laid siege to the new lord-lieutenant, Lord Camden, with supporting fire provided by his brother Mornington. He first hoped to be made secretary at war in the Irish government, which would have tripled his income at a stroke, but was soon forced to admit to Camden that: 'I see the manner in which the Military Offices are filled and I don't wish to ask for that which I know you can't give me.' This being the case, he changed his line of attack, now aiming for a civil office in the Treasury or Revenue boards, with the hand-wringing assurance that 'nothing but the circumstances under which I labour would induce me to trouble Your Excellency's Government'.[36] When this assault also failed, Mornington proposed him as surveyor-general of the ordnance, an unhelpful shot as the post was already held by Kitty's uncle, Captain Thomas Pakenham. Camden actually offered Wesley the post, and although he felt obliged to turn it down, the Pakenhams were not best pleased.

Firmly rebuffed, Wesley returned to his regiment, now at Southampton under orders to sail for the West Indies. He was pursued by a well-meaning letter from Lord Camden, who would be sorry to lose him but:

> approve of your determination to accompany your reg't to the West Indies, as I am convinced that a profession once embraced should not be given up. I shall be very glad if I can make some satisfactory arrangement for you against your come back, but if a vacancy should happen in the Revenue Board I fear the Speaker's son must have the first.[37]

The 33rd embarked for the West Indies but a providential storm drove the fleet back to port after seven unpleasant weeks. Wesley was first quartered in Poole, but then went to convalesce in Dublin as his old agues returned. In the meantime, in the spring of 1796 with one of those sudden changes for which Whitehall is not unknown, the 33rd was sent, not to the West Indies, but to India.

Wesley, promoted colonel by seniority with effect from 3 May 1796, was determined to follow it, but there were arrangements to be made first. He resigned his seat and left advice on its management for his successor; received an assurance from Dublin Castle that it 'should be very happy to relieve his mind from the embarrassment it feels on account of some pecuniary arrangements which he was obliged to leave unsettled'; but was pressed by his agent to ensure that Lord Mornington would deal with the £955 4s 8d of outstanding bills if something unpleasant happened. His future adversary Napoleon, now a *général de division* and just appointed to command the army of Italy, always rated luck as a great military virtue, and there is no doubt that Wesley was lucky that spring. He had escaped a voyage to the West Indies and an unhappy destiny in a yellow fever cemetery, and fortunate in leaving Ireland when he did. For, even in 1796, there was rebellion in the air: Grattan felt it 'creeping in like a mist at the heels of the countryman'. The rebellion of 1798 was to be, as Thomas Pakenham has written, 'the most violent and tragic event in Irish history between the Jacobite wars and the Great Famine'.[38] The 'Year of Liberty' cost perhaps 30,000 men and women their lives, and in its aftermath Britain imposed on Ireland a union whose troubled legacy still persists. It was a good time to leave.

TWO

SEPOY GENERAL

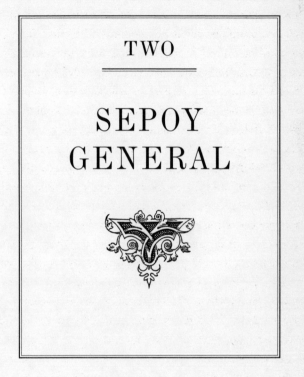

THE INDIA for which Colonel Wesley set sail from Portsmouth in June 1796 was not yet a British possession, though his efforts were to help make it one. In 1600, Elizabeth I had given a royal charter to 'The Company of Merchants of London trading into the East Indies', and eight years later some of its merchants established a trading post at Surat, 150 miles north of modern Bombay. Over the next century the Company's fortunes ebbed and flowed, with occasional conflict with the Dutch, Portuguese and French, who had their own mercantile interests in the subcontinent. It continued to jockey for favour with the Moghul emperor in his capital, first in Agra and then in Delhi, as well as with local rulers whose dependence on the emperor was often little more than nominal.

Madras was settled by the Company in 1639; in 1687 Bombay superseded Surat as the Company's headquarters in western India; and in 1690 one of its agents founded the future city of Calcutta. These three great trading bases, termed presidencies, were run by a governor and council answerable to the Company's court of directors in London, backed by locally recruited soldiers stiffened with British redcoats. It was a short step from defending trading bases to extending British power into the hinterland, and in 1757 Robert Clive defeated the ruler of Bengal at Plassey, a battle in which the deft bribery of opponents was at least as important as firepower. After Plassey the East India Company was a major political power in India, and in 1773 the Regulating Act acknowledged the fact by instituting a governing council in Calcutta, with three of its five members nominated by the British government. The council was presided over by a governor-general, who enjoyed ill-defined authority in both Madras and Bombay. It was indicative of the vast riches to be gained in India that the first governor-general, Warren Hastings, amassed a personal fortune of perhaps £200,000 at a time when a prosperous merchant in England might house and feed his family and servants for £350 a year.[1]

Not all young men who took the passage to India hoped to do quite as well as Hastings, but it was easy for a junior clerk to turn a small investment into a huge fortune without much effort and to return home as a nabob, a figure pilloried by playwrights and novelists as vulgar, corrupt and obscenely wealthy. Sir Philip Francis won £20,000 at cards at a single sitting, and a Mr Barwell lost a staggering £40,000. In 1777 William Hickey, an engaging young rake sent to India to make his fortune, complained that no man worked harder than he did, staying at his desk from eight in the morning till one in the afternoon with only half an hour off for breakfast. Although he was not a rich man by Calcutta standards, he maintained sixty-three servants, as well as 'a handsome phaeton and a beautiful pair of horses, and also two Arabian saddle horses, my whole establishment being of the best and most expensive kind'.[2] Charles Danvers died in 1720 after only three years in India at a salary of £5 a year, but left enough money to have a lavish funeral. He modestly asked the governor 'that I may have as many great guns fired as I am years old, which is now almost twenty-one' and the rest of his estate was to be spent on rice, distributed daily to the poor at his burial place.[3]

Although there were financial risks, for a cargo might go to the bottom or be snapped up by pirates, privateers or enemy warships, the climate and disease were infinitely more dangerous. Europeans who survived the sea voyage – followed, at Madras, by a scarcely less hazardous passage through the surf – risked death from cholera, typhoid, dysentery and sunstroke, snakes, tigers, enraged 'fanaticks', resentful servants and merciless duellists, and undermined their constitutions by eating and drinking to excess. The walls of Indian churches are heavy with marble plaques and Latin tags lamenting death in its many forms, and cantonment cemeteries, so many of them sinking silently back into jungle, are a chilling reminder of human frailty. William Hickey could not resist making a joke of one tombstone:

> Mynheer Gludenstack lies interred here
> Who intended to have gone home last year.

The British cemetery at Seringapatam was established in 1805, not long after the British took the place, and now lies forgotten behind the Fort View Hotel. The tombs inside range from enormous obelisks, one commemorating the garrison commander and another the colonel of the Swiss Regiment de Meuron (a long way from his valleys), to more modest slabs. A sergeant's wife, dead at twenty-two, lies there with her child, and the wife of a private in HM's 9th Lancers evidently had enough money to bestow on her husband in death a status that had eluded him in life. Some died shortly after their arrival in India or, more poignantly still, in the world itself. Others – a retired park-sergeant here and colonel's widow there – had lived on to a ripe old age. There were indeed fortunes to be made in India, but more than half of the Europeans who went there in the eighteenth century died prematurely.

Colonel Wesley, travelling in a fast frigate, caught up with his regiment at the Cape, and he sailed on in the Indiaman *Princess Charlotte*, whiling away his time with his extensive library. It was weighted heavily towards Indian themes, and included Orme's *Indostan*, *Sketches of the Hindoos*, Raynal's *Histoire des Indes* and *Statutes Relative to the East India Company*, as well as Persian and Arabic grammars. There was a good deal of military history, including a book on the Flanders campaign, fifteen volumes on Frederick the Great and Major General Lloyd's formalistic *Reflections on the General Principles of War*. Chapman's *Venereal Disease* might have been a sensible precaution, while nine volumes of *Woman of Pleasure* and ten of the *Aventures du Chevalier du Faublas* catered for lighter moments. He landed in Calcutta in February 1797 and called on the governor-general, Sir John Shore, who found in him 'a union of strong sense and boyish playfulness', and predicted that he would distinguish himself if the opportunity arose.

Wesley lost no chance to chase the opportunity. Both Holland and Spain had now joined the war against Britain, and in August 1797 he was sent on an expedition to the Philippines. He drew up a list of hygiene precautions to be observed by the men. Hammocks were to be scrubbed at least once a fortnight, men were to wash their legs and feet every morning and if possible to have water thrown over them every day. He had agreed to take the Rev. Mr Blunt as chaplain to the 33rd, but during the voyage that gentleman got 'abominably drunk, and in that disgraceful condition exposed himself to both soldiers and sailors . . . talking all sorts of bawdy and ribaldry . . .' When Wesley, on another vessel, heard what had happened he tried to console Blunt, explaining that 'what had passed was not of the least consequence as no one would think the worse of him for little irregularities committed in a moment of forgetfulness', but Blunt's depression could not be lifted and 'he actually fretted himself to death'.[4]

The expedition was recalled when it reached Penang, and Wesley had returned to Calcutta by November. After his return William Hickey dined with him and John Cope Sherbrooke, the 33rd's second lieutenant colonel, at a party consisting of 'eight as strong-headed fellows as could be found in Hindustan'. After twenty-two bumper toasts, they drank steadily till two in the morning: Hickey never experienced 'a more severe debauch'.[5] However, Wesley had by now heard news likely to ease even the worst hangover: his brother Mornington was being sent out to Calcutta as governor-general of British India. Richard was climbing as hard as he could, pressing Pitt for a marquessate, improving his coat of arms by judicious quarterings, and changing the spelling of the family name back to a form used until the seventeenth century. On 19 May 1798 Arthur, now down at Madras, signed himself Wellesley for the first time in a letter to Lieutenant General George Harris, commander-in-chief there, announcing that the new governor-general had just arrived. The three brothers, for Henry had also come to serve as Mornington's private secretary, sailed on to Calcutta. Arthur first acted as unofficial chief of staff to Richard, and was then sent to Madras with the 33rd to press ahead with preparations for war.

The impact of Richard's arrival as governor-general on Arthur's career can scarcely be overstated. India contained many more senior officers, but as the governor-general's brother, he enjoyed great advantages in a world where patronage counted for so much. Mere influence could never cause the dull to shine, but it could give a bright man the opportunity to make his way. That is precisely what it did for Arthur Wellesley, and we should not be astonished that it caused great resentment amongst the less well-connected.

We might be more surprised by the level of Arthur's own confidence. Andrew Roberts is right to observe that while it was possible to write a long book on Napoleon's early career, not much could be said of Arthur Wesley until he took the 33rd to Flanders. By 1798, however, he was not only confident in his profession, but was capable of helping his brother hustle the governor of Madras along the road to war. His correspondence reveals the importance of the family nexus, in which Henry played an important role as go-between, but also shows not the least glimmer of self-doubt. Experience was soon to teach Arthur Wellesley that he might be let down by others – Richard amongst them – but he had utter confidence in himself and he never lost it.

Mornington had arrived already convinced that British India should be expanded. This was not simply a matter of personal ambition, although it could only accelerate his rise, but it would also contribute to the public good, enhancing the Company's trading position, damaging French interests and, in a paternalistic sense, bringing good and settled government to more of the native population. He acted quickly to re-establish Britain's influence over the Nizam of Hyderabad, nominally a liegeman of the Moghul emperor, who ruled a huge tract of central southern India. This was accomplished by the end of October 1798, leaving Mornington free to concentrate on a more dangerous target – Tipoo Sultan, the Tiger of Mysore.

Tipoo was the son of Hyder Ali, a Muslim who had seized the largely Hindu and vast southern state of Mysore. He had fought the British before and in 1790–92 he had been defeated by a previous governor-general, Lord Cornwallis, and was compelled

AFGHANS

MARATHA CONFEDERACY

NEPAL

• Delhi

• Agra

Oudh

Bengal

• Indore

Calcutta

• Baroda

• Surat

Nagpoor

Bombay

Aurungabad •

• Poona

Hyderabad

Hyderabad

Circars

Goa •

Masulipatam

Mysore

Bay of Bengal

Mangalore •

Seringapatam •

Arcot • Madras

Cannanore •

Pondicherry

Arabian Sea

Tanjore

Travancore Carnatic

British India – March 1805

CEYLON

British since 1796, but not part of India

British territory 1796

Territory added by the Wellesleys by July 1805

0   100   200   300   400 miles

N

British India March 1805

to cede part of his territory. Unabashed, Tipoo had a mechanical model depicting a British officer being mauled by a tiger, which made the appropriate growls when set in motion. His habit of keeping his captives chained upright in a dungeon that flooded regularly, leaving them up to their necks in water, did not endear him to the British. Neither did his warm relations with the French, to whom he was Citizen Tipoo. Although French power in India had been broken during the Seven Years War, French agents and military advisers were active in several Indian courts and the prospect of a French revival was disconcerting. Less than a month after his arrival, Mornington read a proclamation by the governor of French Mauritius announcing an alliance between Tipoo and France.

In contrast to the views of his adversaries, Tipoo is affectionately remembered in Madras as a devout Muslim who practised religious toleration; a ruler anxious to enhance the economic strength of his state; an intellectual with a lively scientific interest; and a brave man who did not flinch from a death he might easily have avoided. His interest in technology had led him to develop rockets that resembled large versions of the familiar firework. Some of them were small enough to be carried in a quiver on a man's back, and others were carried in carts fitted with adjustable frames from which they could be fired. The larger ones probably had a range of a thousand yards, and although they were inaccurate, they were terrifying to troops who were not used to them.

Arthur Wellesley and the 33rd sailed from Calcutta to Madras in August 1798. It was a dreadful voyage: their ship, the Indiaman *Fitzwilliam*, ran into a shoal and only the exertions of the soldiers got her out. The water aboard was so bad that although Wellesley himself was only afflicted with the flux, fifteen of his soldiers died. While still in Calcutta he had been trying to persuade Lord Clive, the newly arrived governor of Madras, that Mornington was not set on an immediate and unwarranted war, but after he reached Madras he worked hard to draw Clive into the war party. The governor was nicknamed 'Puzzlestick' by the Wellesleys, although Arthur wrote that 'I doubt whether he is as dull as he appears, or as people think he is.' Arthur found this sort of work uncongenial, and told Henry that he would consider becoming governor of Ceylon if there was no war. Then, gradually, Clive yielded to the pressure. Wellesley wrote to Henry that:

> Now that he has begun to find out that he has no difficulty in transacting the business of the government, he improves daily, takes more upon himself, and will very shortly have less need for the opinions and abilities of those who have long done the business of the country.[6]

Clive's senior civil servant, Josiah Webb, continued to oppose war, arguing that the British were less prepared for what would necessarily be a more extensive campaign than the one in which Lord Cornwallis had beaten Tipoo in 1790–92, but Wellesley argued that proper preparation would overcome many of the difficulties. Meanwhile, relations between Mornington and Tipoo worsened, with the governor-general writing sharply to the sultan that:

> You cannot imagine me to be indifferent to the transactions which have passed between you and the enemies of my country; nor does it appear necessary, or proper, that I should any longer conceal from you the surprise and concern with which I perceived you disposed to involve yourself in all the ruinous consequences of a connexion, which threatens not only to subvert the foundations of friendship between you and the Company, but to introduce into the heart of your kingdom

the principles of anarchy and confusion, to shake your
own authority, to weaken the obedience of your subjects
and to destroy the religion which you revere.[7]

Arthur's own role in the war that now seemed almost inevitable
was at first unclear. Detailed military preparations were in the
hands of Colonel Henry Harvey Ashton of HM's 12th Regiment
and Lieutenant Colonel Barry Close of the Company's service.
The former was a few days senior to Wellesley, and was described
by a subaltern as:

> a great fox-hunter, a patron of the fancy, and a leading
> member of sporting circles. He had many good points
> about him; he was generous and brave, but he had a
> most inveterate disposition to quizzing, which involved
> him in many personal encounters, whereby he obtained
> the reputation of a professed duellist.[8]

Wellesley turned the 33rd over to his second-in-command, Major
John Shee – not a wholly satisfactory arrangement, for in March
the following year he wrote sharply to Shee that he had seen some
of the regiment's soldiers away from their battalion as it formed
up, some of them without their muskets. Shee's response was
intemperate and offensive, and Wellesley warned him that he
would show any similar letter to the commander-in-chief. However, he concluded that:

> I have no intention whatever of doing anything which
> can have any effect unpleasant to your feelings, and that
> the best method of coming to such an understanding as
> we ought to live upon is, to inquire before you act in
> consequence of anything that passes. Of this you may be
> certain, that however my attention may be engaged by

other objects, whenever I find it necessary I shall interfere in everything that concerns the 33rd.[9]

When Wellesley joined General Harris's staff he was over-shadowed by Ashton and Close. Then, in December 1798 Ashton was seriously wounded in a duel with his senior major. Wellesley rode from Madras to Arnee, in the army's forward concentration area, to take command. Ashton lived long enough to give him his grey Arab charger Diomed: then, on 23 December 1798, he died. Wellesley, now in charge of the troops in the Arnee–Vellore–Arcot area set about the careful logistic preparation that was to become his hallmark. It is 250 hot and jungly miles from Madras to Mysore as the crow flies, and more on the primitive roads along which the army would have to travel. The force had both British and Indian units, and both relied heavily on purchasing food in local bazaars, which were soon exhausted by the unprecedented demand. Wellesley encouraged merchants to bring in goods from a wide area, and arranged for them to accompany the army when it moved, because it would be impossible for such a large force to live off the land. Contracts were agreed with 'brinjarries', described by Wellesley as 'a class of carriers who gain a livelihood by transporting grain and other commodities from one part of the country to another. They attend armies, and trade nearly in the same manner as they do in common times of peace.' They maintained their own bullock-trains, so that the army could be supplied with grain without the need to buy its own bullocks.

Lastly, when the army reached Seringapatam, the modern fortress close to Mysore, it would need heavy siege guns to batter the walls, and by early 1799, Wellesley had assembled two 24-pdrs, thirty 18-pdrs and eight long 9-pdrs, complete with 1,200 rounds per gun. Daily battalion drill was instituted, and Wellesley ensured that battalions were combined into brigades and gained experience of drilling together. There was even target practice with live ammunition.

Mornington arrived in Madras on 31 December 1798. He had originally hoped that General Sir Alured Clarke, commander-in-chief of all British troops in India, would command the expedition, but the situation in the north was unstable and so Clarke had been left in Calcutta. The honest and hardworking George Harris, commander-in-chief of the Madras army, was offered the command, but did not immediately take it. Modesty and lack of self-interest, combined with a recognition of the very real difficulties confronting the force, caused him to delay, but eventually he accepted because he considered it his duty to do so. Arthur Wellesley was no less aware of the difficulties, and on 2 January 1799, he told his brother Henry that the proposals made to Tipoo ought to be moderate, because he doubted if the war could be won in a single campaign, primarily because of the shortage of grain. He was somewhat more optimistic a week later, although he complained bitterly that he had been sent two Company's officers to help, 'one of them ... so stupid that I can make no use of him, and the other such a rascal that half my occupation consists of watching him'.[10]

Although the governor-general was no soldier, he seriously considered accompanying the army, and got Henry to consult Arthur on the matter. Arthur firmly advised him against it:

> it appears to me that your presence in the camp, instead of giving confidence to the General, would in fact deprive him of the command of the army ... if I were in General Harris's situation and you were to join the army, I should quit it.
>
> In my opinion, he is at present awkwardly situated,

and he will require all the powers which can be given him to keep in order the officers who will be in this army. Your presence will diminish his powers, at the same time that, as it is impossible you can know anything of military matters, your powers will not answer this purpose . . .[11]

Arthur's loyalty to Harris was rewarded by particular praise for his 'masterly arrangements in respect to supplies'. However, Harris told Arthur that he was reluctant to commend him publicly because 'others would be displeased and jealous', and Arthur himself admitted that, because of his relationship with the governor-general, others in the army thought him 'very little better than a spy'.[12]

The governor-general took his brother's wise advice, and remained in Madras whence, on 3 February 1799 he ordered an advance into Tipoo's territory, with Harris moving up from the east with more than 20,000 troops, 4,300 of them European, while a smaller force from the Bombay army under Lieutenant General James Stuart advanced eastwards from the Malabar coast. Harris reached Amboor on 18 February, and was joined there by a contingent of the Nizam of Hyderabad's army. There were four Hyderabad infantry battalions under Captain John Malcolm, with a mixture of British and Indian officers, a large force of Moghul cavalry – 'some good, some bad', wrote Wellesley – under Captain Patrick Walker, and thirty-six guns. The Company provided six infantry battalions, four from Madras and two from Bengal. The force was commanded by the Nizam's chief minister (and perhaps son), Mir Allum. It was proposed to provide him with a senior adviser, and to stiffen his force with a British battalion. Wellesley and the 33rd were the logical choices, not least because Mir Allum, aware that Wellesley was the governor-general's brother, actually asked for him.

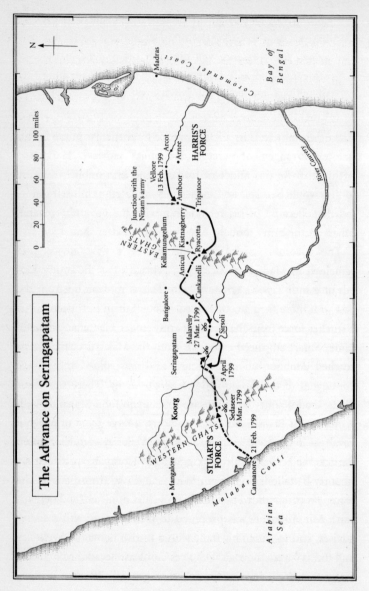

The Advance on Seringapatam

The arrangement did not please everybody. Three of the four major generals in Harris's army enjoyed substantial commands, but the fourth, David Baird, commanded a brigade far smaller than the Hyderabad force. Baird was a brave but tetchy Scot, one of whose officers called him 'a bloody old bad-tempered Scotchman'. He got on badly with Indians, and his temper had not been improved by his long imprisonment by Tipoo in the previous war. Hearing that he was kept shackled to another prisoner, Baird's mother observed that she was sorry for the man who was chained to her Davie. Baird complained to Harris that he should have been given the Hyderabad appointment, but Harris stuck to his decision.

The advance resumed on 21 February. The army was still in British-controlled territory, and the road had been carefully prepared. Nevertheless, progress was slow, perhaps ten miles a day, with a day's halt every three, and it was not until 6 March that the main force at last entered Tipoo's territory. When Cornwallis had invaded along the same route eight years earlier, Tipoo had defended Bangalore, but this time he demolished its defences and his troops fell back westwards, burning the crops as they went. This was a sound strategy, if a harsh one, for if there was no fodder for the bullocks in Harris's army, the expedition could not succeed: it was the failure of supply that had forced Cornwallis to abandon his advance on Seringapatam in 1791. Tipoo's irregular cavalry – Wellesley thought them 'the best kind in the world' – hung about Harris's columns as they advanced, ready to exploit any gaps in the line of march, and making it impossible for all but the strongest of foraging parties to leave the main body.

On 10 March, enemy cavalry attacked Wellesley's rearguard near Kellamungellum and overran a half-company of Madras infantry. Wellesley personally led the decisive counter-attack and was never pressed as hard afterwards. It was now clear that the main route to Bangalore was so badly ravaged that even the brinjarries were finding it hard to feed their bullocks, and Harris wisely swung south-west towards Cankanelli, heading directly for Seringapatam, and moving across country that Tipoo's men had not had time to burn. Progress was still painfully slow, largely because of pay disputes amongst the Company's bullock-drivers. There was good news from the west, however. On 15 March, Harris heard that Stuart's column had beaten off a full-scale attack at Sedaseer, and that Tipoo's army had recoiled eastwards. Harris's force continued to trudge forwards across flat, fertile land laced with groves of trees known as topes.

Early on 27 March 1799, Harris set out for Malavelly, a straggling village six miles away from his previous camp; it contained abundant water and so was to be that evening's campsite. It is unusually difficult to be sure of what happened, for contemporary accounts are unclear, and Malavelly itself has since straggled more widely. But what seems certain is that a large part of Tipoo's main army, with two heavy guns, had taken up a position on a low ridge west of the village, blocking the main road. Although the quartermaster-general's men were already laying out the camp in Malavelly, Harris decided to give battle as soon as he could, for if he defeated this section of Tipoo's army, there would be less of it to defend Seringapatam. His force moved with its British contingent to the north of the road, and the Hyderabad army to the south; both columns preceded by cavalry and infantry outposts, the latter, 'the pickets of the day', drawn from all the infantry regiments.

The British force swung north-west of Malavelly, shaking out from column of march into line as it did so, though with natural obstacles ensuring that instead of all three leading brigades being side by side, they advanced with one up and two back. The Hyderabad army, perhaps five miles further south, also swung into line, each battalion moving in column, with its individual companies in column, one behind the other, with enough space between them to deploy into battalion line when the time came. HM's 33rd was to the right front, near the main road, and the Company's battalions were echeloned back to its left, each about 200 yards behind the one on its right. The Hyderabad battalions probably formed a reserve. Wellesley, mounted on Diomed, galloped along his line, checking that the spacings were correct and noting that the 33rd was now just ahead of the leading British brigade, across the road to its right. As he ascended the gentle ridge held by Tipoo's men, he ordered his battalions to form line of battle, and quickly the advancing force completed its deployment into a long two-deep line.

Thus far Tipoo's position had been marked by occasional puffs of white smoke as the cannon fired, but now a large force of infantry, 2–3,000 strong, came down the hill, making straight for the 33rd. What followed was a repeat of what had happened at Boxtel in 1794, and was the precursor of what was to occur in dozens of future encounters. Wellesley ordered the 33rd to halt, and then gave the order to fire. Although the Mysore troops 'behaved better than they have ever been known to behave', the measured volleys were too much for them, and although they 'almost stood the charge of bayonets of the 33rd', they took to their heels. On the other side of the road, Tipoo's cavalry charged Baird's brigade, but this was only to gain time so that the rest of his army could retreat, and it slipped away before Harris's jaws could close around it.

Harris continued his advance on 28 March, swinging south to cross the broad River Cauvery not far from Sirsoli and then turning north to approach Seringapatam, neatly outflanking Tipoo's field army as he did so. Tipoo, his confidence already shaken by defeats at Sedaseer and Malavelly, withdrew into the fortress. Seringapatam lies on an island in the Cauvery. At that time of year the river was almost dry, and both of its branches, the North and South Cauvery, could be crossed on foot with little difficulty. But things were very different in the rainy season, when the water was too deep for fording but too fast-flowing for boats to be used easily. With the change of seasons approaching, Harris needed to take the place by the end of May.

I first saw Seringapatam from across the South Cauvery just east of the main river's fork, and it looks hugely impressive despite the passage of two centuries. White granite walls, their tops pierced with splayed brick-lined embrasures, rise thirty feet from a broad, wet ditch, invisible until an attacker is right on top of it. An inner belt of fortifications would have given the garrison some respite against an attacker who had penetrated the outer defences, and the main gates – the Bangalore gate to the east, the Mysore gate to the south, and the Water gate fronting the North Cauvery – are still entered through wide tunnels between layered defences. The tower of the Hindu temple and the twin towers of the mosque rise above the defences, and a scattering of palm trees lends an exotic air to the place.

Although the design of Seringapatam shows some Western influence, we cannot expect Tipoo's French military advisers to have been hugely enthusiastic about it. Whereas European engineers, following the precepts of the great Vauban, strove to conceal most of their masonry behind a gently sloping earth glacis so that the attacker's guns would have little to shoot at, the long, high walls of Seringapatam offered a vulnerable target. And though some of the fortress guns were mounted on high works jutting out from the front of the main line of the wall, these were not well developed enough to be bastions – the great arrowhead-shaped

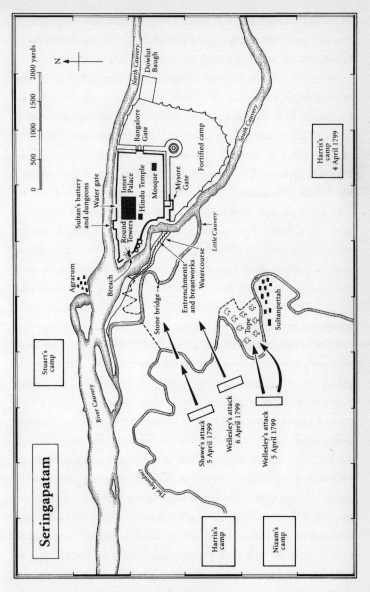

Seringapatam

defences that were the essence of European artillery fortification. The former offered only a poor prospect of bringing flanking fire to bear on an attacker assaulting the main line of the wall.

On 5 April 1799, the British completed their march, having taken thirty-one days in all to cover what they had measured as 153.5 miles from the Madras frontier. Harris proceeded to encamp south of the Cauvery, two miles west of Seringapatam. His army was too small to surround the place and mount a formal siege, and, with time of the essence, he planned to breach the fortress's south-west face rather than attempt to secure a footing on the island further east. That day Wellesley wrote optimistically to the governor-general that 'we are now here with a strong, a healthy and a brave army, with plenty of stores, guns, &c., &c., and we shall be masters of this place before much more time passes over our heads'. He added that the fatigue, heat and bad water had given him a bowel complaint, 'which did not confine me, but teased me much'.[13]

He was teased a good deal more that night. On the afternoon of the 5th, Harris ordered him to carry out a night attack on the village of Sultanpettah and a nearby grove known as Sultanpettah Tope, using his own 33rd and two Madras battalions, while Lieutenant Colonel Shawe of HM's 12th and two other Madras battalions launched a similar attack further north. The two features stood astride an aqueduct, slightly south of the army's route to Seringa-patam, and would have to be cleared before the main attack could begin. The ground as it stands today gives little real clue to the operation. The village and the grove have gone, and the aqueduct (Wellesley called it a nullah) is now a full-blown drainage canal, steeply banked, with lush paddy-fields below it. Even then the ground was confusing, and Wellesley, on horseback amongst the outposts when the message to attack arrived, asked Harris to meet him in front of the lines to clarify the order, suggesting that 'when you have the nullah you have the tope'. Harris did not come forward – in fairness, he had much else to do – and at sundown Wellesley attacked a position he had not been able to reconnoitre with troops who had also not seen the ground.

He led the 33rd forward in column, with the Madras battalions behind. As they approached the nullah, almost dry at that time of year, they were engaged by Tipoo's rocket men and by musket fire, but carried the nullah with little difficulty. There Wellesley dismounted, and led the grenadier and light companies of the 33rd forward, while Major Shee brought the rest of the battalion on. The patchwork of paddy-fields, dykes and bamboo clumps at the bottom of the slope, previously screened by the banks of the nullah, would have made no sense to the attackers, while they themselves would have been silhouetted against the sky as they climbed over the bank to begin their descent. If Tipoo's infantry could not cope with the 33rd in open field, things were different here, and there was fierce hand-to-hand fighting: Lieutenant Fitzgerald, already hit in the arm by a rocket, was bayonetted and mortally wounded, and eight men of the grenadier company were captured. While the two forward companies fought for their lives, Shee took the remaining companies back across the nullah. Such was the confusion that five of Wellesley's companies eventually joined Shawe to the north, where they helped secure the few gains of another largely unsuccessful attack, while Captain Francis West of the grenadiers emerged further south, where the Hyderabad outposts held the front line.

Wellesley himself got back to the watercourse, where he seems to have remounted and cantered along it, trying to restore order. He was hit on the knee by a spent musket-ball at some stage in the proceedings and, finding that there was little he could do, rode to Harris's headquarters to report his failure. Harris wrote that he 'came to my tent in a good deal of agitation to say that he had not carried the tope. It must be particularly unpleasant to him.' Wellesley, exhausted as much from the expenditure of nervous energy as from the physical effort, lay down on a nearby mess table and went to sleep. The news was far from unpleasant to Wellesley's critics, who resented his closeness to the governor-general and authority over the Hyderabad contingent. Captain George Elers of the 12th, who had fallen out with Wellesley by the time he wrote his memoirs, declared that: 'Had Colonel Wellesley been an obscure officer of fortune, he would have been brought to a court-martial and perhaps received such a reprimand for bad management as might have induced him to have resigned His Majesty's service.'[14]

Yet even Wellesley's bitterest opponents could hardly claim that it was a major setback. There were less than twenty-five British casualties, and the following day Wellesley launched a fresh attack with a larger force, and took the whole position without losing a man. However, the whole scrambling affair left its mark. Wellesley resolved 'never to attack an enemy who is prepared and strongly posted, and whose posts have not been reconnoitred by daylight'.[15] He was also well aware of having lost control of his force, and his almost pathological need to remain in control was reinforced by the incident.

Lieutenant General Stuart's detachment of the Bombay army, which had marched on Seringapatam from the west, arrived on the 14 April, escorted by a force sent out by Harris to meet it. Stuart's force made camp north of the Cauvery, north-west of Seringapatam. After dark on the 17th, both the Madras and Bombay forces launched preliminary attacks, the former securing the Little Cauvery and the latter taking the ruined village of Agrarum and throwing up a battery which, in the event, was just too far west for effective bombardment of Seringapatam. On the morning of the 21st, the Madras force established a battery on newly captured ground between the Little Cauvery and the South Cauvery. Stuart's men were also busy, and threw up batteries to engage the western walls. On the morning of the 26th, British guns took on Tipoo's cannon, and by midday had silenced those facing them. That evening and the next morning, Wellesley, the duty brigade commander, cleared Tipoo's men from the whole area between the Little Cauvery and the South Cauvery, enabling batteries to be established only 400 yards from the walls. They were ordered to concentrate their fire on an area between the westernmost 'bastion' and a pair of towers further south. The gunners' objective was to cut a cannelure – a long groove – towards the base of the masonry, so that the wall and rampart behind it would slide forward, leaving a rough slope of earth and rubble. A breach was deemed practicable when a man could ascend it with his musket and accoutrements without needing to use his hands.

When a practicable breach was established, Major General Baird, who had volunteered for the task, was to lead an assault delivered by two columns, one from Stuart's force and the other from the Mysore army. A third column, under Wellesley, would remain in reserve, to be committed only if there was a significant check. The assault was delivered on the afternoon of 4 May 1799, and although the unexpected strength of the inner defences caused a delay, the attackers fanned out once they were through the breach and were soon fighting deep inside Seringapatam against resistance that was fast collapsing. When it seemed clear that the attack had succeeded, Wellesley posted a guard from the reliable Swiss Regiment de Meuron to secure the breach. Other soldiers helped recover wounded from the river-bed and the breach itself, and the remainder were stood down. Wellesley walked up the breach, with its carpet of dead, and from the top he could see chaos as some soldiers dealt with embers of resistance while others set about looting and drinking. Most of the 33rd was drawn up outside Tipoo's palace, where surrender negotiations were going on. Although it had now been discovered that thirteen British prisoners, including the men of the 33rd captured at Sultanpettah, had been murdered – either by having their necks broken or by having nails driven into their skulls – the occupants of the palace were to be spared, provided that resistance ceased.

Tipoo, however, was not amongst them. Then Wellesley heard that he had been killed in the fighting at the Water gate, and walked the short distance to the northern wall, where he found a long tunnel beneath the ramparts choked with dead. A well-dressed body was dragged out, and Wellesley himself checked the man's pulse: it was Tipoo, and he was indeed dead. Witnesses had seen a short, fat officer play a conspicuous part in the defence, standing to fire at the attackers while retainers passed him loaded weapons. He had been hit several times, and seemed to have been killed by a close-range musket shot through the temple: some said that a British soldier had fancied the jewel in his turban. The Tiger of Mysore had snarled defiantly to the last.

Leaving the grenadiers of the 33rd to protect the palace, Wellesley went out to his brigade, marched it back to camp, washed – he had been in the same clothes for sixty hours in hot weather, and was always a fastidious man – and went to bed. He must, however, have been able to hear shots, yells, and drunken singing from Seringapatam, and the episode reinforced something he already knew. The British soldier had many virtues, not least cold, almost canine, courage and determination, but if discipline wavered and drink was at hand, brave soldiers could turn into drunken animals.

The attackers lost 389 killed or wounded in the assault, and though reports of the number of Mysore dead vary, 8–9,000 were buried. The disparity suggests that the attackers, their mood hardened by the scenes at the breach and the discovery of the murdered prisoners, were not inclined to give quarter. When we later consider Wellesley's inflexible view of discipline, we must remember the sounds that drifted through that sultry night as the victors remorselessly looted and raped in Seringapatam.

Early the next day, Wellesley was ordered to take command of Seringapatam. Baird had already asked to be relieved because he was physically exhausted – although he later claimed to have cancelled this request – and Wellesley, although not, strictly speaking the next brigade commander for duty, was appointed, probably because Barry Close, Harris's adjutant-general, had a high opinion of him. Wellesley went straight to Baird's headquarters in Tipoo's summer palace, outside the fort, and told Baird that he had been superseded. Baird, breakfasting with his staff, snapped 'Come, Gentlemen, we have no longer any business here.' 'Oh,' replied Wellesley, 'pray finish your breakfast.'[16] Wellesley later told John Wilson Croker that:

> I never inquired the reason for my appointment, or for Baird being laid aside. There were many other candidates besides Baird and myself, all senior to me, some to Baird. But I must say that I was the *fit person* to be selected. I had commanded the Nizam's army during the campaign, and had given universal satisfaction. I was liked by the natives.

He added that:

> Baird was a gallant, hard-headed, lion-hearted officer, but he had no talent, no *tact*; had strong prejudices

against the natives; and he was peculiarly disqualified from his manners, habits &c., and it was supposed his temper, for the management of them.

Although Baird fiercely resented his supersession, in 1813 he told Sir John Malcolm that he had long since forgiven Wellesley, and: 'His fame is now to me joy, and I may also say glory, and his kindness to me and mine has all along been most distinguished.'[17]

As soon as Wellesley was in command, he went into Seringapatam to restore order: four soldiers were hanged and others flogged. He was soon writing to Harris that 'plunder is stopped, the fires are all extinguished, and the inhabitants are returning to their houses fast'. He asked Harris 'to order an extra dram and biscuit for the 12th, 33rd and 73rd regiments, who got nothing to eat yesterday, and were wet last night' and emphasised that the place needed a permanent garrison with its own commander. Harris decided that Wellesley was the man for the job. The governor-general had already declared that when Tipoo was beaten, his policy would be one of conciliation, and Wellesley had made a very good start. A commission with military and civilian members had been appointed at the start of the campaign to run affairs in captured territory, and after the fall of Seringapatam a new commission was set up, its members including Arthur and Henry Wellesley.

Although Arthur's direct responsibilities were at first confined to Seringapatam island, he was soon not only head of the commission, but, as the main armies withdrew, the senior military officer in the region. When the commission was dissolved he retained power, warning the governor-general that he would not accept 'any person with civil authority who is not under my orders'. Lieutenant Colonel Barry Close, who he regarded as 'the ablest man in the Company's army' was sent down as Resident, an arrangement which worked well. A five-year-old boy, the closest surviving descendent of the line of Hindu rajahs which had been overthrown by Hyder Ali, was appointed ruler of Mysore, with Purneah, an able man who had served Hyder Ali with distinction, as his chief minister.

Arthur Wellesley had played a principal part in winning a significant victory and had gone on to wield exceptional power for a thirty-year-old colonel. He had also been paid £4,000 of the prize money distributed when the proceeds of the victory were divided up, the shares varying with rank: Harris received £150,000, a British soldier £7, and a sepoy £5. Although Arthur had still not received the allowances to cover his campaign expenses, he immediately offered to repay Mornington 'the money which you advanced to pay my lieutenant-colonelcy, and that which was borrowed from Captain Stapleton on our joint bond'.[18] Richard generously replied that: 'I am not in want of money and probably never shall be: when I am, it will be time enough to call upon you.'[19] But the governor-general was not at his best. Although his hoped-for marquessate had arrived at last, he was Marquess Wellesley of Norragh – in the peerage of Ireland. It was, as he called it, a 'double-gilt potato'. 'As I felt confident there had been nothing Irish or pinchbeck in my conduct or its results,' he wrote, 'I felt an equal confidence that there should be nothing Irish or pinchbeck in its rewards.'[20]

Arthur dealt with the myriad of military and political issues that crossed his writing-desk in Tipoo's cool and spacious summer palace, whose wonderful murals – some of which depicted the British being roundly beaten by Hyder Ali and his French allies – were restored on his orders. He denied a request from a French priest to have 200 Christian women who had been carried off by Tipoo 'in the most indecent and tyrannical manner' returned to their homes. This refusal was, he admitted, unjust, but they were currently living with Tipoo's family, and as the Company had undertaken to protect the family, sending the women home would have been a breach of faith. He pondered the composition of courts, civil and military, though the demonstrative nature of justice was never far from his mind: 'the criminals shall be executed after the facts have been clearly ascertained by an examination of witnesses . . .'[21] He dealt sternly with officers who stole or accepted bribes, and although they sometimes had reason to complain of the slowness of the rajah's government, 'they had none to ill-use any man'. One senior officer whose conduct towards the Indians had caused complaint was warned that 'he must either act as he ought, or he shall be removed from his command'.[22] Yet Wellesley was moved to pity by the case of one of the Company's lieutenant colonels, convicted of 'very serious crimes' before a general court-martial and stripped of his commission. Wellesley observed that when he had repaid the Company the money he owed it, he would be entirely destitute. Wellesley begged the governor of Madras 'to give him some small pension to enable him to support himself, or . . . recommend him for some small provision . . . on account of his long services and his present reduced situation'.[23]

His chief concern, though, was with the assortment of freebooters – 'polygars, nairs, and moplahs' – in arms around the state. His most obdurate opponent was Dhoondiah Waugh, a tough mercenary who had escaped from Tipoo's custody just before Seringapatam fell, recruited a substantial following from amongst Tipoo's former soldiers and other malcontents, and proclaimed himself 'King of the Two Worlds'. He was beaten in 1799 and escaped northwards into Maratha territory, but was back again the following year. In May 1800, Wellesley himself mounted a full-scale campaign against Dhoondiah, his well-organised transport system enabling him to move across a desolate area. Even so there were difficult moments. On 30 June, he told Barry Close that he was a day later than planned in crossing the River Toombnuddra, and its sudden rise delayed him on the south bank for ten days. As no supplies could be brought in, the army ate much of the corn it had with it, and was now held up. 'How true it is,' he mused, 'that in military operations, time is everything.'[24] He systematically took Dhoondiah's fortresses and finally caught up with him at Conaghull, right up on the borders of Hyderabad, on 10 September.

Although Wellesley, pursuing with two regiments of British cavalry and two of Indian, was badly outnumbered, he formed up his little army in a single line and led a charge that routed Dhoondiah's army. Wellesley reported to the adjutant-general in Madras that: 'Many, amongst others, Dhoondiah, were killed; and the whole body dispersed, and were scattered in small parties over the face of the country.'[25] He could be magnanimous in victory. Dhoondiah's young son, Salabut Khan, was found amongst the baggage. Wellesley looked after him, and when he departed from India, he left money for the boy's upkeep with the collector of Seringapatam. Salabut, 'a fine, handsome, intelligent youth', eventually entered the rajah's service and died of cholera in 1822.

In May 1800, Arthur had been offered command of a force to be sent to capture Batavia in the East Indies from the Dutch, but he told his brother that although he would welcome the appointment, it would not be in the public interest for him to leave Mysore until 'its tranquillity is assured'. With Dhoondiah beaten, however, he was able to accept the command and, after assembling a staff, he departed for Ceylon, where he arrived on 28 December. Arthur soon heard that the expedition was to go to Egypt instead, and he duly ordered it to concentrate in Bombay. He was on the way there himself when he heard that his brother, who had anticipated 'great jealousy from the general officers in consequence of my employing you', had been pressed to supersede him with Major General Baird. This was not as unreasonable a decision as Arthur maintained. He was still only a colonel, albeit a senior one, and the governor-general told him privately that 'you must know that I could not employ you in the chief command of so large a force as is now to proceed in Egypt without violating every rule in the service . . .' There were limits to how far Richard could go on his behalf. Baird had been infuriated by his supercession by the governor-general's brother at Seringapatam, and made this very clear in three inter-views with Richard Wellesley. In her sympathetic anecdotal biogra-phy of Arthur, Muriel Wellesley suggests that Richard had no alternative but to act as he did: 'He must either sacrifice his brother, or lose the confidence of those he governed, which he inevitably would do once the stigma of favouritism and partiality were to become attached to him.' There were times when Arthur, like Achilles, was capable of sulking in his tent, and this was one of them.

Right or wrong, he was deeply hurt, and now began his letters to the governor-general not as 'My dear Mornington', but as the coldly official 'My Lord'. He was franker in a letter to their brother Henry:

> I have not been guilty of robbery or murder, and he has certainly changed his mind . . . I did not look, and did not wish, for the appointment which was given me; and I say that it would probably have been more proper to give it to somebody else; but when it was given to me, and a circular written to the governments upon the subject, it would have been fair to allow me to hold it till I did something to deserve to lose it.[26]

Although he was appointed Baird's second-in-command, Wellesley remained in Bombay when the expedition set sail. Although he assured Henry that Baird's conduct towards him was 'perfectly satisfactory', he first suffered from fever, followed by an attack of 'Malabar itch', which obliged him to undergo a regimen of nitrous baths. He knew that the episode would not redound to his credit, and when he felt well enough, he returned to Mysore. Captain George Elers observed that he had begun to grey at the temples and did not laugh as explosively as before. Responsibility followed by disappointment had marked him: 'He may already have forgotten how to play.'[27]

But even now, in the depths of his disappointment, he recovered something of his sparkle. Elers wrote that he kept a 'plain but good' table, and had an excellent appetite, with roast saddle of mutton served with salad as his favourite dish. He was abstemious, drinking only four or five glasses of wine with dinner and 'about a pint of claret' afterwards. 'He was very even in his temper,' wrote Elers, 'laughing and joking with those he liked . . .' He could even smile in the face of adversity. Riding hard for Seringapatam with Elers and a tiny escort through dangerous country, he joked that if they were captured: 'I shall be hanged as being brother to the Governor-General, and you will be hanged for being found in bad company.' Hearing that there had been a promotion of colonels to be major generals, he called for a copy of the Army List, but found that he was not included. He admitted ruefully that his only ambition was 'to be a major general in His Majesty's service'.

When Wellesley returned to Mysore, India was on the verge of another major conflict, this time between the British and the Maratha Confederacy, now the East India Company's principal rival on the subcontinent. The Hindu Marathas controlled the great mass of central India, bordered by the Ganges in the north and Hyderabad in the south, running from the Arabian Sea to the Bay of Bengal, and eventually including Delhi. In 1761 they had been beaten with great loss at Panipat, just outside Delhi, by the Afghan, Ahmad Shah Durrani, Muslim ruler of Kabul. However, they enjoyed a revival after Panipat and in 1778–82, the East India Company fought an inclusive war against them. Thereafter the Company was preoccupied with Mysore, but by 1800 the Maratha state had fragmented into what were, in effect, independent principalities, themselves uniting the fiefs of smaller semi-independent chiefs. The Peshwa Baji Rao, nominally the most senior, ruled at Poona, although his writ ran only around the frontiers of Hyderabad and Mysore. The most powerful of the maharajas was Daulat Rao Scindia, who controlled the northern Maratha lands from his capital at Ujjein, while at Indore, Jeswant Rao Holkar ruled a central slab of land between the Narmada and Godavari Rivers. The Bhonsla Rajah of Berar, with his capital at Nagpur, dominated the south-east Maratha lands. The Gaikwar of Baroda, fifth of the great princes, ruled territory in the west, around the Gulf of Cambay, but was to throw himself onto the Company's protection and play no part in the coming conflict.

The fragmentation of Maratha power was both risk and opportunity for the Company. On the one hand growing instability meant there was a chance of war breaking out while the Company was busy elsewhere – it was for this reason that Sir Alured Clarke had been left in Calcutta when Mornington began his campaign against Tipoo. But, on the other, the Company might be able, as it had elsewhere, to exploit friction between local rulers. Their chance came in 1800, when Holkar defeated the Peshwa and Scindia at Poona. Scindia fell back into his own territory, but the Peshwa fled to Bassein, in British territory, and signed a treaty agreeing to give the Company control over his foreign affairs and to accept (and pay for) a garrison of six of the Company's battalions in return for the Company's help in restoring him to his throne.

The task of restoring the Peshwa was given to Arthur Wellesley in November 1802. He had just heard that he had been gazetted major general on 29 April that year, (news had only reached him in September), and given an appointment on the Madras establishment, where Lieutenant General Stuart, who had led the Bombay army column that fought at Seringapatam, was now commander-in-chief. As he had told Barry Close, soon to be political Resident with the Peshwa, in September 1801, 'before long we may look to war with the Mahrattas'. He had already made a lengthy analysis of the terrain he might have to cover, highlighting the problems of providing food and water and crossing the many rivers that would lie across his path. As usual he delved into detail. He would need 10,000 gallons of arrack (native spirit) for his European troops, and this should be carried in 6 gallon kegs, 'well fortified with iron hoops'. There would also have to be 90,000 lbs of salt meat, 'packed in kegs well fortified, 54lbs in each keg, besides pickle, &c.; and the same quantity of biscuits in round baskets, containing 60lbs each; these baskets to be covered with waxed cloth'.[28]

Major General Wellesley moved off in March 1803, his own army numbering just under 15,000 men, with a Hyderabad force of nearly 9,000 also under his command. He was well aware that his task was to restore the Peshwa but not to bring about a wider war with the Marathas as he did so. In fact, there was no resistance. The careful preparations ensured that the march of some 600 miles was swift, and rigid discipline ensured that local inhabitants were not alienated by plundering. His leading cavalry reached

Poona on 20 April, but the Peshwa would not re-enter his capital till 13 May, when the stars were propitious. Wellesley observed that he was 'a prince, the only principle of whose character is insincerity'. He made heavy weather of re-establishing himself, but at the same time was already negotiating with the other Maratha princes. In May, Holkar raided into Hyderabad territory, replying civilly to Wellesley's letter of remonstrance, stating that the Nizam of Hyderabad owed him money. The Nizam was in fact mortally ill, which induced Stuart in Madras to send troops to Hyderabad to help maintain order. This added to the political tension between the Marathas and the Company. Although open war was still not inevitable, Scindia was striving to draw the other Maratha chiefs into a coalition against the British.

Wellesley, as usual, was preoccupied with his logistics. His line of communication ran back down to Mysore, and although he did his best to ensure against its collapse when the monsoon came – locally-made coracles, 'basket boats', were stockpiled at all likely river-crossings – it would be much easier if he could open a shorter line to Bombay. However, the authorities there lacked his own attention to detail, and sent him pontoons for river-crossing at the moment when the weather broke, and the wagons carrying them foundered on the very first day. Stuart generously told the governor-general that he had no wish to take command, for Wellesley's 'extensive knowledge and influence . . . and his eminent military talents' made him ideally suited for the appointment in which, Stuart was sure, his army would render 'very distinguished services'. Accordingly, in June 1803, an order from Mornington gave Wellesley full military and political authority in central India, and he immediately ordered Colonel John Collins, British Resident at Scindia's camp still on Maratha territory, now close to the Nizam of Hyderabad's fortress of Ajanta, to ask Scindia precisely what he objected to in the treaty of Bassein. Wellesley was prepared to make minor concessions and was anxious not to fire the first shot in a new war. On 25 June, he told Colonel James Stevenson, his principal subordinate, that: 'It will be our duty to carry out the war, with activity, when it shall begin, but it is equally so to avoid hostilities, if we possibly can . . .'[29] On 3 August, Collins reported that Scindia and the Rajah of Berar would give no direct answer to his demands, and had left for the Nizam's nearby fortress of Aurungabad. Welles-ley at once announced that he was obliged to go to war 'in order to secure the interests of the British government and its allies'.[30]

The Maratha armies looked formidable on paper. The core of Scindia's invading force was his regular infantry, about 15,000 strong, which was trained and led by European officers and organ-ised in brigades called 'compoos', including some cavalry and a few guns. Colonel Pohlmann, once a sergeant in a Hanoverian regiment in British service, commanded the largest, with about 7,500 men; the Begum Somroo, widow of a German mercenary who had become one of Scindia's vassals, had recruited a slightly smaller force, commanded on her behalf by Colonel Saleur, and Colonel Baptiste Filoze, of Neapolitan-Indian ancestry, com-manded a third. Scindia's army had about eighty field pieces and a few heavier guns. His irregular troops included 10–20,000 infan-try, and there were something between 30–60,000 light cavalry.

The governor-general had tried to persuade British subjects serving the Marathas to relinquish their posts, promising them employment if they did so and prosecution for treason if they refused. Some were certainly reluctant to fight. 'John Roach Englishman and George Blake Scotsman lately commanding each a gun in the service of the Begum' informed Wellesley that they 'left camp by permission upon remonstrance against being employed to fight' and told their countrymen all they knew.[31]

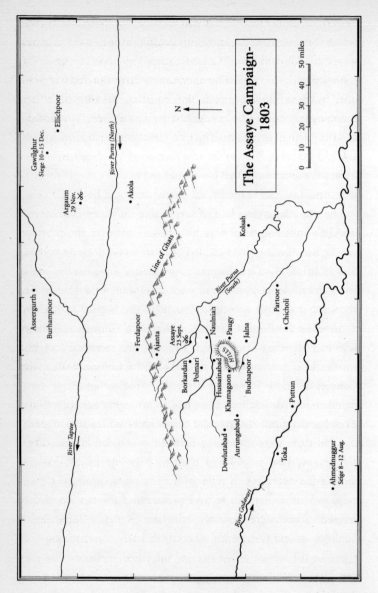

The Assaye Campaign 1803

Stewart, an officer of Pohlmann's compoo, also joined the British as soon as he could, as did Grant, brigade major (chief of staff) to one of the compoos. But some certainly stayed to fight, for Wellesley told Colonel Collins that some of his wounded had been killed by the cavalry attached to the compoos, and a British officer in enemy service had been heard to say to another: 'You understand the language better than I do. Desire the jemadar [native junior officer] of that body of horse to go and cut up those wounded European soldiers.'[32]

Wellesley had already decided that he must act boldly. He told Colonel Stevenson that 'the best thing you can do is to move forward yourself with the Company's cavalry and all the Nizam's and dash at the first party that comes into your neighbourhood . . . A long defensive war would ruin us and will answer no purpose whatever.'[33] On 8 August 1803, he broke camp and marched to Ahmednuggur, the nearest Maratha-held fort. It was held by one of Scindia's regular battalions under French officers and about 1,000 reliable Arab mercenaries, but Wellesley believed that this was too small a force to hold the fort and the surrounding town (the *pettah*), although both were walled. He determined to carry the town by assault, using ladders to scale the walls, without preliminary bombardment. The 78th Highlanders led the assault, and when they were beaten back, a lieutenant of the grenadier company, Colin Campbell – who was to die a general in 1847 – hung his claymore from his wrist with a scarf to climb the better, and laid about him when he topped the wall. Other units entered elsewhere, and in twenty minutes the town was taken. One of the Peshwa's officers summed it all up:

> The English are a strange people, and their General a
> wonderful man. They came here in the morning, looked

at the *pettah* wall, walked over it, killed the garrison, and returned to breakfast! What can withstand them?[34]

The fort capitulated on the 12th once Wellesley's guns had breached the wall and the assaulting columns were formed and ready.

With Ahmednuggur in his hands, Wellesley snapped up all Scindia's possessions south of the Godavari, and then crossed the river with an army of 2,200 Europeans and 5,000 sepoys, with 2,200 light cavalry from Mysore and 4,000 of the Peshwa's cavalry. He reached Aurungabad, on the edge of the Nizam's territory, on 29 August, and rode on to meet Colonel Collins, encamped just to the north. Collins told him that he need not worry about the Maratha horse – 'You may ride over them, General, whenever you meet them' – but his regulars were a different matter altogether. Collins had seen Scindia's army at close quarters for five months, and declared that: 'Their infantry and the guns attached to it will surprise you.'[35]

Wellesley was at Aurungabad, and Stevenson, with more than 10,000 men, was at Kolsah, a hundred miles away to the east. At first Wellesley feared that the Maratha cavalry, up on the frontier between these two forces, would use its superior mobility to raid deep into the Nizam's territory. After nearly a month of shadow-boxing Wellesley and Stevenson met at Budnapoor on 21st September, and agreed a plan by which the two armies, moving separately, would manoeuvre in order to catch Scindia's main army in or around Borkardan. The first phase went well enough, and Wellesley reached Paugy and Stevenson Khamagaon on the 22nd September. On the following day, Wellesley's force, which as usual had left camp well before dawn so as to complete most of its marching before the heat of the day, reached Naulniah just before midday. Borkardan was another ten miles on, and camp was already being laid out when a cavalry troop brought in some brinjarries who reported that the Maratha army, with three compoos and abundant cavalry, was not at Borkardan at all. It was much closer, on the far bank of the River Kaitna, under the command of Colonel Pohlmann.

Wellesley went forward with a strong cavalry escort and reached a spot from which he could see the Marathas, in all perhaps 200,000 strong, in the process of breaking camp. As he later told the governor-general, 'it was obvious that the attack was to be no longer delayed'.[36] If he waited for Stevenson, the Marathas would slip away, but if he attacked at once they must either fight, or flee and abandon their guns. He quickly discarded the option of a frontal assault, and instead led his army parallel with the river as far as the village of Peepulgaon. Just across the river lay the village of Waroor, and he decided that the villages would not have been built so close together without 'some habitual means of communication' between them: there simply had to be a ford.

I visited the battlefield in September 2001. The monsoon was late, but the heavens had finally opened when I flew in to Aurungabad the day before. Although two four-wheel drive vehicles took us out to the battlefield through the smoky early morning bustle of village India, the rivers had all risen alarmingly and the tracks were pure mud. North of Peepulgaon we borrowed a tractor and trailer, and slithered our way to the River Kaitna, looking, like Wellesley two hundred years earlier, for a ford. We found it just where Wellesley had expected it to be, between the two villages. I have long felt that there is a particular merit to viewing a battlefield from horseback: that extra few feet of height improves the view, and horses can go where most vehicles cannot. Rani, a tricolour Kathiawari horse with the breed's signature ears – furry equine radars that curve round to cross above the horse's head

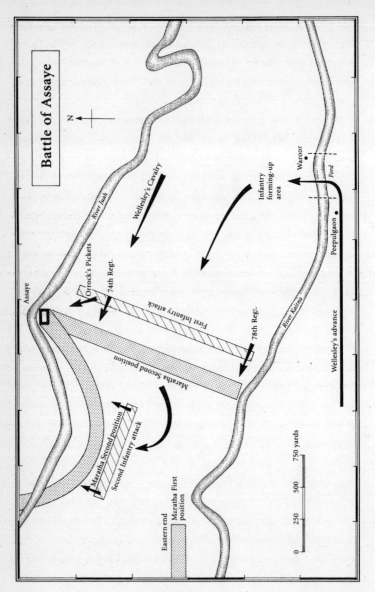

The Battle of Assaye

RIGHT Arthur
Wellesley's father,
Garrett, Earl of
Mornington, in
characteristic pose.

BELOW Richard,
Marquess Wellesley,
Arthur's ambitious
and flamboyant
oldest brother,
c 1820.

BELOW RIGHT
Anne, Countess
of Mornington.

Arthur Wesley as lieutenant colonel of the 33rd Regiment, aged about 26. He gave the portrait to his brother Richard, who pronounced it 'admirable; much the best which exists of you; the likeness is perfect, and conveys the true expression of your countenance.'

OPPOSITE ABOVE Sepoys of the East India Company at the close of the 18th century: a native officer (left), infantryman (centre) and artilleryman (right).

BELOW *The storming of Seringapatam.* The artist has painted the scene with the South Cauvery, almost dry at the time of the siege, at his back. Although distances are foreshortened, the breach is pretty well correctly positioned between the 'bastion' at the western tip of the defences and two round towers further south-east.

RIGHT Tipoo Sultan, Tiger of Mysore. He died bravely in 1799 when Seringapatam was stormed: it was said that he was killed by a soldier who fancied the jewel in his turban.

BELOW This heroic painting shows Major General Baird, who had led the assault on Seringapatam, superintending the discovery of Tipoo's body at the Water Gate. It was in fact Wellesley who pronounced Tipoo dead, and the scene was a good deal less decorous than that depicted here.

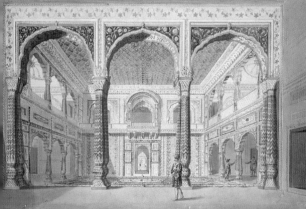

ABOVE Tipoo in happier times. Large murals around the summer palace, restored on Wellesley's orders, show scenes from Tipoo's campaigns – the capture of David Baird amongst them.

ABOVE Tipoo's summer palace after its capture: Wellesley was to rule Mysore from here.

RIGHT One of Tipoo's rocket-men lighting his missile.

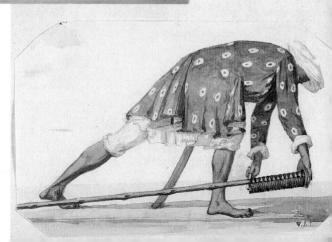

ABOVE Wellington at Salamanca (1812), a battle widely regarded as his masterpiece. The Lesser Arapile rises behind him, and on the right Major General Le Marchant's heavy cavalry launch their victorious charge.

LEFT Wellington sat to Goya for this study for a portrait soon after his entry into Madrid in 1812. It shows how the strain of the campaign had affected Wellington: while Goya was at work Wellington roundly rebuked Dr James McGrigor, his chief medical officer, for disobeying orders.

BELOW Wellington, unusually dressed in his general's uniform rather than a simple frock coat, making his formal entry into Madrid in 1812.

PREVIOUS PAGE
This near-contemporary print catches something of the flavour of Assaye, Wellington's hardest battle. Here he is shown encouraging his Indian (left) and British (right) infantry in their attack on the Marathas. One of his chargers was killed and another, the grey Arab Diomed, badly wounded that day.

and seem capable of 360-degree movement – was not at her best after three hours in the back of a truck. As I nudged her down the muddy slope into the fast-flowing Kaitna, my spirits, cast down by the weather and worries about more floods, lifted.

Crossing the Kaitna on Rani emphasised the sheer difficulty of Wellesley's plan. He had to bring most of his army parallel with the river, across the front of a superior force, and then swing from column into line and attack. He was in view of the Marathas for much of the time: an 18-pdr solid shot took off the head of one of his orderly dragoons near the river, and as his army crossed, Pohlmann was swinging his own thirteen regular battalions and approximately one hundred guns through 45 degrees to face the new threat. This would have been relatively simple for his infantry, but the move must have been difficult for the Maratha gunners, for it is heavy going even on tracks. The ground is now quite flat and featureless, with some scrub and trees between the fields. To the north the River Juah flows parallel with the Kaitna, and the mud-walled village of Assaye on the Juah, invisible from Wellesley's crossing-point, anchored Pohlmann's left flank. Maratha horse south of the Kaitna hovered round the rear of Wellesley's army, kept off by his own irregular Indian cavalry.

Once he was across the Kaitna, Wellesley could see enough of the ground to realise that there was not much space for all his infantry, and recognised that the strongly held Assaye would be best left alone until the battle was won in open field. He first formed up with two lines of infantry just west of Waroor; the first, preceded by Lieutenant Colonel William Orrock, who commanded the pickets of the day, contained three battalions with guns in the gaps between them, and the second another three. His cavalry, four regiments under Lieutenant Colonel Patrick Maxwell, stood further back, out of range of Assaye. Wellesley briefed his commanding officers in person, starting with Orrock on the right of the line and then galloping southwards on his bay charger to speak to the remainder. Colin Campbell of the 78th testified to the importance of Wellesley's personal leadership.

> The General was in the thick of the action the whole time ... I never saw a man so cool and collected as he was ... though I can assure you that until our troops got the order to advance, the fate of the day seemed doubtful.[37]

An artillery duel was already in progress, and the Maratha guns had the better of it. Wellesley reported that: 'Our bullocks, and the people who were employed to draw them, were shot, and they could not all be drawn on, but some were, and all continued to fire as long as the fire could be of any use.'[38] An unknown cavalry officer described it as 'a dreadful and destructive cannonade ... never was artillery more destructively served or better defended'.[39]

The infantry went forward in good order, the second line moving up on the right of the first as it did so. The 78th Highlanders, down by the Kaitna, met the Marathas first, and the disciplined musketry of the attackers unsettled Pohlmann's infantry, most of which did not stand to meet the charge. The Company's battalions, their men elated by the victory, pushed too far in pursuit and might have fallen victim to the watchful Maratha horse, but the 78th quickly reformed and stood ready to beat them off.

Wellesley had lost his charger during this phase of the battle, and mounted the grey arab Diomed to ride fast up to the northern flank where the firing was intense. He found that Orrock had mistaken his orders, and instead of attacking parallel with the rest of the line, had gone straight for Assaye. HM's 74th, the next battalion on his left, had taken the same line. Both marched

Colonel Patrick Maxwell's last charge at Assaye. Wellington's British and Indian cavalry played a key role in the battle, but Maxwell, their commander, was killed.

steadily into the fire of infantry and guns acknowledged by seasoned veterans to be the most severe they had ever seen. 'I do not wish to cast any reflection on the officer who led the pickets,' wrote Wellesley. 'I lament the consequences of his mistake, but I must acknowledge that it was not possible for a man to lead a body into a hotter fire than he did the pickets on that day against Assaye.'[40] Pohlmann's infantry and cavalry then attacked the pickets and the 74th, and although the latter formed a rough square behind the hastily piled bodies of enemy dead, the situation was desperate. An officer wrote that:

> The pickets and the 74th regiment were charged by a wonderful fine body of cavalry and infantry. The pickets lost all their officers except Lt Colonel Orrock and had only about 75 men left. The 74th out of 400 men of whom

only about 100 are likely to survive. Every officer of this corps except Major Swinton and Mr Grant the quarter-master were either killed or desperately wounded.[41]

This was the crisis of the battle, and Patrick Maxwell, with the cavalry behind the threatened flank, rose to meet it, charging with three of his regiments and making 'dreadful slaughter'. They hurtled on, crashing into 'an immense body that surrounded the elephants carrying some of the Maratha chiefs'. Some even crossed the Juah. With his cavalry victorious but scattered, Wellesley quickly regrouped, using the steady 78th and the one uncommitted cavalry regiment to deal with some Maratha horse, which had ridden down amongst his own guns, immobile and exposed once the infantry had advanced. As he led this attack, a Maratha piked Diomed in the chest, and Wellesley mounted his third charger of the day.

By now Pohlmann's army had been pushed back into a semi-circle with its left in Assaye and its right across the Juah. Maxwell had returned to the field, and Wellesley ordered him to charge the eastern end of Pohlmann's line while he took the re-formed infantry against its centre and right. Maxwell was hit by canister as he led his men forward, and his death sapped their confidence. Most accounts suggest that they did not charge home and sheered off in front of the Maratha line. However, a cavalry officer main-tained that 'we succeeded however in getting possession of their cannon, retaining them till our line of infantry came up'. Perhaps he was referring to guns standing in Pohlmann's second position, in which case his remark would make sense, for the attacking infantry would indeed have passed through these. But there is no doubting the impact of the infantry attack or the role the 78th played in it. Although its men had marched about 25 miles since dawn and fought a hard battle on a hot day, they marched on against the third Maratha position with as much confidence as they had against the first. Pohlmann's men did not wait for them, but fled across the Juah. They left 'the whole country strewn with the killed and wounded, both European and natives, ours as well as the enemy's'.[42] The cavalry, exhausted by its efforts, was in no condition to pursue.

Wellesley spent the night with some other officers in a farm near Assaye. The battle had cost him 1,584 killed, wounded and missing, and perhaps 6,000 Marathas had been killed or wounded. The Marathas had lost all their guns. Fifteen years later a cavalry officer told Wellesley that he remembered him congratulating a brave Indian sergeant at the day's end, promoting him 'with that eloquent and correct knowledge of the native language for which you were celebrated'. He may have had his tongue in his cheek, for Wellesley apparently said '*Acha havildar: jemadar*', – 'OK sergeant: lieutenant' – scarcely the apogee of linguistic ability. The incident may in fact testify to Wellesley's deep mental and physical exhaustion. He thought the battle 'the bloodiest for the numbers that I ever saw', and later told Stevenson that 'I should not like to see again such loss as I sustained on the 23rd of September, even if attended by such a gain.'[43] That night he had a recurring nightmare that 'they were *all* killed'. Years later when he was asked what was the best thing he ever did in the way of fighting, he replied with the single word 'Assaye'.

I finished my day on the battlefield near Assaye itself, surrounded by eager children selling canister shot and musket balls and pointing out the fragments of Maratha iron guns, some of them destroyed by the British after the battle. Patrick Maxwell lies beneath a huge peepul tree, and although words are no longer visible on his headstone, his name is well remembered. It could so easily have been Arthur Wellesley, for the price of leadership had been heavy that day and, not for the last time in his career, Wellesley felt the finger of God upon him.

Assaye did not end the war. Stevenson, who had marched on the sound of the guns, joined Wellesley shortly afterwards, and a hospital for the wounded was established within the fortifications of Ajanta. In the weeks that followed, Wellesley at first continued his 'two army' strategy, manoeuvring with Stevenson to take more of Scindia's fortresses and pushing the Rajah of Berar back towards his capital. On 29 November 1803, with his armies united, Wellesley attacked the combined forces of Scindia and Berar at Argaum. He launched a frontal assault into cannon fire 'not to be compared with that of Assaye'. With the infantry only 500 yards from the Maratha line, his own guns came into action, shaking the opposing infantry badly before the measured volleys ended what cannonballs had begun. A short firefight ended with the rout of the Maratha infantry, while on each flank the Maratha horse was driven off by British and Indian cavalry. The battle cost Wellesley 361 casualties – only 46 of them fatal – while the Marathas lost at least 5,000 men and, again, all their guns. Elsewhere the war was going in favour of the British, and on the Delhi front Lieutenant General Gerard Lake (later Lord Lake) had beaten Scindia in a battle just as important as Assaye. On 15 December 1803, Wellesley stormed the powerful stronghold of Gawilghur, and this defeat induced Scindia and the Rajah of Berar to make peace, giving up territory and agreeing to disband their forces.

Holkar had not become involved in the war, but soon realised that its peace terms could only limit his influence, not least because his armies relied on plunder which could no longer be obtained if neighbouring states were under British protection. In April 1804 a new war broke out, this time with Holkar as its chief protagonist on the Maratha side. Mindful of the fate of Scindia's regulars at the hands of better-trained troops, he relied on more traditional Maratha tactics, and south of Delhi he ran circles round Lake (who was not able to bring the war to a successful conclusion till the end of 1805), and roundly defeated Lieutenant Colonel William Monson in late August 1804. Lake told the governor-general that he did not want Wellesley's help in the north, and that he should be sent to command in his old stamping-ground, the Deccan. But Wellesley, now back at Seringapatam, no longer felt equal to the challenge.

There were several reasons for this. First, he believed that his victories had been squandered by the governor-general and his council. He disapproved of the weakening of native princes, which could only result in increasing demands being placed upon the Company, as he described in April 1804.

> I have always been of the opinion that we have weakened
> Scindia more than is politic; and that we shall repent of
> having established a number of these little independent
> powers in India, every one of whom will require the
> support of the British government, which will occasion
> a constant demand of employment of troops, a loss of
> officers and men, and a claim of money.[44]

He had predicted that war would break out again, and was 'dispirited and disgusted' at the way things had been handled. Next, his military appointment was 'of an ambiguous nature': he was still on the staff at Mysore, for although the Duke of York, commander-in-chief of the British army, had promised him an appointment, there was no sign of one. Worse, he felt tired, ill and desperately homesick, 'anxious to a degree which I can't express to see my friends again'. 'I have served as long in India,' he affirmed in June 1804, 'as any man ought who can serve anywhere else.'[45] He certainly bore the scars of India. Sir Jonah Barrington, a judge who described him as 'ruddy faced and juvenile in appearance' in 1793, thought that in 1805 he was 'looking so sallow and wan, with every mark of what is called a worn out man'.[46] And there was a political undercurrent. His brother's days as governor-general were coming to an end – he was to be replaced by the aged Lord Cornwallis in mid-1805 – and without powerful support, it was not hard to see that the victor of Assaye might have his wings clipped by the senior and disappointed. On 8 June 1804, after obtaining Lake's permission to depart, he formally applied for leave to return home, though matters were not finally settled till early the following year.

But as he prepared to go, there were consolations. He was appointed a Knight of the Bath on 1 September 1804. A pleasing story tells of the order's star being quietly pinned to his coat by his old friend Sir John Cradock while he slept, though he himself wrote, in a tone reflecting the dejection of that phase of his life, that the insignia was 'kicking about the *Lord Keith* which arrived about ten days ago and discovered by a passenger looking for his own baggage'.[47] He was not only a knight, but rich, with a personal fortune of over £42,000. He told Major Merrick Shaw, his secretary, that 'I am not rich in comparison with other people but very much so in comparison with my former situation, and quite sufficiently for my own wants', admitting that he was now 'independent of all office or employment'.[48] His officers from the Maratha campaign gave him a silver dinner service worth £2,000, now in Apsley House, and the gentlemen of Calcutta, a sword worth half as much. The officers of the 33rd sent their thanks, and his reply characteristically enjoined them 'to adhere to the system of discipline, subordination, and interior economy which you have found established in the regiment, and, above all, to cherish and encourage among yourselves the spirit of gentleman and of soldiers'.[49] The inhabitants of Seringapatam had written fulsomely as soon as his departure was mooted.

> May you long continue to dispense to us that full stream of security and happiness, which we first received with wonder . . . and, when greater affairs shall call you from us, may the God of all castes and all nations deign to hear with favour our humble and constant prayers for your health, your glory, and your happiness.[50]

Wellesley embarked on Admiral Rainier's flagship HMS *Trident* on 10 March 1805. The first leg of the voyage took him, portentously, to the little island of St Helena, where he stayed in the Briars, which was briefly to house Napoleon while Longwood was being prepared for him. He had found the voyage enormously restoring to his health, and suggested that he would have become seriously ill had he remained in India. At St Helena he heard the sad news that Stevenson, his tireless collaborator, had died on the way home, probably without hearing that he had been promoted to major general. *Trident* dropped anchor off Dover on 10 September, and Wellesley was home at last.

'I understood as much about military matters when I came back from India as I have done ever since,' remarked Wellesley ten years later.[51] Although, like so many of his aphorisms, this contains a whiff of exaggeration, it is still hard to understate India's influence on him. First, it had shaped his habits. He advised Henry 'to live moderately, to drink little or no wine, to use exercise, to keep the mind employed, and, if possible, to keep in good humour with the world'.[52] Despite bouts of a variety of diseases, ranging from tropical fevers to the Malabar itch, he tried to keep fit, and always walked '40 paces back and forth in front of his tent' soon after rising. He was a fine practical horseman, covering 45 miles a day on the way to Gawilghur. His attention to detail was as remarkable as it was remorseless. He did not believe in lingering in bed – 'when it is time to turn over, it is time to turn out' – and as soon as he was up, he would be in the saddle or at his desk. He made a rule of doing 'the business of the day in the day', and kept all his books and papers in a single cart.

His dress was already taking a familiar shape: white pantaloons tucked into Hessian boots, scarlet tunic, and black cocked hat. He was fond of silver-hilted curved swords with Indian or Persian blades; slightly flashy, to be sure, but infinitely more practical in a brawl – he probably fought hand-to-hand at both Sultanpettah and Assaye – than the slim straight-bladed sword decreed by regulations.

There was an early warning of trouble to come. Wellesley had a healthy sexual appetite, and Captain Elers thought that he 'had a very susceptible heart, particularly towards, I am sorry to say, married ladies'. Elizabeth Longford believed that he was 'more likely to make aphorisms than to make love', but acknowledges that there might have been something more serious between Wellesley and the wife of Captain John William Freese of the Madras Artillery. His conduct 'shocked his censorious aide-de-camp, Captain West, not to mention an officious married lady, the natural daughter of an earl, a situation guaranteed to make anyone starchy'.[53]

India had also formed his views on tactics. A shaky opponent was best dealt with by a sudden attack, before he had time to collect himself. 'Dash at the first fellows that make their appearance and the campaign will be ours' was his watchword for the Assaye campaign.[54] In September 1804 he told Colonel Murray that he should attack the Maratha infantry 'before you think of doing anything else.' But he should avoid allowing the Marathas to mount a formal attack of their own, because their powerful artillery would do so much damage. Defensive operations settled nothing, and although a commander might have to withdraw if faced by impossible odds or because he had outrun his supplies, it ought always to be with a view to striking again. Drill and discipline underpinned tactics. Wellesley had believed this when he came to India, and his views had been reinforced by his experience there: Assaye and Argaum were both won as much by discipline and cohesion as by courage. In June 1804 he ordered a parade of all his native infantry at six in the morning, and listed points of detail for the attention of commanding officers, pointing out that alignment on the colours was easiest if the sergeant between the colours followed his commanding officer's footsteps precisely, and substantial changes of direction were to be achieved by 'echelon march of divisions' rather than by wheeling. This was not drill as an end in itself, but the precise adjustment of the machinery of war.

He valued the acquisition of intelligence highly, and usually began the process well before the outbreak of war. He maintained a network of professional spies called *hircarrahs*, paid them well and looked hard at the information they provided. Commanders were warned not to listen to gossip:

> Major Walker sends out Hircarrahs who tell him what they please; he writes the whole down and sends it off to Mr Duncan by whom it is circulated. Major Walker discovers that his Hircarrahs have told him falsehoods; but I doubt if they are punished, or rewarded when they do well.[55]

And when in doubt officers should check for themselves. An officer who complained that intelligence was poor was told sharply that:

'you are mounted on a damn good horse and have two eyes in your head'.[56] Lastly (though Wellesley might have put it first), war was, start to finish, a matter of logistics. It was here that his keen eye for detail was sharpest, here that his emphasis on preparation was most pronounced. A general who could command an army in the Deccan, with its lines of communication running over 300 miles across major rivers down to the Madras presidency, was as well prepared as any commander could be for the rigours of the Iberian Peninsula.

There were political lessons too. Wellesley's dispatches show the pains he took to keep his superiors, political and military, apprised of what he did, for in the topsy-turvy world of Indian politics, he was finished if he lost their confidence, even if they did not enjoy his own. He often found himself campaigning with allies who were incompetent or unreliable, and here he plied consummate tact, although, as his private correspondence reveals, with much effort. There were areas where he would brook no compromise. While he treated the commanders of his Indian auxiliary cavalry in a 'gentleman-like' manner, he was merciless if they broke his rules. In December 1803 he told Colonel Murray that: 'If my Maratha allies did not know that I should hang any one found plundering, not only should I have starved long ago, but most probably my own coat should have been taken off my back.'[57] He set his face firmly against the 'sweeteners' that were routine in Indian political life. When an officer told him that the Rajah of Kittoor had offered 10,000 gold pagodas to be taken under British protection, he was 'surprised that any man in the character of a British officer should not have given the Rajah to understand that his offer would be considered as an insult . . .'[58] In politics, as in war, the subcontinent was admirable preparation for the Peninsula.

THREE

FALSE
STARTS

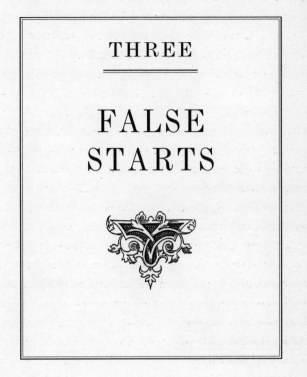

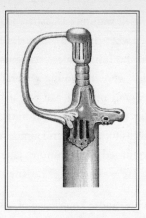

MAJOR GENERAL SIR ARTHUR WELLESLEY was home, at least as far as home went. His mother was still living off Cavendish Square, but there was little intimacy there, and on the wider stage, his Indian victories cut no ice in London. He had already heard that Richard was to be replaced as governor-general, and was well aware that the whole 'Wellesley system' of expanding British power in India would need defending in Whitehall and the City. He had returned to find that William Pitt, the prime minister, had just brought together the Third Coalition against Napoleon. It was expected that Britain would provide some sort of expeditionary force, though there were the usual wild rumours as to where it might be sent, and Wellesley was anxious for a command. Although he did not need money in the way he had before he left for India, the prospect of idleness appalled him.

On 12 September 1805, he called on Lord Castlereagh, a Dublin-born acquaintance from his Irish past, at the Colonial Office in Downing Street. Castlereagh had recently been appointed secretary of state for war and the colonies, an office he held in 1805–6 and again in 1807–9; both crucial periods in Wellesley's career.

Wellesley found himself waiting in Castlereagh's outer office with a short naval officer who, 'from his likeness to his pictures and the loss of an arm', he immediately recognised as Nelson. The admiral had no idea who the young general was, and 'entered into a conversation with me, if I can call it conversation, for it was almost all on his side, and all about himself, and, really, in a style so vain and silly as to surprise and almost disgust me'. Nelson left the room and returned a few minutes later, having found out who Wellesley was. He was a changed man, and talked:

> with a good sense, and a knowledge of subjects at home and abroad, that surprised me equally and more agree- ably than the first part of our interview had done; in fact, he talked like an officer and a statesman . . . I don't know that I ever had a conversation that interested me more.

He later reflected that 'if the Secretary of State had been punctual, and admitted Lord Nelson in the first quarter of an hour, I should have had the same impression of a light and trivial character that other people have had . . .' Nelson left to join HMS *Victory* the following day, and sailed off to fight at Trafalgar. The two men never met again.[1]

Wellesley saw a good deal of Castlereagh over the next few weeks, defending Richard's achievements to the Secretary-of-State. As Elizabeth Longford puts it, 'while Castlereagh resisted the advo- cate's pleas, he came to believe in the advocate's personality and skill'.[2] On several occasions Wellesley went riding with Pitt, now fading fast, and spoke out on behalf of 'our late system in India', and advised on the conduct of the war against France. He found Pitt 'too sanguine . . . he conceived a project and then imagined that it was done, and did not enter enough into details'. Pitt, for his part, was favourably impressed by the general who 'never made a difficulty, or hid his ignorance in vague generalities. If I put a question to him, he answered it distinctly; if I wanted an explanation, he gave it clearly; if I desired an opinion, I got from him one supported by reasons that were always sound.'[3] He argued against one especially hare-brained scheme for mounting a two-pronged attack on the Spanish colony of Mexico, with one expedition striking out from Jamaica and the other moving from Madras by way of the Philippines and Australia, pointing out that even if the two forces duly converged in Mexico, the United States would not be likely to view with equanimity the old world's sudden resurgence in the new.

With connections like this, it would have been surprising if Wellesley had not obtained a command, despite the hostility of Horse Guards. The Duke of York, commander-in-chief, had made it clear that he thought Harris had been wrong to give Wellesley the Mysore command in place of Baird, and to the end of his life, he maintained that Wellesley was ambitious and untrustworthy. Nevertheless, Wellesley was appointed to command a brigade in an expedition to be sent to north Germany in the distant hope of collaborating with the Prussians. But on 2 December 1805, Napoleon trounced the Austrians and Russians at Austerlitz, and devastated the coalition. Pitt presciently told an assistant to roll up a map of Europe, as it would not be wanted for ten years, and went home to die. Wellesley found himself back in England, commanding a brigade at Hastings. With Nelson's victory at Trafalgar and the break-up of Napoleon's camp at Boulogne, this was scarcely an embattled coastline, and although he famously declared that 'I have eaten of the King's salt, and, therefore, I con- sider it my duty to serve with unhesitating zeal and cheerfulness, when and wherever the King or his Government may think proper to employ me', he was bored and sidelined.[4] However, in January 1806, he was appointed the Colonel of the 33rd Regiment, a real honour for a junior major general, and happily told his friend Lieutenant Colonel John Malcolm that: 'The regiment which they have given me, and [employment on] the Staff, have made me rich.'[5]

He spent some of his new money on re-entry into politics. Castlereagh advised him to contest Rye, a pocket borough 'where the government interest was paramount', because it would enable him to protect Richard's 'character and service from unjust aspersions', and he was duly elected in April 1806.[6] But the government was not in a strong position. After Pitt's death the 'Ministry of All the Talents' took office, with Lord Grenville as prime minister and Charles James Fox as foreign secretary. 'We are not actually in opposition,' lamented Wellesley, 'but we have no power.'[7] Still, there was plenty of work to be done in the House. Another MP, James Paull, a successful merchant who had returned disgruntled from India, led the attack on Richard Wellesley, and there were many, inside parliament and outside it, who were inclined to follow. The opulence of the marquess's lifestyle had astonished his successor, who complained that there were so many sentries inside his residence that 'if I show my head . . . a fellow with a musket and fixed bayonet presents himself before me'. Opponents attacked Richard's dealings with Indian princes, his role in bringing about the Maratha wars, and claimed that that he had wasted public money. They hoped to see him impeached, and there was every chance that his fall would damage Arthur, for amongst the contested expenditure was a grant of 30,000 rupees paid to Arthur in the Deccan. In parliament, Arthur, seeking a quick decision rather than a long campaign, demanded that specific charges should be brought in place of generalised accusations, thereby greatly contributing to his brother's survival in public life.

Meanwhile Arthur was taking a decisive step in his private life. Despite his subsequent love affairs, he had never forgotten Kitty Pakenham. In 1801 Colonel William Beresford wrote from Dublin to ask 'if Miss Pakenham is an object to you or not', adding that she looked as well as ever. Arthur was also corresponding with Olivia Sparrow, one of Kitty's closest friends, and assured her that: 'Notwithstanding my good fortune, and the perpetual activity of the life which I have led, the disappointment, and the object of it, and all the circumstances, are as fresh upon my mind as if they had passed only yesterday.' He added that 'the merit of your friend is still felt', and begged to be remembered to her 'in the kindest manner'. Kitty, for her part, was desperately anxious that Arthur should not feel '*obliged* to renew a pursuit, which perhaps he might then not wish or my family (or some of them) take kindly'.[8] However, on the basis of the news enthusiastically relayed by Mrs Sparrow, she was confident enough to break off her engagement to Colonel the Hon. Galbraith Lowry Cole, second son of the Earl of Enniskillen. Cole was as downcast by the rejection as Wellesley had been years before. One of his brothers thought that there was 'not the smallest chance' of his marrying. 'Since that love affair with Kitty Pakenham,' he wrote, 'Lowry seems like a burnt child to the fire . . .'[9]

There is no evidence that, at this stage, Wellesley was driven by a sense of obligation, for he had ample opportunity to withdraw. But he assured Mrs Sparrow that he had come home 'for one purpose only', and in November 1805 professed himself 'the happiest man in the world' when Kitty agreed to marry him. It is hard to disagree with Joan Wilson, Kitty's biographer, that it is 'almost unbelievable' that no meeting was then arranged between them. Kitty was desperately worried by Arthur's departure for Germany: her Aunt Louisa wrote that 'she coughs sadly and looks but ill'. She was engaged to a man who was too busy to come and see her, and although she publicly maintained confidence in 'the very first of human creatures', the episode put her under a strain that was all too evident when they eventually did meet again – on their wedding day. The wedding took place on 10 April 1806 in the Longford's Dublin drawing-room, with the Reverend Gerald Wellesley officiating. Arthur was not impressed by the first sight of his bride in ten years, muttering to Gerald: 'She has grown ugly, by Jove!' In contrast, Kitty's friend Maria Edgeworth found him 'very handsome, very brown, quite bald [in fact close-cropped] and a hooked nose'. Arthur went back to his brigade after a week's honeymoon, leaving Gerald to escort Kitty to 11 Harley Street, which was to be their London home. When she was presented at court, the kindly Queen Charlotte called her a 'bright example of constancy', and asked if she had ever written to Wellesley during his long absence. 'No, never, Madame,' replied Kitty. 'And did you never think of him?' enquired the Queen. 'Yes, Madame, very often.' There was no mention of Olivia Sparrow's tireless efforts.

The marriage was a mistake. Wellesley later told his close friend Harriet Arbuthnot that: 'I married her because they asked me to do it & I did not know myself. I thought I should never care for anybody again & that I shd be with my army &, in short, I was a fool.'[10] This holds little water. There is no trace of any external pressure on him, and if he did not know himself at thirty-seven, he had left it precious late. The real reasons seem more complex. First, deeply in love with Kitty, he had been downcast by her brother's rejection of his suit: he was not a man to take a rebuff lightly, and the incident rankled, just as his supersession by Baird had. Second, absence had indeed made the heart grow fonder. Towards the end of his time in India, he was desperately anxious to get back home, and would not be the last returning warrior to fasten his hopes on the girl he left behind him, and to hope for more from a relationship than it could ever deliver. He had been warned that she was 'much altered', but replied that it was her mind he cared for, and that would not alter. By the time he saw just how much she had changed, it was too late for an honourable retreat. If Kitty's mind had remained as he imagined, there might still have been some hope. But it was soon evident that she did not run the household as crisply as her husband had run the 33rd Regiment, and there were many 'domestic annoyances' as he was drawn into difficulties with servants or the accounts. When they had first met, he had appreciated her sharp wit, and saw her at the centre of an admiring circle. Now the roles had changed. He was dominant and admired, she nervous and unsure. Arthur had accomplished his mission and purged the Pakenham family's rejection of his suit. Now he had other things to do, and, assuming that his new wife would understand his own fierce commitment to duty, he took no time to get to know her. It was a disastrous beginning.

Arthur's brigade did not interfere with his parliamentary duties, and with Henry's help, he was to slip deftly from one economical seat to another, representing Mitchell in Cornwall after the 1806 election and Newport, Isle of Wight, in 1807. But he was not truly comfortable in politics. He later told Croker that he was mistrusted by Horse Guards because:

> In the first place, they thought very little of anyone who had served in India . . . Then because I was in Parliament, and connected with people in office, I was a politician, and a politician can never be a soldier. Moreover, they looked upon me with a kind of jealousy, because I was a lord's son, 'a sprig of nobility', who came into the army more for ornament than use.[11]

He told Richard that he longed for military employment: 'it is such an object to me to serve with some of the European armies that I have written to Lord Grenville upon the subject; & I hope that he will speak to the Duke of York'.[12] He had no illusions about the jobs he might get, assuring Richard that: 'I don't want a Chief Command if it cannot be given to me ... I should be very sorry to stay at home when others go abroad, only because I cannot command in Chief.'[13] The war was not going well. Napoleon beat the Prussians in the double battle of Jena-Auerstadt in October 1806 and went on to occupy Berlin. However, in July, Lieutenant General Sir John Stuart had beaten the French General Reynier in a scrambling little battle at Máida, in southern Italy. It was hardly Austerlitz, but it did help persuade Arthur, sent a detailed report of the action from a friend who was there, that French columns could indeed be seen off by a British line.

In March 1807 the government, unsettled by the death of Fox, fell, and the king summoned the sick and drowsy Duke of Portland to form a new administration. The Duke of Richmond was to be lord-lieutenant of Ireland, and Arthur was offered the post of chief secretary for Ireland with a salary of £6,566 a year. He accepted it only on the condition that he would be allowed to relinquish it at short notice if a command became available, and duly moved with Kitty and their month-old son, Arthur Richard, to the chief secretary's house in Dublin's Phoenix Park.

Ireland had changed greatly since his last visit. As a result of the rebellion of 1798, Pitt had become convinced that constitutional union between Britain and Ireland was the answer to the Irish question. The government deployed all its patronage of 'jobs, places and peerages' to gain support, for the union was opposed by most ascendancy politicians as well as by nationalist parliamentarians like Grattan. In 1800, the Irish parliament voted itself into oblivion, and a reduced number of Irish constituencies were thenceforth represented at Westminster. But the viceroy and his court survived, and 'above all the Castle continued; with its complex machinery of patronage and contacts, manipulated politically by the Chief Secretary and administratively by the Under Secretary . . .'[14] The balance of power was still 'invincibly Protestant', and 'the wretched cabins remained eternally unaltered, with the same ragged families inside, the same sprouting weeds on the roof, and the same holy pictures on the walls . . .'[15] Arthur recognised that 'a good use of the patronage of the government' was essential to the preservation of power, and no sooner had he arrived than he found himself marshalling that patronage in the Tory interest for the 1807 elections. He saw that there was no prospect of altering the laws that bore down upon the Catholics – the king's steadfast resistance to any such reform had finished the previous 'Ministry of All the Talents' – but he told Lord Fingall, a Catholic nobleman, that they would be enforced 'with mildness and good temper'.[16]

Above all, he believed that the union was deeply unpopular. 'Show me an Irishman,' he declared later, 'and I'll show you a man whose anxious wish is to see his country independent of Great Britain.'[17] He thought that no political concession would alter this spirit, and that the Irish looked eagerly towards a French invasion, which would enable them to throw off the English yoke. He argued then, as he was to argue at Westminster twenty years on, that the worst thing that could befall any country was civil strife. The political supremacy of Britain over Ireland had to be maintained at all costs, and steps taken to deal with a French descent. 'I lay it down as decided that Ireland,' he wrote, 'in a view to military operations, must be considered as an enemy's country . . .'[18]

In the spring of 1807, Wellesley heard that the government was planning an expedition to Denmark, and forced Castlereagh's hand by declaring that he would not stay in Ireland whether or not he was given a command. On 24 July, he told the Duke of Richmond that he had been offered a post if the expedition did go ahead. 'I don't know, and I have not asked,' he wrote, 'whether I am to return to my office when this *coup de main* will have been struck or will have failed.' He concluded that he had not mentioned the expedition to the nervous Kitty, and did not propose to do so 'till it will be positively settled that we are to go'.[19] It was not a coup which aroused much support in England. The victorious Napoleon, who had just concluded the Treaty of Tilsit with the Tsar, had decreed that European ports were closed to British trade. Although the combined French and Spanish fleets had been badly mauled at Trafalgar, the neutral Portuguese and Danish fleets might yet fall into French hands and make an invasion of Britain possible. George Canning, the foreign secretary, asked Denmark to place her fleet under British protection for the remainder of the war and when the steadfast Danes refused, sent an expedition under Lieutenant General Lord Cathcart to take it by force. This looked uncommonly like theft, and Charles Napier, one of the martial brothers who were to distinguish themselves in the Peninsula, echoed public opinion when he wrote 'Poor Danes!'

Wellesley commanded one of Cathcart's divisions, and was given a steady brigadier called Richard Stewart as his second-in-command, 'a kind of dry nurse', as Wellesley put it. He landed an advance guard near Copenhagen on 16 August 1807, and the rest of the army followed to lay siege to the Danish capital. When a relief column appeared, he was sent to deal with it and good-humouredly put Stewart in his place by saying 'Come, come, 'tis my turn now.' By 3 September he had cleared the whole island of Zeeland of Danish regulars and militia, at a cost to his division of only 6 killed and 115 wounded. The city surrendered on 8 September after a brief bombardment, which Wellesley disliked, arguing that 'we might have taken the capital with greater ease'.[20] He helped negotiate the terms of a capitulation that gave the British the Danish fleet of eighteen ships of the line, and allowed a British occupation force to remain until the fleet had been towed to British ports and damage to British property had been repaired. On 14 September he asked Cathcart for permission to return home. He had been 'very uncertain and very indifferent' over whether he should retain the chief secretaryship, but now found that he had not been replaced and that 'there is much to do in Ireland. The *long nights* are approaching fast, and if I am to have any concern in the government of that country, it is desirable that I should be there.'[21] Cathcart made no objection, and he returned to England at the end of the month.

Although the Copenhagen expedition taught Wellesley little, it had one important legacy. Major General Thomas Grosvenor had taken his favourite mare on the expedition, Lady Catherine, sired by John Bull out of a mare by the Rutland Arabian. She was found to be in foal and was sent home, and at Eaton Hall, home of Grosvenor's cousin, Earl Grosvenor, she foaled a strong chestnut colt called Copenhagen. He was bought by the Hon. Charles Stewart, Wellesley's adjutant-general in the Peninsula, who sold him to Wellesley. He became Wellesley's favourite charger, and survived the Peninsula and Waterloo, where he came close to braining his master with an ill-tempered kick when he dismounted after the battle. Copenhagen retired to Stratfield Saye, and was a great favourite with Kitty, who used to feed him bread, so that he regularly approached lady visitors 'with the most confiding familiarity'. He died in 1836 and lies buried at Stratfield Saye beneath a Turkey Oak in Ice-House Paddock. 'There may have been many faster horses, no doubt many handsomer,' said Wellesley, 'but for bottom and endurance I never saw his fellow.'[22]

The autumn saw Wellesley back in Dublin, where Kitty was heavily pregnant: she gave birth to their second son, Charles, on 16 January 1808. Wellesley busied himself with tithes, education, police reform and corn exports, and still hoped that it might be possible 'to obliterate, as far as the law will allow us, the distinction between Protestants and Catholics'. He strove to promote 'mild government' and criticised absentee landlords, but it was clear that serious reform was out of the question, and he longed to be away from Dublin and back on campaign.

He was summoned to Westminster, where he received the thanks of parliament for his work in Denmark. He spoke out again in support of Richard, and defended the army's conduct in Denmark and the taking of the Danish fleet. He continued to advise the government on the many military projects that floated into view and then sank beneath the waves of impracticability. First there was to be an expedition to Sweden. Then there was talk of a Franco-Russian descent on India against which preparations must be made. And then nationalists in Spain's South American colonies were to be encouraged to rise up with British support. Wellesley did not approve of 'revolutionising any country for a political object' and disapproved of republican constitutions 'too regularly constructed to ever answer any practical effect'. Besides, it would not do to stir up in Caracas what one sought to put down in Cork. However, he had been promoted lieutenant general on 25 April, and was now senior enough to be given command of a force of 9,000 men earmarked for an expedition to South America, where it would assist the Venezuelan patriot Francisco de Miranda, then living in exile in London. The precedents were not encouraging, for Lieutenant General John Whitelock, forced to surrender his own tiny expedition at Buenos Aires, had just been court-martialled and cashiered. But once again fate intervened, and Wellesley was given a new objective, a good deal nearer home.

Seizure of the Danish fleet may have shocked the tender-hearted in Britain, but it had also irritated Napoleon, who now determined to secure the Portuguese fleet. Spain, its government effectively in the hands of the first minister Manuel Godoy, was an unenthusiastic ally of France, and Godoy agreed to give a French army under General Andoche Junot free passage across Spain to reach Portugal. Junot struck in November 1808, and covered the last 300 miles of his journey in just fourteen days, narrowly missing the Portuguese court. The Portuguese regent, Prince John, had been encouraged by Britain to withstand the French. He hesitated, but was eventually evacuated to the Portuguese colony of Brazil while the fleet fled to Britain. Although the Portuguese initially welcomed the French, they were soon alienated by the invaders' behaviour. Oporto declared itself independent of France and elected a junta, headed by its bishop. There were risings elsewhere, which confined the French to Lisbon and a handful of fortresses, and the junta in Oporto appealed for British help.

Napoleon was also strengthening his grip on Spain, now full of French troops ostensibly sent there to support Junot. Popular pressure forced the corrupt and conservative King Charles IV to abdicate in favour of his son Ferdinand. But Napoleon wanted to be rid of the Bourbons altogether, and he lured the whole royal family to Bayonne. There, Charles declared that he had abdicated against his will, compelling Ferdinand to step down in his favour.

He promptly surrendered the crown to Napoleon, who proclaimed his brother Joseph King of Spain. On 2 May 1808, even before this process was complete, the inhabitants of Madrid attacked the French garrison. Although the rising in the capital was brutally repressed, it sparked off a general insurrection throughout the country. Many civilian officials and military officers argued that it was folly to fight the French, but improvised provincial juntas took on the leadership of what Spaniards call the 'War of Liberation'.

'That unlucky war ruined me,' Napoleon acknowledged frankly in later life, because:

> it divided my resources, obliged me to multiply my efforts, and caused my principles to be assailed ... it destroyed my moral power in Europe, rendered my embarrassments more complicated, and opened a school for the English soldiers.[23]

He believed that intervention in Spain was correct both from the strategic point of view, for the British would have moved in to fill any vacuum, and because the Spaniards themselves deserved better government. It was, he maintained, his methods that let him down. His constant intervention placed Joseph, personally quite popular with many of his subjects, who spoke of him as 'Uncle Joe', in an impossible position. In 1809 Joseph offered to abdicate, complaining that 'I have no real power beyond Madrid, and even in Madrid I am every day counteracted.' Napoleon was reluctant to delegate authority, and in mid-1811, he maintained six separate armies in Spain, under commanders who usually got on badly, not only with one another but also with their subordinates. For the French, the war in Spain was indeed an ulcer, always irritating and ultimately debilitating.

British historians often tend to depict the Peninsular War as an Anglo-French conflict in which the Spanish occasionally appear as tardy and incompetent British allies. The truth is very different. French invasion of the Iberian Peninsula provoked a fierce nationalist reaction that involved many men who would normally have played no role in politics. A French cavalry officer thought that the Spaniards were motivated solely by 'religious patriotism'. They had neither discipline nor knowledge of the laws of war, and 'had but one sentiment, to revenge, by every possible means, the wrongs the French had done to their country'.[24] One French officer saw a hospital in which four hundred men had been hacked to pieces and fifty-three buried alive, and on another occasion a single French soldier was left alive, though with his ears cut off, to testify to the murder and mutilation of 1,200 of his wounded comrades: the experience drove him mad.

Women fought too: the young Augustina Zaragoza famously rallied her countrymen during the sieges of Zaragoza in 1808 and 1809. Ensign John Mills of the Coldstream Guards thought her very ugly, 'dressed in a jacket, turned up with red ... She had half-boots, and pantaloons ... I had forgot to mention, a huge cutlass, which hung by her side.'[25] The juntas kept regular armies in the field, though often with much difficulty, and in July a French corps was captured at Bailén in the south. But where the Spanish could not wage war on a large scale, they fought it on a smaller one, and it is no accident that this form of war is still known by the Spanish word for 'little war' – guerrilla. Guerrilla leaders included priests, noblemen and smugglers. They fought not only the French but also the Josefinos, those of their countrymen who had thrown in their lot with Joseph Bonaparte, and the conflict took on many of the uglier aspects of a civil war. British officers who served in Spain noted that their reception ranged from wild excitement to silent hostility. John Mills wrote from Madrid that: 'The men and women (particularly the latter) hug us in the street and call us their preservers', while there was 'universal gloom' in Valladolid. Although Joseph's Spain remained at war with Britain, in June 1808, the juntas sent representatives to London where, like their Portuguese counterparts, they asked for British assistance.

George Canning declared that 'Britain would proceed upon the principle that any nation in Europe which stirs up with a determination to oppose [France] immediately becomes our ally.'[26] Wellesley told the cabinet that this was 'a crisis in which a great effort might be made with advantage', and emphasised that his own force at Cork could easily be sent to the Peninsula rather than to Venezuela. Before the end of the month, he was 'closing the government in such a manner that I may give it up, and taking the command of a corps for service'.[27] The Venezuelan patriot, Miranda, became so agitated when Wellesley told him the news in a London street that 'he was so loud and angry, that I told him I would walk on first a little that we might not attract the notice of everybody passing'. 'You will be lost, nothing can save you,' shouted Miranda. 'That, however, is your affair; but what grieves me is that there was never such an opportunity thrown away.'[28]

Wellesley handed over his Irish responsibilities to John Wilson Croker, MP for Downpatrick, and prepared to take his little army to Portugal. One evening the two men were musing over the port in the Wellesleys' Harley Street dining-room after Kitty had retired upstairs to the drawing-room. Conversation on the Dublin Water Bill palled, and Sir Arthur fell silent. Croker asked him what he was thinking about. Wellesley replied:

> Why, to say the truth, I am thinking of the French that
> I am going to fight. I have not seen them since the

campaign in Flanders, when they were capital soldiers, and a dozen years of victory under Bonaparte must have made them better still. They have, besides, it seems, a new system of strategy which has out-manoeuvred and overwhelmed all the armies of Europe. 'Tis enough to make one thoughtful, but no matter: my die is cast, they may overwhelm me, but I don't think they will out-manoeuvre me. First, because I am not afraid of them as everyone else seems to be; and secondly, because, if what I hear of their system of manoeuvres is true, I think it a false one against steady troops.[29]

He said his farewells, staying with his sister Anne, now married to Charles Smith of Hampton, her first husband having died in 1794, and with the home secretary Lord Hawkesbury. On his way to Holyhead to catch the Dublin packet, he called on the Ladies of Llangollen, who gave him a Spanish prayer book from which he could study the language. His mind was already running in the groove of military detail. The troops at Cork were to be landed frequently from their transports as 'it will tend much to the health of the men and make them feel less unpleasantly the heat and confinement', and 'small tin kettles' were to be procured for the coming campaign.[30]

On 12 July 1808 he sailed in HMS *Donegal*, soon shifting to the faster HMS *Crocodile*. It took him a week to reach La Coruña, where he heard encouraging news of Spanish successes, and told Castlereagh that: 'It is impossible to convey to you an idea of the sentiment which prevails here in favour of the Spanish cause.'[31] He was to be reinforced by a contingent from Gibraltar under Major General Sir Brent Spencer, designated his second-in-command, to whom he outlined his strategy in a letter written aboard *Crocodile* off the mouth of the Tagus on 26 July. Whether or not the Spanish prospered in their struggle, 'nothing we can do can be so useful to them as to get possession of and organise a good army in Portugal ... whether Spain is to continue or to fail, Portugal is an object, and your presence here is most necessary'.[32] This plan, in so many respects a classic example of an expeditionary strategy that combined sea-power with a reluctance to engage a major land power in a theatre where its strength could be concentrated, formed the basis of his conduct during the whole Peninsular war, and was to influence him during the Waterloo campaign of 1815. British command of the sea would guarantee a line of communication to Portugal, and a firm base there would enable the British to operate in Spain, taking as much or as little of the war as they chose. Wellesley also told Spencer that:

> I did not know what the words 'second-in-command' meant ... that I alone commanded the army ... that ... I would treat ... him ... with the most entire confidence, and would leave none of my views or intentions unexplained; but that I would have no second-in-command in the sense of his having anything like superintending control ...[33]

The question of command was soon raised once more. Wellesley stopped briefly at Oporto, where he made arrangements with the bishop for the supply of oxen and mules to the army. Then, after discussions with Admiral Sir Charles Cotton, he prepared to land his army amidst the thunderous surf of Mondego Bay, a hundred miles north of Lisbon, for the Tagus estuary contained not only French-manned vessels, but also a Russian fleet whose attitude was uncertain.

In Mondego Bay, Wellesley received a letter from Castlereagh containing both good news and bad. The army in Portugal was to be increased by the addition of 15,000 men, including a force under Lieutenant General Sir John Moore, which had previously been dispatched to Sweden. Both the king and the Duke of York had already complained that Wellesley was too junior to command the expedition, and its reinforcement made his supersession inevitable. He was told that Sir Hew Dalrymple was to be sent out to command, with Sir Harry Burrard as his second-in-command; and four more lieutenant generals, all senior to Wellesley, were to make their way to Portugal. Sir Arthur sent a courteous reply to Castlereagh, thanking him for his support and emphasising that he would do his best to ensure the army's success regardless of his own position, and would not hurry ahead with operations before his seniors arrived 'in order that I may acquire the credit of the success'. He was, however, more candid in a latter to the Duke of Richmond: 'I hope that I shall have beat Junot before any of them arrive, and then they may do as they please with me.'[34]

His first steps were entirely characteristic. A General Order stressed that Portugal was friendly territory and its inhabitants were to be treated accordingly. Their 'religious prejudices' were to be respected, with officers removing their hats, soldiers saluting and sentries presenting arms when the Host passed them in the streets. A stirring proclamation to the people of Portugal announced that his men had landed 'with every sentiment of faith, friendship and honour', and were wholly committed to 'the noble struggle against the tyranny and usurpation of France'.[35] He met Major General Bernadino Freire, the local Portuguese commander, arranged for his men to be given 5,000 muskets and sets of infantry equipment, and appointed Lieutenant Colonel Nicholas Trant, British military agent in Portugal (described by Wellesley as 'a very good officer, but as drunken a dog as ever lived') as his liaison officer with Freire.

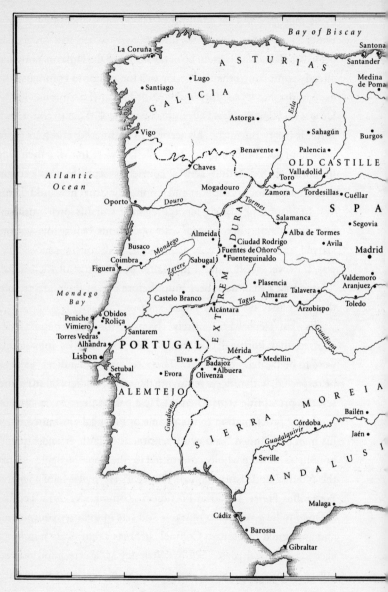

The Iberian Peninsula

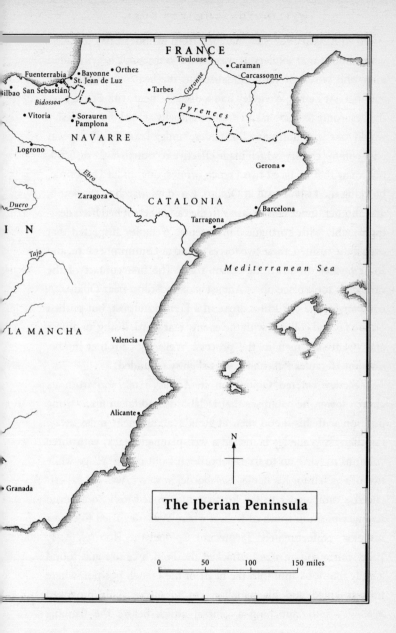

The Iberian Peninsula

0   50   100   150 miles

On 10 August Wellesley marched from Mondego Bay to Leiria with some 15,000 soldiers. It was a hard journey for heavily laden men who were not yet acclimatised to the heat of a Portuguese summer. At Leiria, Wellesley had a disagreement with Freire over the best route to Lisbon, and it was eventually agreed that Wellesley would take with him 1,600 Portuguese under Trant. Wellesley was badly off for cavalry, which made effective reconnaissance difficult, but knew that he faced two French armies, one under Delaborde, blocking the Lisbon road at Obidos, two days march to the south, and another under Loison, away to the east, where it had been dealing roughly with Portuguese insurgents. Wellesley suspected that even if they united, these two forces would not outnumber him, and so he pushed on down the Lisbon road. The first contact of the campaign took place on 15 August 1808 at Brilos, near Obidos. A company of the 95th Rifles drove in a French outpost, but pushed on too far and collided with the enemy rearguard, losing an officer and twenty-six men in the process. Wellesley's brother-in-law, Captain Hercules Pakenham, was slightly wounded.

Wellesley entered Obidos on 16 August 1808, and from its church tower, he could see that Delaborde had taken up a strong position with his 4,000 men at Roliça, about eight miles away. On the 17th, Wellesley launched a well-planned attack, with three columns moving up to fix Delaborde in front of the village while two others felt for his flanks. Delaborde, however, was too experienced a campaigner to fall for that, and pulled back to an even stronger position south of Roliça, where Wellesley tried to repeat his ploy. Unfortunately, Lieutenant Colonel the Hon. G. A. F. Lake, commanding 1/29th, attacked the French centre and found a gully that took him into the heart of the French position where he was killed and his battalion cut to pieces. This provoked Wellesley into launching a general attack before the flanking columns were in position, and Delaborde conducted a skilful fighting withdrawal, though he had to abandon three of his five guns. It was hardly a crushing victory but it was certainly a promising start, and stands as an early rebuttal of the myth that Wellesley was simply a defensive general.

There were now reinforcements off the coast, and on 18 August Wellesley sent orders for them to proceed to the Maceira estuary, fifteen miles south-west of Roliça, and marched his army there to cover the landing. His army was now 17,000 men strong. Burrard – Dalrymple's second-in-command – had also arrived, and on the 20th, Wellesley met him aboard his ship. Burrard, with a better idea of French strength, ordered Wellesley to keep the army where it was until it was joined by Sir John Moore's force, which was to land in Mondego Bay. Wellesley rode back to the army, drawn up astride the Maceira on two long ridges with the village of Vimiero to their front.[36] In the small hours of 21 August, he heard that Delaborde and Loison, now united under the command of Junot, were approaching not from the south, but from the east, and after dawn he shifted troops from the western ridge to reinforce those on the eastern, and threw two brigades forwards onto the flat-topped Vimiero Hill, just south of the village.

The first French blow fell on the brigades on Vimiero Hill. They were drawn up with four companies of 2/95th and the whole of 5/60th, all armed with rifles, on the forward slope of the hill, forming a strong skirmish line, with the other five battalions further back, three just behind the crest and two deeper, in reserve. The hill was attacked by two large French columns, each about thirty men broad and at least forty deep, marching behind a screen of skirmishers and supported by field guns. The French skirmishers were checked by the British riflemen, who did not fall back until the main columns came into play. It was not until the riflemen retired that they unmasked the British guns, which had time to get off only a round apiece before column met line.

The first battle on Vimiero Hill that morning was a microcosm of what was to happen elsewhere that day, and on a dozen other dry, red-earthed Peninsular battlefields over the next few years. The northern French column encountered 1/50th drawn up in a line two deep, so that every one of its 800 muskets could bear. The first volley crashed out at 100 yards, and was followed by repeated volleys at 15-second intervals as the range shortened. As the firefight went on, the flanks of the 50th gradually edged forward, like a rather flat letter U, to enfold the head of the column. The slightly convex curl of the slope meant that the 50th had been engaged neither by skirmishers nor by artillery before the column arrived. Columns, whatever their nationality, could indeed break lines that were already weakened and disconcerted before the column came up to administer a shock, which was as much psychological as it was physical. But an intact line was another matter and faced with this one, General Thomières, the French brigade commander, attempted to deploy from column into line to meet fire with fire. The drill movement was a familiar one, but this was neither the time nor the place to carry it out, with soldiers out of breath from toiling up the hill, galled by the fire of skirmishers and artillery, and now under sustained close-range musketry. It is no reflection on French bravery to say that they could neither deploy nor stand, but broke away down the hill with the riflemen running out to shoot at them as they fell back.[37]

Successive attacks, spreading out against the whole of Wellesley's eastern flank, were just as gallantly launched, but fared no better, and now British guns, firing shrapnel for the first time in Europe, were reaching out to rake columns long before they came into

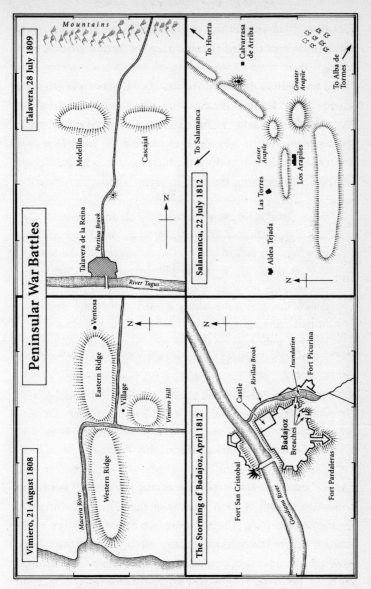

Peninsular War Battles

contact with the line. Rifleman Benjamin Harris of the 95th, busy with his Baker rifle in the skirmish line, saw 'regular lanes opened through their ranks as they advanced, which were immediately closed up again as they marched steadily on. Whenever we saw a round shot go through the mass, we raised a shout of delight.'[38] As one of the attacks ebbed back Wellesley, on hand at the crucial spot, as was so often the case, launched the 20th Light Dragoons and some Portuguese cavalry in a counter-attack. Sergeant George Landsheit charged with the 20th.

'Now, Twentieth! Now!' shouted Sir Arthur, while his staff clapped their hands and gave us a cheer, the sound of which was still in our ears when we put our horses to their speed. The Portuguese likewise pushed forward, but through the dust which entirely enveloped us, the enemy threw in a fire which seemed to have the effect of paralysing altogether our handsome allies. Right and left they pulled up, as if by word of command, and we never saw more of them till the battle was over. But we went very differently to work. In an instant we were in the heart of the French cavalry, cutting and hacking, and upsetting men and horses in the most extraordinary manner possible, till they broke and fled in every direction, and then we fell on the infantry.[39]

The 20th cut their way through the fleeing infantry but were soon checked by a wall of fresh infantry and, worst of all, two fresh regiments of cavalry. The regiment lost almost a quarter of its strength before reaching the relative safety of the British lines. Amongst the dead was Lieutenant Colonel Taylor, shot through the heart. Benjamin Harris, lying exhausted amongst the dead and wounded, was almost killed as the Light Dragoons thundered past.

'I observed a fine, gallant looking officer leading them on in that charge,' he wrote in his *Recollections*.

> He was a brave fellow, and bore himself like a hero; with his sword waving in the air, he cheered the men on, as he went dashing upon the enemy, and hewing and slashing at them in tremendous style. I watched him as the dragoons came off after that charge, but saw him no more: he had fallen. Fine fellow! His conduct indeed made an impression on me that day that I shall never forget.[40]

Wellesley was less favourably impressed. His dispatch to Burrard reported that the 20th Light Dragoons had met French cavalry 'much superior in numbers' and been badly cut up. But pride of place went to the 36th Regiment. 'I cannot avoid adding that the regular and orderly conduct of this corps throughout the service, and their gallantry and discipline in action, have been conspicuous,' he wrote.[41] Wellesley felt his cavalry had made a bad start by galloping off in pursuit of their enemies after an initial success, and he was to see the same thing happen again, most notably in the action at Maguilla in June 1812, which prompted him to complain of:

> the trick our officers of cavalry have acquired of galloping at everything, and their galloping back as fast as they gallop upon the enemy. They never consider their situation, never think of manoeuvring before an enemy; so little that one would think they cannot manoeuvre, excepting upon Wimbledon Common; and when they use their arm as it ought to be used, viz., offensively, they never keep nor provide for a reserve.[42]

Although Wellesley had never been a real cavalry officer, despite his brief passage through the Light Dragoons, he was a keen

foxhunter and had led the decisive cavalry charge against Dhoondiah Waugh – when he himself had no reserve – and so knew
from personal experience just how hard it was to keep control of
excited horsemen. It was precisely this lack of control that was
the basis of his dissatisfaction with the cavalry. He prized those
qualities of order, regularity, and thus reliability that he had
praised in the 36th Regiment. He could never maintain the same
control over his cavalry, and in his dispatches he not only paid
them less credit than they deserved (the fine outpost work carried
out by hussars and light dragoons in the Peninsula often went
unremarked), but also gave ample ammunition to historians who
did not bother to look further.[43]

By midday the battle was won. All the French attacks had failed,
with the loss of about 2,000 men and at least 13 guns to Wellesley's
loss of 720 men. Junot's army was in no state to resist a co-ordinate
counter-attack. Sir Harry Burrard had arrived on the eastern ridge,
and generously left the conduct of the battle to Wellesley. But if
Junot was to be pursued, it could only be Burrard's decision.
Wellesley galloped across to him, and said:

> Sir Harry, now is your chance. The French are completely
> beaten; we have a large body of troops that have not yet
> been in action. Let us move on Torres Vedras. You take
> the force here straight forward; I will bring round the
> left with the troops already there. We shall be in Lisbon
> in three days.[44]

But Burrard would have none of it, and ordered the army back
to its bivouacs. He was himself superseded by Sir Hew Dalrymple,
who arrived from Gibraltar the next day.

Neither contemporary public opinion nor subsequent history
has dealt kindly with Dalrymple and Burrard, and we must not

let the fact that they came close to prejudicing Wellesley's career
as gravely as their own induce us to write them off as amiable old
buffers. Dalrymple had been commissioned in 1763 at the age of
thirteen, but had not been on active service until the Flanders
campaign of 1793. He had made the best of a difficult job as
governor of Gibraltar despite the intricacies of Spanish politics
and lack of clear orders from the government. Burrard, commissioned into the Coldstream Guards in 1772, had exchanged
into the 60th Regiment to serve in North America, and transferred
to 1st Foot Guards on his return. He sat sporadically in parliament
for the family seat of Lymington, served in the Flanders campaign,
commanded a brigade on the 1799 Helder expedition, and was
Cathcart's second-in-command at Copenhagen. Both felt uncomfortable with arrangements. Dalrymple had not been formally
replaced at Gibraltar, and had been given the Portuguese command 'for the present'. Moreover, in a personal letter, Castlereagh
urged him 'to make the most prominent use' of Wellesley, who
'has been for a length of time in the past in the closest habits
of communication with His Majesty's Ministers . . .' Dalrymple
suspected that 'something seemed to lurk under this most compli-
cated arrangement:' he might be superseded himself, possibly by
the Duke of York, or blamed if anything went wrong.[45]

Burrard was even more uneasy. He arrived off the coast to find
Wellesley determined to take on the French, and feared that if
Junot was able to unite his forces, he would outnumber the British.
'I begin to be apprehensive,' he wrote after Roliça, 'that if he
[Wellesley] should meet with a superior force he will have nothing
to fall back on.' He himself had been captured in 1798 when his
brigade, landed on the Flanders coast as part of a large-scale
raid, was captured when the surf rose, preventing the navy from
evacuating it. He had good reason to mistrust operations against

an aggressive enemy across a difficult coast. When Wellesley had met him aboard HMS *Brazen* on the 20th, as we have seen, Burrard took counsel of his fears and 'decided that the army should halt' until Moore's corps could join them from the north and guarantee their superiority. He wrote to Moore, ordering him to re-embark at Mondego Bay and land at Maceira: it would take time, but risk nothing. He was rowed ashore on the morning of Vimiero, and met on the beach by a messenger from Wellesley who told him that battle had been joined. He arrived on the field in time to see the French repulsed, and 'directed him [Wellesley] to go on with an operation he had so happily and so well begun'. But nothing he saw altered his decision not to advance.

When Dalrymple arrived on the 22nd, he met Wellesley on the beach, superintending the embarkation of his wounded. Sir Arthur immediately began 'to represent to him the necessity for an immediate advance', leading Dalrymple to suspect that he was trying to circumvent Burrard, and inducing him to point out that he had only just arrived and was in no position to make a judgement. Dalrymple rode up to Vimiero, past carts bringing the wounded down to the beach and houses that had been converted into temporary hospitals. A meeting with Burrard, to which Wellesley was eventually invited, emphasised the army's logistic difficulties, for 'future supplies ... depended on the victuallers, and the victuallers on the weather'. No decisions had been reached when word arrived that the whole French army was advancing, and Dalrymple ordered Wellesley to take up his earlier defensive positions. However, at about 2.00pm a French patrol reached the outposts of the 50th escorting General François Etienne Kellermann with a flag of truce. He had come to suggest an armistice.

Junot had concluded that his position was impossible in the long term, and hoped to negotiate the evacuation of his army from

Portugal. The three British generals regarded this as a favourable outcome for the campaign, all the more so, in Wellesley's case, because the chance of inflicting a major defeat on Junot had now passed. The British discussed terms amongst themselves, and then negotiated with Kellermann. Dalrymple was later to argue that 'Sir Arthur Wellesley appeared to me to bear the prominent part in this discussion', something Wellesley always denied. Kellermann eventually dictated the fair copy of the agreement, and, probably recognising that Wellesley's personal reputation and high standing with the government would make it hard for Britain to repudiate the agreement, suggested that Wellesley, his equal in rank, should sign it.[46] Wellesley, waiting in another room, was called in by Dalrymple, who asked him whether he had any objection to signing the instrument. Wellesley said that he would sign anything Dalrymple wished him to sign, observed that it was 'a very extraordinary paper', but proceeded to put his name to it.

The Convention of Cintra, which elaborated the terms of the original armistice, was a triumph for the French. They were to be returned to France by the Royal Navy without becoming prisoners of war, and were to take with them 'their arms and baggage, with their personal property of every kind'. The Russian squadron at Lisbon was to sail unmolested, and no reprisals were to be taken against Portuguese who had supported the French. In these latter respects, the British generals were clearly acting beyond their powers, and Wellesley was unhappy enough with the Convention to write, the very next day, to beg Castlereagh not to blame him for it, for it had been negotiated by Dalrymple. Although he agreed that the French should evacuate Portugal, he felt the terms too generous. He spent the rest of the summer dealing with the French evacuation, but felt that he had 'been too successful with this army ever to serve with it in a subordinate situation, with satisfaction

This is the Convention that Nobody owns, that saved old Junots Baggage and Bones, altho Sir Arthur (whose Valour and skill began so well but ended so ill,) had beaten the French who took the Gold that lay in the City of Lisbon.

A contemporary cartoon ridiculing the Convention of Cintra. A smug General Junot looks on while Wellesley unwisely signs the convention which allowed the French to take their plunder home with them.

to the person who shall command it, and of course not to myself'.[47] After declining a suggestion that he should go to Spain to formulate plans for its defence, on 5 September 1808 he told Castlereagh that 'it is quite impossible for me to continue with this army' and asked to resume office in Ireland, to be given an appointment on the staff, or simply to remain unemployed.[48]

Wellesley's worst fears about the Convention of Cintra were realised. The French achieved a very generous definition of private property. In Junot's case this included a bible from the royal library, which his wife later sold for 85,000 francs, and Junot's paymaster general removed £25,000 from the Portuguese treasury. In England, initial press reports had paid handsome tribute to Wellesley's achievements at Roliça and Vimiero. But when news of the Convention broke in early September, the mood changed. Castlereagh thought that there must be 'base forgery' in his copy of it, and the prime minister found the terms so poor that he thought it 'impossible that any English officer could have sanctioned them.'[49] Wellesley came in for the lion's share of the blame, and the efforts of his Tory friends to help simply attracted the fire of the opposition and its friends in the press, who, fresh from their attacks on Richard, now assailed Arthur too. The *Chronicle* begged that 'if the Wellesleys must be employed, for God's sake, let it henceforth be in regulating the police of the City of Dublin, or in enforcing the residence of the Irish clergy'. There was even a squib mocking:

> This is Sir Arthur (whose valour and skill
> began so well but ended so ill)
> Who beat the French, who took the gold
> That lay in the city of Lisbon . . .

Lord Byron caught the mood of the moment, declaiming in *Childe Harold* how 'Britannia sickens, Cintra! At thy name.' The City of London's Court of Common Council demanded a public enquiry, and the government promptly recalled both Dalrymple and Burrard (Wellesley had already returned), giving command in the Peninsula to Moore. On 1 November 1808, it announced its intention to hold an enquiry.

A board of seven general officers appointed 'to enquire into the Convention &c in Portugal' met in the great Hall of the Royal Hospital at Chelsea on 14 November under the presidency of General Sir David Dundas. The board examined a mass of written documents and heard evidence from witnesses. The proceedings became, as Michael Glover observed, 'a duel between Dalrymple and Wellesley', and on 22 December, the board presented its findings to the king. Wellesley's operations were 'highly honourable and successful', and given the 'extraordinary circumstances under which two Commanding Generals arrived from the ocean and joined the army, the one during, and the other immediately after a battle, and those successively superseding each other, and both the original Commander within the space of twenty-four hours . . .' it was not surprising that victory at Vimiero was not followed up. The board was then pressed to elaborate its views in more detail, and although three of its members affirmed that they disapproved of the Convention, the majority approved of it.

This concluded official proceedings. The government saw off a political assault, first ensuring that Wellesley was awarded the thanks of parliament for Vimiero and then voting down an opposition move to censure the Convention. Dalrymple was not helped by the fact that he was a Scot, and there was a marked anti-Scottish feeling in London, a legacy of deeper eighteenth-century undercurrents but given recent momentum by the impeachment of Henry Dundas, Viscount Melville, for 'gross maladversion and breach of duty' at the admiralty in 1805. And by now the public was losing interest, for there was fresh news from the Peninsula. Sir John Moore had driven deep into Spain, but was opposed by superior forces under Napoleon himself, and had made a painful retreat in the depths of winter, reaching the port of La Coruña on 11 January 1809. Moore was mortally wounded in a battle outside the town, and his survivors were evacuated by the Royal Navy. The opposition hailed him as a victim of governmental incompetence, and the heat was off the Wellesleys.

Sir Arthur himself was back in Dublin Castle, snapping at the questing Lord Enniskillen that there were no sinecures left in Ireland and urging 'patience and [good] temper' on Kitty.[50] Poor Kitty had already been complaining to her cousins of Arthur's coldness and neglect, and with reason. Wellesley seems to have been a regular customer at Mrs Porter's establishment in Berkeley Street, and asked her to approach the notorious courtesan Harriette Wilson for him. Harriette alleged that they became lovers, and although there are serious inconsistencies in her account, there are also flashes of pure Wellington. During the Cintra enquiry, she told him that: 'They say you will be hanged, in spite of all your brother Wellesley can say in your defence.' 'They must not work me in another such campaign,' he riposted, 'or my weight will never hang me.' However, he was more fortunate than Dalrymple, who was dismissed from his post at Gibraltar that month and not restored to favour till 1814, when he was awarded a baronetcy. It is perhaps a reflection of the government's uneasy conscience that this was 'given free of all the usual charges'. Burrard returned to duty with the guards in London, but was dogged by bad luck. He lost one of his three boys with Moore at La Coruña, and another, an ensign in 1st Foot Guards, died storming San Sebastian in 1813: he himself died at Calshott Castle that same year.

With Moore's death and the wounding of Sir David Baird at La Coruña, command of British forces in Portugal devolved upon Lieutenant General Sir John Cradock, and the government was gloomy about his prospects. On 7 March Wellesley sent Castlereagh a memorandum on the defence of Portugal. He argued that a British army of not less than 30,000 men, well supplied with artillery and cavalry ('because the Portuguese military establishment must necessarily be deficient in these two branches'), working closely with the Portuguese army, which should be restructured under British command, could defend Portugal even if Spain remained in French hands, and its presence would lend valuable support to the Spanish.[51] The government took the hint, and proposed to the king that Wellesley should be appointed, arguing that, as it was unlikely that substantial reinforcements would be sent to Portugal, Wellesley's lack of seniority did not matter. The king, previously hostile to Wellesley, had welcomed him at a levée the previous year, where he told a deputation from the City's Common Council that 'it is inconsistent with the principles of British justice to pronounce judgement without previous investigation'. Having stood by Wellesley in adversity, the king remained supportive as his fortune changed. The fact that the Duke of York had had to resign temporarily as commander-in-chief because of the indiscretions of his former mistress, Mary Anne Clarke, may have helped. Whatever the reason, Wellesley was being given a second chance.

FOUR

PENINSULA

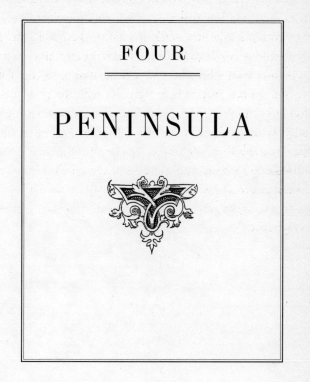

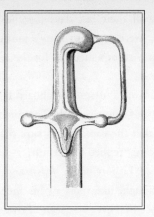

THE LETTER formally appointing Wellesley to command in Portugal arrived on 6 April 1809, and warned him that the defence of that country was his primary concern: he was not to mount operations in Spain without the government's authority. He set about his preparations, moving Kitty to Malvern Wells, organising aides-de-camp and horses, and, if Harriette Wilson is to be believed, calling on her twice. Although he would have to accept the subordinate commanders given him by Horse Guards, he might have expected that Lieutenant General Henry, Lord Paget, would be sent out to command the cavalry. Paget had distinguished himself on the Coruña campaign, and was probably the best senior cavalry officer in the army. However, on 6 March, he ran away with Arthur's sister-in-law, Lady Charlotte Wellesley, wife of his brother Henry, although he had several children and Charlotte four of her own. This upset ensured that Paget could not serve under Arthur, at least for the moment. Lastly, just before he sailed, Kitty lent her brother Henry money to pay his gambling debts and could not settle her household accounts. A disappointed tradesman approached Sir Arthur, who was furious. The episode did not simply spoil their last days together but, in Elizabeth Longford's words, 'were to haunt Kitty's journal during the long months ahead, and Arthur's memory for the rest of their married life'.[1]

Wellesley sailed from Portsmouth aboard HMS *Surveillante* on 14 April in the teeth of a howling gale. That night an aide-de-camp came to tell him that the captain was sure that the vessel would founder: 'In that case,' replied Sir Arthur, 'I shall not take off my boots.'[2] He reached Lisbon on 22 April and found the city in carnival mood, though, like most of his men, he found it 'the most Horrible Place that ever was seen'. Private William Wheeler of the 51st Regiment was even more derogatory:

> What an ignorant superstitious, priest-ridden, dirty, lousy set of devils are the Portuguese. Without seeing them it is impossible to conceive there exists a people in Europe so debased. The filthiest pig sty is a palace to the filthy houses in this dirty stinking city, and all the dirt made in the houses is thrown into the streets, where it remains baking for months until a storm of rain washes it away.[3]

Mindful of the pain of his own recent supercession, Wellesley relieved the torpid Cradock, an old friend, as gently as he could, suggesting that 'it might possibly be more agreeable and convenient to you to see me here than with the army', and in 1819 he was instrumental in gaining him a peerage.

Wellesley's plight was not encouraging. Marshal Soult had over-run northern Portugal: he was at Oporto with perhaps 20,000 men, and was supported by Marshal Ney in Galicia with as many more. Marshal Victor had an even larger army at Mérida, in the Spanish province of Extremadura, ready to enter Portugal by the valleys of the Tagus to the north, or the Guadiana to the south.

Although Wellesley's friend Lieutenant General Sir William Beresford had been appointed to command the Portuguese army with the rank of marshal in that service, it would take time, and a generous admixture of British officers and equipment, for his army to reach full efficiency. As always logistics would drive operations, and Wellesley was busy assembling oxen, mules and horses.

Within two days of arriving, he had decided to leave a detachment to watch Victor, while a larger force, under Beresford, would prevent Soult from moving eastwards to join him. Meanwhile Wellesley, with almost 20,000 men, would head for Oporto to deal with Soult. Although he did not manage to trap Soult south of the city as he had hoped, he reached the Douro on 12 May. However, Soult had blown up the bridges and secured almost all of the boats in the area, and was strongly posted behind the wide river. Wellesley heard that there was a damaged ferry four miles upstream that could be brought back into service, and sent a brigade to cross there. Four intact wine barges, their presence disclosed by a patriotic barber, were brought across from the northern bank. They could take perhaps 600 men an hour into Oporto itself, and the troops could hold out in the walled bishop's seminary on the river as the force built up. Wellesley launched the operation at 10.30 that morning with the laconic words 'Well, let the men cross.'

By the time the French reacted, the seminary was securely held, and its garrison was supported by the fire of Wellesley's guns from the southern bank. After two attacks were beaten off, the French abandoned Oporto, and with it 70 guns and 1,500 of their men in the hospital. In the next week, Wellesley proceeded to elbow Soult out of northern Portugal. Indeed, had it not been for the gallant seizure of a damaged bridge over the Cavado near Salamonde by a party of hand-picked grenadiers under Major Dulong, briefed for the task by Soult in person, a great part of the French army might have been captured. As it was, the results of the campaign were impressive: Soult had lost 4,000 men and all his guns and baggage; Wellesley had less than 500 casualties.

On 18 May Wellesley had been told by Major General Mackenzie that Victor had crossed the border from Spain, and swung south to face him. The rumour proved false, however, and Wellesley was able to pause at Abrantes to repair damaged wagons and gun-carriages. He also needed to repair discipline, having told Castlereagh on 31 May that his army was 'a rabble who cannot bear success any more than Sir J. Moore's army could bear failure'.[4] On 17 June 1809, he wrote more fully from Abrantes, saying that it was 'impossible to describe the irregularities and outrages committed by the troops'. He argued that men were induced to do their duty by fear of punishment and hope of reward. But his own powers were very limited: real authority lay with Horse Guards. He had 'not the power of rewarding, or promising a reward to a single officer in the army', complaining that he had no patronage for the 'incitement of the Officers under my command'. His ability to punish was also sharply circumscribed: regimental courts-martial were not severe enough, and he was in urgent need of more provost staff – he wrote admiringly of the French *gendarmerie* – to help preserve order.[5]

Even before he moved against Soult, Wellesley had written to both the junta of Extremadura in Spain and to Don Gregorio de la Cuesta, captain general of the province, warning them that his first task was to secure Portugal. Having done so, he would then move by way of Elvas, the Portuguese fortress opposite Badajoz on the Spanish side of the frontier, to join Cuesta's army in an attack on Victor. It was decided that the two armies would meet in the Guadiana valley east of Badajoz, and on 10 July 1809

Wellesley rode to meet Cuesta in the village of Miravete, not far from the Tagus bridge at Almaraz. It was one of those meetings that went wrong from the start. Cuesta was expecting him early in the afternoon, and had formed up part of his army for his ally's inspection. But Wellesley's guide got lost, so they arrived long after dark. Cuesta was roused and the guard of honour turned out to be inspected by torchlight. Wellesley concluded that, however brave the Spanish might be, they were neither well-equipped nor well-drilled.

In a quotation so finely-tuned that it is used by almost everybody who writes about the subject, Philip Guedalla describes how: 'Composed in equal parts of pride and failing health, [Cuesta] was the embodiment of Spain at its very worst – old, proud, incompetent and ailing . . .'[6] Rising seventy, and knocked about when his own cavalry had ridden over him at Medellín not long before, Cuesta travelled in a large coach drawn by nine mules, and was hoisted into the saddle when battle seemed imminent. Wellesley complained repeatedly of the impossibility of persuading him to honour any agreement, and later told John Hookham Frere, British envoy to the central junta, that his troops had nothing to eat while the Spanish army had plenty. The situation was intolerable.

So it was; but it was not straightforward. Cuesta had been commissioned long before Wellesley was born, and did not take kindly to being hustled in his own country by a young general to whom he could not speak except through an interpreter. He knew (though apparently Wellesley did not), that Hookham Frere had proposed to the junta that Wellesley should assume overall command of the Anglo-Spanish force, and that Cuesta should be replaced by another Spanish general. Also, the interpreter was Cuesta's chief of staff, Major General Odonoju, his family name once O'Donohue, who was a descendent of one of the 'wild geese',

Irish Catholics who had taken service in Spain after the Protestant William III's victory in Ireland in 1691. Guedalla suggests that Odonoju was 'a friendly reminiscence of Dublin'. But it is more likely that his relationship with Wellesley was coloured by less comfortable overtones as a son of the ascendancy met a dispossessed scion of an older Ireland.

After a long and difficult discussion it was agreed that Wellesley, with 35,000 men, and Cuesta, with 20,000, would meet on 21 July at Oropesa, thirty miles west of Talavera, where Victor was posted with over 20,000 Frenchmen. General Sebastiani had another French army, 22,000 strong, about 75 miles south of Madrid, but Cuesta had ordered a Spanish force under General Venegas to fix Sebastiani in that area, and to report if Sebastiani managed to disengage. This plan would allow Wellesley and Cuesta to attack Victor before he could be reinforced, and it began well. On the 22nd, the allied advanced guards pushed the French back through Talavera, and Victor took up a position on the little river Alberche, which joins the Tagus near Talavera, to its east. Wellesley and Cuesta agreed that on the 23rd, the Spanish would attack from the west while the British turned Victor's flank from the north. The British were ready to attack before dawn, but there was no sign of the Spanish; when Wellesley rode south to find the old gentleman, he was told that the Spanish were too tired to fight that day. Cuesta agreed to move on the 24th, but Victor slipped away during the night.

Things now went from bad to worse. Cuesta pursued Victor towards Toledo only to discover that Sebastiani, playing agile bull to his arthritic matador, had dodged Venegas and joined Victor, who had also been reinforced from Madrid: Joseph Bonaparte had arrived to take command in person with Marshal Jourdan as his chief of staff. Wellesley had not followed the Spanish. He had got wind of Sebastiani's approach, and, more seriously, was so short of food because 'the people of this part of Spain are either unwilling or unable to supply' it, that he had to warn Castlereagh that 'till I am supplied . . . I cannot continue my operations in Spain'.[7] He even considered withdrawing into Portugal, but it was clear that he could not do so now: Cuesta was recoiling westwards, with the French in hot pursuit. Wellesley pushed two of his four divisions across the Alberche to support his allies, and on the 27th, begged Cuesta, by some accounts on bended knee, to cross the river so that both armies could fight side by side on its western bank.

At last Cuesta consented, and Wellesley and Odonoju agreed final dispositions. The Spanish would hold the southern end of the line, by far its strongest section, their right flank anchored on the Tagus and the walled town of Talavera, as far as a prominent hill called the Pajar de Vergara. From there, the British would hold the west bank of the Portina brook, no obstacle in itself, but a useful guide to alignment, and their line was to run northwards, along the eastern edge of the Medellín hill, towards the mountains. While the armies were redeploying, Wellesley rode to a stoutly-built farmhouse just east of the Alberche, dismounted in its court-yard and ascended the stone tower that gives the house its present name, Las Torres. French skirmishers, who had crossed the river quietly, surprised some of his troops nearby, and, probably because he was concentrating on his telescope, which narrowed his field of view, he did not see them until it was almost too late. Wellesley pounded along the upstairs corridor from the tower and leapt down the stairs to escape. He jumped onto his horse and was away with the shots of the skirmishers popping away behind him. Years later, he told Gleig that he was grateful to the grooms, who had 'behaved with perfect steadiness. They took no notice of what was passing outside, but sat upon their horses, holding ours

... If the French had been cool, they might have taken us all ...'[8]

No sooner was he safe than there was heavy firing from the south. The leading French dragoons, trotting forwards through the 'olive trees, much intersected by banks and ditches' in front of the Spanish line, firing their pistols at sentries and stragglers here and there, were greeted by a volley from the Spanish infantry, fired at an impossible range. 'If they will but fire as well tomorrow then the day is our own,' observed Wellesley to an aide, 'but as there seems nobody to fire at just now, I wish you would stop it.'[9] Then 'nearly 2,000 ran off ... (not 100 yards from where I was standing) who were neither attacked, nor threatened with an attack, and who were frightened only by the noise of their own fire'. The carriages of Cuesta and Odonoju were swept away in the torrent, and the fugitives paused only to plunder the British baggage.

Wellesley's men were still not in position when night fell, and he was busy bringing in the last of his divisions from across the Portina. He had intended to place his best division, under Major General Rowland Hill (known affectionately to his men as 'Daddy') on the key ground of the Medellín on his left, but a staff officer positioned them too far west, and led them to believe that they were in the second line. By now Wellesley was just behind the Pajar, receiving reports, when he saw muzzle-flashes to the north and heard the sound of heavy firing. He mounted and rode off to find out what was happening, though the darkness and confusing reports made this difficult. It transpired that a strong French division had crossed the Portina in three columns, and although the night and the broken ground caused them to lose alignment, they had surprised some of Wellesley's King's German Legion (KGL) – first-rate troops raised in the French-occupied kingdom of Hanover – and briefly seized the crest of the Medellín hill. Major General Rowland Hill could see the dark mass of troops, but thought that 'it was the old Buffs [3rd Regiment of Foot] as usual making some blunder', so rode across with a staff officer to put them right. As he reached the crest, a French skirmisher grabbed him and almost dragged him from his horse, and his staff officer was shot dead. Although his mount was hit, he managed to get back to his division, threw a brigade into battalion columns and sent it against the Medellín. The crest was taken by the 29th Regiment, and the position secured; both sides had lost about 400 men in the action. Wellesley spent the night up on the hill, rolled in his cloak, and was about at first light preparing to meet the attack he knew would come.

At 5.00 on the morning of 28 July 1809, a single French gun fired from the summit of the Cascajal, across the Portina from the Medellín, signalling the start of a general bombardment. Between fifty and sixty guns concentrated their fire on the Medellín, where Wellesley ordered his men to fall back behind the crest and lie down, so that most round-shot hissed harmlessly overhead. The smoke hung so thickly that it was hard to see what was happening, but the sound of musketry down on the brook told that riflemen and light companies in front of the main line were taking on the French skirmishers. Behind the latter marched three huge columns of French troops, each sixty men across and twenty-four deep, coming on steadily to the sound of fife and drum.

The imposing spectacle affected even Hill, causing him to swear, one of the two occasions on which he ever did so: 'Damn their filing: let them come on anyhow.'¹⁰ As the columns advanced, Wellesley's infantry moved over the crest and stood ready to meet them. The northernmost column, containing troops who had attacked the previous night, advanced onto unoccupied ground just north of the Medellín and was not seriously engaged; the other two met the British line and were driven back by its volleys.

The British followed up, taking prisoners, but some of them pushed too far across the Portina and were checked by fresh French units on the far side.

There followed a long pause, during which French and British infantry went down to the Portina to get water – in one of those unofficial truces that were so common in the Peninsula – for it was already a very hot day. Sergeant Anthony Hamilton of the 43rd Light Infantry saw how both sides took the opportunity to get their wounded away to the rear and then, 'shaking hands, they mutually expressed admiration of the gallantry displayed by their opponents'.[11] Wellesley used the lull to adjust his position, for he could see that a more general attack would come next. He moved some guns, a British cavalry brigade, Bassecourt's Spanish infantry division, and a Spanish cavalry division to the northern end of his line, between the Medellín and the mountains. French artillery recommenced fire at about 1pm, 80 guns now pounding the line between the Pajar and the Medellín, and about 30,000 infantry then came on in thick columns.

As they met the line, it was the same story as the morning's battle, with disciplined British firepower breaking the French columns as they tried to deploy into line. Yet the ending was different: as the columns melted back, Sherbrooke's division, in the front line just north of the Pajar, went forward in pursuit. One of its brigades, Campbell's, re-formed just east of the Portina, but the other three – including the Guards – carried on. Fugitives from the French first line passed through the second, comprising most of the uncommitted French infantry, which immediately counter-attacked. Many of the British had not reloaded their muskets and were in disorder after the advance; they had little chance. Even so, they fought back hard. The Guards lost a quarter of their strength, but there was not one unwounded prisoner. Campbell's brigade, which might have stood, found its field of fire masked by retreating British and it too was swept away. The French saw their chance, and perhaps 10,000 infantry in columns, accompanied by dragoons and artillery, began to move up to exploit the huge gap in Wellesley's line.

When he saw Sherbrooke's men advance, Wellesley – who described the move as 'nearly fatal to us' – began to shift troops to fill the space behind them. He dared not take much from the Cascajal, but chose a single battalion, 1/48th, the biggest in the army, to close the gap. He ordered a cavalry brigade to move up from the rear, and directed Mackenzie's division, down by the Pajar, to edge northwards. Wellesley had chosen his instrument well. The 48th, gallantly led by Lieutenant Colonel Charles Donnellan, who still dressed in the style of the eighteenth century, with tricorne hat and white buckskin breeches, first swung its companies back like gates on their hinges to allow fugitives to pass through, and the line was re-established. As the British survivors passed through, they rallied with a cheer, and the new line stopped the French attack with yet another demonstration of those terrible volleys. Donnellan was mortally hit, but handed over command with old-fashioned courtesy: 'Major Middlemore, you will have the honour of leading the 48th to the charge.' The infantry pushed forward to the line of the brook, and Cotton's cavalry brigade charged the southernmost French column, which broke.

When Sir Walter Scott later asked Wellesley to have a history of Talavera written, he replied that 'it would be as easy to write the account of a ball as of a Battle! Who was the Partner of Who? Who footed to each other? Who danced down all the couples?'[12] Most historians write that the battle had now passed its crisis, and what followed was a cavalry charge which further diminished the standing of British horsemen in Wellesley's eyes. Wellesley, however, thought that the charge took place *before* the first attack of the afternoon was repulsed and Sherbrooke's advance. Whatever the precise timing, the events were clear enough. French columns had advanced north of the Medellín. They were composed of men who had fought the previous night and that morning, and were now past their best, so Wellesley decided to use his cavalry to check them.

The first line of horsemen, the 23rd Light Dragoons and the 1st Hussars KGL, charged the French infantry, who formed squares as they approached. The light dragoons, already travelling at speed, found a dry watercourse, visible only at the last moment, in their path. Some jumped it, but others came to grief. The survivors re-formed, charged the squares alongside the German hussars, and then went on to attack fresh French cavalry to the rear. The 23rd lost almost half its officers and men in the action. However, Wellesley wrote approvingly of the charge in his dispatch, arguing that it 'had the effect of preventing the execution of that part of the enemy's plan . . .'[13]

By late afternoon, it was apparent that the French plan had indeed failed, and that night Joseph's army withdrew across the Alberche 'in the most regular order', though it left twenty guns behind. Wellesley acknowledged 'the great loss we have sustained of valuable Officers and soldiers in this long and hard fought action fought with more than double our numbers'. He had lost 5,365 men, over a quarter of his entire force, and although the French had suffered over 7,000 casualties, it was a far smaller proportion of their army. The battle had reinforced his conviction that his personal supervision was essential if things were to go well, and that only the firmest discipline could hold the army together in the face of a numerous and aggressive enemy. The 48th set a clear example: not only was it mentioned twice in Wellesley's dispatch, but he also did his best to ensure the promotion of Major Middlemore despite predictable unhelpfulness from Horse Guards.

Although Talavera was unquestionably a victory, it was not one which could be exploited. At first Wellesley thought, 'We shall certainly move towards Madrid, unless we are interrupted by some accident on our flank.' That accident materialised in the form of a thrust from the north by a powerful French army under Soult, and early August saw brisk manoeuvring in the valley of the Tagus before Wellesley began a long retreat to Badajoz. The alliance was under even more pressure, with Wellesley writing furiously to Castlereagh on 8 August that the 'disgrace' of the loss of the hospital at Talavera, with all its wounded, should be laid squarely at Cuesta's door.

Richard, Marquess Wellesley, had just replaced John Hookham Frere as envoy to the central junta, and Arthur lost no opportunity to warn him that supplies were still not forthcoming, and 'the army will be useless in Spain, and will be entirely lost, if this treatment is to continue . . .'[14] 'A starving army is worse than none,' he warned. 'The soldiers lose their discipline and their spirit. They plunder even in the presence of their officers.'[15] On 4 September 1809, a General Order warned against plundering, but with so little effect that a sterner version, three days later, reiterated threats of punishment and told officers that their lack of attention contributed to the 'disgraceful and unmilitary practices of the soldiers'.[16] The Spanish armies suffered two serious defeats in September, confirming Wellesley's belief that he could not hope to remain there. He advised his brother to warn the junta against calling a parliament, because the *Cortes*, 'a new popular assembly', could do nothing but harm. At this stage Spain needed 'men of common capacity', not another talking-shop.

As he fulminated against plundering and ordered the commandant of Elvas to ensure that all men sent forward up the long line of communication had two good shirts and two pairs of shoes, Wellesley received some good news. He was to be given a viscountcy for Talavera, but there had been no time to consult him over the title, so his brother William had made the decision for him. He wrote:

> After ransacking the Peerage and examining the map, I at last determined upon Viscount Wellington of Talavera and Wellington, and Baron Douro of Welleslie in the county of Somerset – Wellington is a town not far from Welleslie ... I trust that you will not think that there is anything unpleasant or trifling in the name of Wellington ...

Arthur told him that he had chosen 'exactly right', but Kitty was not pleased, confiding to her diary that 'I do not like it for it recalls nothing', and it was small compensation for her agonies of worry. 'Surely heaven will protect the good, brave man,' she wrote later, '. . . with all my soul I wish he was at home.' The title was gazetted on 4 September 1809, and on the 16th Arthur signed a letter about 'biscuits and cash balances' to John Villiers, ambassador in Lisbon, as Wellington, adding: 'This is the first time I have signed my new name.'[17]

Wellington, as we may now call him, at last, was not to fight another battle for more than a year. In the interim, he was busy both politically and militarily. Firstly, he set about securing Portugal. In a memorandum of 20 October 1809, he told Lieutenant Colonel Richard Fletcher, his chief engineer, that, while the French could not attack him at the moment, they would do so when reinforced. He knew that Napoleon had beaten the Austrians, and was now free to concentrate on the Peninsula. Lisbon and the Tagus were crucial to the defence of Portugal, and their possession would also permit the British army to be re-embarked if all else failed. Fletcher was ordered to carry out wide-ranging surveys – Wellington listed twenty-one specific tasks – with a view to the construction of three lines of fortification covering the segment of Portugal between the Tagus and the sea. Rivers were dammed and roads broken up to disrupt the French advance, while forts, so close that their fields of fire could interlock, were built on high ground, with lengths of trench and rampart between them. The first line ran twenty-nine miles from Alhandra on the Tagus, through the town of Torres Vedras, to the coast just south of the Ziandre estuary. The second was some six miles further south, and the third, which was centred on Fort St Julian on the Tagus, covered an embarkation beach. Next, Wellington redoubled his efforts to increase the value of the Portuguese army, beginning the process of incorporating a Portuguese brigade in each of his divisions, and ensuring that the Portuguese *ordenanza*, the militia, was properly organised, and was prepared to destroy crops, food stocks, mills and ovens when the French advanced.

Thirdly, he had to deal with the backwash of British politics. Lord Portland's government, weakened by the failure of an expedition sent to the disease-ridden island of Walcheren off the coast of Holland, fell in 1809 amidst such recrimination that Castlereagh fought a duel with George Canning. Neither found themselves in the new Tory administration headed by Spencer Perceval. Lord Liverpool took over from Castlereagh as secretary of state for war, and Richard Wellesley replaced Canning at the foreign office. William Wellesley-Pole went off to be chief secretary of Ireland, and Henry Wellesley (unhappily denying that he was the father of his wife's latest child), took over as British representative to the central junta. Wellington suspected that the new government would not last for long, but had decided that he would serve under 'any administration that may employ me', and opined that 'the Spirit of Party in England' was to blame for 'all the misfortunes of the present reign'.[18] He was more right than he knew, for in the opposition's eyes, he was simply part of the hated clan jobbing in Spain as they had in India, and as one hostile politician observed, 'the Wellesleys will now be beat if they are attacked properly . . .'

Wellington was not helped by the fact that the opposition was well represented in the army. His second-in-command, Sir Brent Spencer, a great favourite at court, was drawn into indiscretions at the royal dinner parties he attended when on leave. His adjutant-general, Charles Stewart, was 'a sad *brouillon* and a mischief-maker'. Even the redoubtable Robert Craufurd of the Light Division, who had been forgiven by Wellington for receiving a well-merited rebuff by the French up on the River Coa, was a notable 'croaker', complaining about the conduct of the campaign. There was no censorship of mail, and officers of all ranks wrote frank letters home. Some could not understand why they had not gone on to Madrid and ended the war, and others resented the long period of inactivity. Wellington was exasperated by it all: 'as soon as an accident happens, every man who can write, and has a friend who can read, sits down to write his account of what he does not know . . .'[19]

Whatever might happen in Westminster, it was in Portugal that Wellington expected the next blow. Portuguese peasants toiled under the supervision of his engineers to embellish the landscape with the bastions and ravelins, tenailles and fausse-brayes beloved of classical fortification. The sheer scale of their achievement is striking even today. Above the town of Torres Vedras one of the forts has been well restored, and from its ramparts one can see similar works on the neighbouring hillsides; the term field fortifications somehow does not catch the scope of it all. Much of the army was less onerously employed, and Wellington maintained his unrelenting efforts to make of it the instrument he sought. The commandant of Lisbon was urged not to allow British officers to sit, with their hats on, on the stage at theatres. Lieutenant William Pearse of the 45th had been 'honourably acquitted' of ungentlemanly conduct in a brawl in a brothel, and the court was bidden to reword its verdict as Wellington was sure that there was 'no officer upon the General Court Martial who wishes to connect the term Honour with the act of going to a Brothel'.[20] An officer was told that 'I cannot give leave to any officer whose health does not require his return to England, or who has business to transact which cannot be done by another, or which cannot be delayed', and Wellington trusted 'that I shall be spared the pain of again refusing you'.[21]

Although Wellington was never on quite the same terms with Liverpool that he had been with Castlereagh, they had been friends in private life, which undoubtedly helped, and the formal 'My Lord' which opened Wellington's first letters – like that of 21 November 1809, lamenting that English newspapers contained accurate reports of the strength and disposition of his army – was soon the more comfortable 'My dear Lord'. In January 1810 he reported that his men were 'a better army than they were some months ago', though he feared that 'they will slip through my fingers . . . when I shall be involved in any nice operation with a powerful enemy to my front'.[22]

That powerful enemy materialised in the spring of 1810. Marshal André Massena, with a total of 138,000 men, perhaps half of them in his field army, had been ordered to retake Portugal. He began by seizing the Spanish fortress of Ciudad Rodrigo, which commanded the northern route into Portugal, on 10 July, and followed on to take its Portuguese counterpart, Almeida, on 28 August after a mortar bomb ignited a train of powder from a damaged keg and blew the main magazine sky-high. Then he advanced into Portugal down the Mondega valley harassed by the *ordenanza* as he went. Wellington knew the ground well, and on 26 September blocked the French advance in formidably strong position, a long steep-sided ridge running from the village of Busaco to the Mondego. Busaco is a formidable position: it is hard simply to keep one's feet on parts of the ridge, and toiling up it, even in the cooler days of September, with musket and pack, must have been almost unbearable. The two armies were roughly equal at about 48,000 apiece, and Massena sought to gain local superiority by concentrating his attack, launched early on a foggy morning, on a narrow axis, with Reynier's corps assaulting south of Busaco and Marshal Ney's making for the village itself. He had a brief glimmer of hope when the capable General Foy broke through part of 1/45th and three Portuguese battalions to reach the crest, but Wellington had already ordered a British division to move up and Foy's men were dispatched back down the hill.

Wellington, galloping along the long, straight road that runs through the trees along the top of the ridge, was always ready to direct counter-thrusts, but his divisional commanders had things well in hand. Major General Craufurd of the Light Division launched his own counter-attack with a great shout of: 'Fifty-Second, avenge Moore!' The French lost over 4,500 men to Wellington's 1,252, and did not resume the attack, but slipped past the ridge, through defiles which, owing to a misunderstanding, the Portuguese militia were not watching.

Wellington had to fall back to avoid being cut off from his

base, but he was not sorry to do so because, as he wrote to Liverpool on 30 September 1810:

> This movement has afforded me a favourable opportunity of showing the enemy the description of troops of which this army is composed; it has brought the Portuguese levies into action with the enemy for the first time in an advantageous situation; and they have proved that the trouble which has been taken with them has not been thrown away, and that they are worthy of contending in the same ranks with British troops . . .[23]

The French entered the undefended city of Coimbra on 1 October and continued to follow Wellington, only to have the garrison of Coimbra and the sick in the hospitals there captured in a well-timed raid by the bibulous Colonel Nicholas Trant and his Portuguese. Had Massena but known it, this was a foretaste of what was to come. The weather broke on 7 October, and Wellington's army began to enter the lines of Torres Vedras the following day. The forts were held by Portuguese militia, a corps of Spanish regulars, and 2,500 British marines and gunners, leaving Wellington's field army free to meet any French attempt to break through. Massena stayed up at Sobral for ten days, and then fell back onto a position between Santarem and Rio Major, where his men, skilled at living off the country and with no regard for the plight of the Portuguese, astonished Wellington by somehow finding enough to eat. He told Liverpool that it was 'an extraordinary instance of what a French army can do . . . I could not maintain one division in the district where they have maintained not less than 60,000 men and 20,000 animals for more than 2 months.'[24]

It could not last. Although Massena was reinforced by some 11,000 men under D'Erlon late in December, he was never strong enough to attack the lines, and sickness, hunger and attacks by Portuguese irregulars were costing him 500 men a week. In March 1811, he slid away to the north-west, abandoning most of his vehicles and hamstringing all surplus animals. There was a sharp little action on the River Coa on 3 April, and Massena reached Almeida on the 11th, after a campaign lasting eleven months that had cost him perhaps 30,000 men.

The next phase of the war centred upon the frontier fortresses of Ciudad Rodrigo in the north, and Badajoz further south. The latter had been taken by Soult, thrusting up from Andalusia, in March, and Wellington entrusted Beresford with the task of besieging it while he concentrated on Almeida and Ciudad Rodrigo. Badajoz and Ciudad Rodrigo were three days apart for Wellington at his hard-riding best. That spring Wellington was responsible for a force at Cádiz under the reliable Lieutenant General Sir Thomas Graham, who had just beaten the French at Barossa; Beresford's allied army in Extremadura; and his own force in Old Castile. Each faced an enemy who was potentially stronger, and both Wellington and Beresford relied on lines of communication running back to Lisbon.

There were two major battles at this juncture, both of them hard-won allied victories, as the French sought to raise the sieges of Badajoz and Almeida. On 3 May 1811, Massena attacked Wellington at Fuentes de Oñoro, south of Almeida, and renewed his efforts on the 5th. This was not a carefully stage-managed defensive battle like Busaco, and there were some very dangerous moments. One of them came when the inexperienced 7th Division was caught out in the open by a superior French force. But Robert Craufurd of the Light Division rose brilliantly to the occasion, rescued the 7th, and then extricated his own troops in a remarkable display of disciplined minor tactics.

The battle ended with a bloody fight for Fuentes itself. Private Thomas Pococke of the 71st, an actor who had enlisted after falling victim to stage-fright, described what happened in his own part of the field:

> A bayonet went through between my side and my clothes, to my knapsack, which stopped its progress. The French-man to whom the bayonet belonged fell, pierced by a ball from my rear-rank man. While freeing myself from the bayonet, a ball took off part of my right shoulder wing, and killed my rear rank man, who fell upon me.

He fired 107 rounds that day, and his shoulder was 'as black as coal' from his musket's recoil. The Connaught Rangers played a distinguished part in capturing the village, and Pococke saw them lying 'two and three deep of dead and wounded'.[25] The 79th was also badly cut up in Fuentes, and despite his manifold cares Wellington found time to write to their colonel, whose son had been mortally wounded commanding it.

> You will always regret and lament his loss, I am con-vinced; but I hope you will derive some consolation from the reflection that he fell in the performance of his duty, at the head of your brave regiment, loved and respected by all who knew him, in an action in which, if possible, British troops surpassed every thing they had ever done before, and of which the result was most creditable to His Majesty's arms.[26]

Having failed in his attempt to relieve Almeida, Massena sent word to the city's governor, ordering him to blow up the magazine and escape. Three French soldiers set off with messages, disguised as peasants; two were caught and shot as spies, but the third succeeded. The resourceful governor, Major General Brennier, fired a pre-arranged signal, three salvoes at five-minute intervals, to tell Massena that the order had been received, and led his men to safety on a dark night, crossing an unguarded bridge at Barba del Puerco. Wellington was furious, calling failure to intercept the French 'the most disgraceful military event that has yet occurred to us'. He told Liverpool that he might have prevented it had he been on the spot, but having deployed two divisions and a brigade to prevent the escape of 1,400 men, he was confident that all was well. Then he returned to a familiar theme. 'I am obliged to be every where,' he grumbled, 'and if absent from any operation, something goes wrong.'[27]

He blamed Lieutenant Colonel Bevan of the 4th Regiment, who had been ordered to the bridge. In fact the order had been written out by the notoriously incompetent Lieutenant General Sir William Erskine, who had stuffed it into his pocket with his snuff box and forgot about it. By the time Bevan received the order, it was midnight. Had he broken camp and marched immediately, he could have reached the bridge on time, but he waited till dawn, and it was too late: Brennier was across. Erskine told Wellington that the 4th had got lost – which is what Wellington reported in his dispatch to Liverpool. Bevan begged for an enquiry, but Wellington decided to court-martial him instead. Although a trial might have brought out some of the case in Bevan's failure, he did not wait for it, and blew his brains out. Wellington was widely blamed for Bevan's suicide, but if he sensed the climate, he paid no attention to it. He wrote sharply to Major General Alexander Campbell, a close friend of the Prince Regent's, warning him that the army was full of 'the desire to be forward in engaging the enemy'; but he would do better to show 'a cool, discriminating judgement in action'.[28] He was even more frank when writing to his brother William Wellesley-Pole that: 'there is nothing so stupid as a gallant officer'.[29]

Wellington's conviction that things inevitably went wrong if he was not present was reinforced by events further south. On his orders, Beresford had begun to besiege the powerful fortress of Badajoz on 5 May 1811. His efforts were not simply hampered by the great strength of the place, but by the fact that he was pitifully short of heavy guns, and had to rely on elderly pieces borrowed from Elvas. Beresford soon heard that Soult was on his way to relieve Badajoz, and so he temporarily abandoned the siege and marched out to meet him. The local Spanish army commanders, Blake and Castaños, agreed to fight under Beresford's command, and on 16 May he faced the French on a low ridge near the village of Albuera. Soult pinned Beresford to his position by a frontal feint, and then threw his whole weight against the allied right. Although British sources are often disdainful of Spanish battlefield performance, there is no doubt that the dogged courage of Zaya's division, on Beresford's right, checked the initial French assault, allowing time for Stewart's division to come up.

Stewart's leading brigade arrived just in time to be greeted by a sudden rainstorm, which made many of its muskets useless, and by a determined cavalry charge, which took advantage of the fact: three of its four battalions were cut to pieces, one of them, the Buffs, losing over 80 per cent of its strength. At this point Beresford seems to have lost his presence of mind, and Lowry Cole, prompted by a bright, young staff officer, Henry Hardinge, brought his 4th Division up without orders. There followed one of the most prodigious firefights of the entire period, with Cole's brigades steadily making their way forward, men loading and firing as if in a dream, closing to the centre as musketry and grapeshot winnowed their ranks, and realising that they were making progress because the nationality of the dead on whom they trampled changed from allied to French. It was there that the 57th Regiment

earned its own niche in the military pantheon, with its commanding officer, hard hit, shouting: 'Die hard, 57th, die hard.' Sir William
Napier, Peninsula infantry officer and one of the campaign's most
notable historians, has subjective views on the conduct of the
battle and a low regard for Beresford, but his prose rises to meet
the high drama of the occasion:

> ... then was seen with what a strength and majesty
> the British soldier fights ... Nothing could stop that
> astonishing infantry. No sudden burst of undisciplined
> valour, no nervous enthusiasm, weakened the stability of
> their order, their flashing eyes were bent on the dark
> columns to their front, their measured tread shook the
> ground, their dreadful volleys swept away the head of
> every formation, their deafening shouts overpowered the
> dissonant cries that broke from all parts of the tumult-
> uous crowd ... the mighty mass gave way and like a
> loosened cliff went headlong down the steep. The rain
> flowed after in streams discoloured with blood, and
> fifteen hundred unwounded men, the remnant of six
> thousand unconquerable British soldiers, stood triumph-
> ant on that fatal hill![30]

Beresford had lost 6,000 men (two thirds of them from his
British infantry) and Soult 8,000. His dispatch to Wellington paid
handsome tribute to 'the distinguished gallantry of the troops',
and he reported that 'our dead, particularly the 57th Regiment,
were lying as they had fought in ranks, and every wound was in
front'.[31]

Beresford had written to Wellington the moment Soult appeared,
and Wellington, mistrustful as ever, hurtled southwards, riding so
hard that two of his horses died. But he was too late: Beresford
had fought at Albuera before he arrived. Wellington, seeing that

Beresford was downcast at his losses, did his best to console him by saying: 'You could not be successful in such an action without a large loss. We must make up our minds to affairs of this kind sometimes, or give up the game.'[32] But he was harsher when writing to his brother, Henry, a few days later. The Spanish, although capable of great bravery, were inflexible, and the British had 'suffered accordingly' in assisting them. 'I am not very easy about the results of another action,' he continued, 'should we be obliged to fight one.'[33] At Fuentes, Wellington had faced a superior force marching to relieve Almeida and beaten it, losing less than 2,000 men; Beresford, in spite of a numerical advantage, had lost far more heavily. Wellington visited a hospital near the field, and found it full of wounded of the 29th Regiment. 'Men of the 29th, I am sorry to see so many of you here,' he said. 'If you had commanded us, My Lord,' replied a sergeant, 'there wouldn't be so many of us here.'[34] A Geordie private in 7th Fusiliers had made the same point to his mate George Spencer Cooper on the morning of the battle. 'Whore's ar *Arthur*?' he asked. 'I don't know, I don't see him,' replied Cooper. 'Aw wish he wor here,' said the man. 'And so,' mused Cooper, 'did I.'[35]

Despite allied victories at Fuentes de Oñoro and Albuera, the French still held Badajoz and Ciudad Rodrigo, and could use them as stepping-stones for another invasion of Portugal. That summer Wellington renewed the siege of Badajoz, but made poor progress, and an attempt to storm Fort San Cristobal, an outwork on the northern side of the Guadiana, was bloodily repulsed. William Wheeler survived the assault, and commented on the state of Ensign Dyas – 'a young officer of great promise, of a most excellent disposition, and beloved by every man in the Corps' – and the other survivors. Dyas, was without cap, his sword was shot off close to the handle, the sword scabbard was gone, and the laps of his frock coat were perforated with balls. Indeed everyone who returned bore evident marks of where they had been. Their caps, firelocks, belts etc were more or less damaged. I had three shots pass through my cap, one of which carried away the rosehead and tuft, my firelock was damaged near the lock, and a ball had gone through the butt.[36]

Wellington recognised that he could not take the place with strong French field armies hovering nearby, and he moved north to peck at Ciudad Rodrigo, but the problem was the same: strong French forces were too close to enable him to mount a siege with any real prospect of success. It was not until the end of the year that the tide began to turn in his favour as some of Marmont's troops from Old Castile were sent off to help Marshal Suchet against the Spanish in Valencia. 'Daddy' Hill brought substantial reinforcements from Portugal, demolishing a French force at Arroyos Molinos on his way forwards, and the siege train, with its heavy guns, was not far behind him. On 8 January 1812, the allied army began to besiege Ciudad Rodrigo, in weather so cold that as John Mills of the Coldstream Guards told his mother, 'the water froze in the mens' canteens'.[37]

The attractive town of Ciudad Rodrigo, with its high walls and old Moorish castle, still dominates the surrounding countryside. Its lofty position, once a source of strength, was a weakness in the artillery age, and its walls were far less robust than those of Badajoz. The French had repaired the damage they had done in taking the town in 1810, and built a redoubt on top of the Greater Teson, a hill which dominated the northern defences. The Light Division took it on the night of 8 January, and the allies immediately began working on trenches, establishing batteries of heavy guns which began firing on the 13th. Six days later, there were two breaches in the walls, the greater opposite the Teson hills and the lower slightly to its east. Wellington ordered an assault that night, with Sir Thomas Picton's 3rd Division attacking the greater breach and Craufurd's Light Division the lesser. There were to be subsidiary attacks elsewhere.

The assault began at about 7pm on 19 January. The French defended both breaches stubbornly, and exploded a mine under the greater breach just as the Light Division's leading brigade took it, causing casualties to both sides. But both assaulting divisions, led with selfless determination, were making good progress into the town, and the subsidiary attacks had also entered the place. By now the French garrison was well aware that sustained resistance was not only fruitless, but likely to inflame the attackers, who were not obliged to give quarter to a garrison which had fought on after a practicable breach had been established. John Mills entered the town after the storm and found a scene of things which 'can be neither described nor imagined'. Lieutenant John Kincaid of the 95th had been in the Light Division's storming party, and describes how:

> A town taken by storm presents a frightful scene of outrage. The soldiers no sooner obtain possession of it, than they think themselves at liberty to do what they please ... without considering that the poor inhabitants may nevertheless be friends and allies ... and nothing but the most extraordinary exertions on the part of the officers can bring them back to a sense of duty.[38]

Picton did his best to restore order, swearing like a trooper and belabouring drunken men with a broken musket-barrel, but it was only exhaustion that stopped the pillage. When Wellington rode into the town next morning he saw a bizarre sight as men stumbled past, 'some of them dressed in Frenchmens' coats, some in white breeches and huge jack-boots, some with cocked hats and queues; most of their swords were fixed on their rifles, and stuck full of hams, tongues and loaves of bread, and not a few were carrying bird cages'. 'Who the devil are those fellows?' he asked, and was told that it was the 95th.[39] On this occasion 'no Spanish civilians were killed and only a few molested,' but the portents were not good.

The siege had cost Wellington 568 casualties and the French about the same, though the whole garrison of almost 2,000 was captured. Robert Craufurd was amongst the wounded. His spine had been smashed by a musket ball, and he lingered on in agony for a week, always asking after George Napier, who had commanded his division's storming party and lost his arm. Craufurd was a strict disciplinarian and inspired tactician, but had been one of the many 'croakers' who had complained to their friends in England that Wellington was too cautious. He apologised before he died, and Wellington reflected that 'he talked to me as they do in a novel'. The Light Division buried him in the lesser breach. He had always insisted that the division should never deviate from its line of march, and on the way back from the funeral the leading files found a long marshy pool in their way. They marched straight through the icy, thigh-deep water, and every officer and man followed them in silence. Kincaid recalled how unpopular Craufurd had once been, 'and it was not until a short time before he was lost to us for ever that we were capable of appreciating his merits . . .'

On 29 January 1812 Wellington told Liverpool that he proposed to attack Badajoz as soon as he could, once Rodrigo and Almeida

LEFT Sir Thomas Lawrence's famous 1824 portrait of Wellington at Waterloo was originally painted with a watch in the duke's hand, but he objected that he had not been waiting for the Prussians, and told Lawrence to put a telescope there instead.

BELOW This detail from a vast canvas by Sir William Allen shows Wellington presiding over the repulse of the Imperial Guard.

LEFT Although his pose might have been too theatrical for his taste, this painting catches something of the flavour of Waterloo. As the afternoon wore on the duke rode from square to square, saying: 'Stand fast! We must not be beat! What will they say of this in England?'

BELOW LEFT In a Waterloo battle-piece which unusually mingles accuracy with atmosphere, Denis Dighton shows British guardsmen and French infantry fighting in front of the south gate of Hougoumont.

BELOW In the charge of the Union Brigade, Sergeant Charles Ewart of the Royal Scots Greys captured the eagle of the French 45th Regiment.

RIGHT Waterloo banquets, held at Apsley House on the anniversary of the battle, became annual events. Here the artist has ensured that the faces of all surviving senior officers can be seen and, for good measure, included both himself and his publisher amongst the gentlemen in the background.

BELOW Wellington (right foreground) with the reformed House of Commons behind him. The spectacle provoked him to declare that he had never seen so many bad hats in all his life.

Some cartoonists were not above alluding to the duke's virility. Here the master-general of the ordnance is shown astride a cannon. One lady exclaims: 'Bless us! What a Spanker! I hope he won't fire it at me. I could never support such a thing.' 'It can't do any harm,' retorts her friend, 'for he has fired it so often, in various Countries, that it is nearly wore out.'

In 'Punishment Drill', a cartoon of 1830, the duke is shown carrying the burdens of office – Catholic Emancipation, the budget and the Treasury amongst them – through the mire of politics.

Benjamin Robert Haydon stayed with Wellington at Walmer in 1839 to prepare *Wellington Musing on the Field of Waterloo*. The duke disliked the Lion Mound, erected on the spot where the Prince of Orange was wounded, maintaining that it had spoiled his battlefield.

Wellington was a fastidious man, often shaving twice a day. This dressing-case includes razors, nail-scissors and tooth-brushes. The duke eventually lost his teeth, whose disappearance made him seem hollow-cheeked.

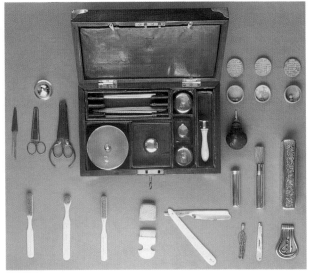

LEFT The King of Prussia presented Wellington with a plate from the Saxon service hand-painted with scenes from his life: here is his London residence, Apsley House.

BELOW LEFT Three of Wellington's many field-marshal's batons: his British baton, designed by the prince regent, is on the right.

BELOW This plate, from the Prussian service, shows the Brussels road crossing the ridge at Mont St Jean.

ABOVE
Wellington's funeral procession passing Hyde Park Corner on 18 November 1852. Apsley House is on the left. Decimus Burton's triumphal arch, on the right, was moved to the top of Constitution Hill in 1882. The huge statue of Wellington, here shown on top of it, was eventually moved to Aldershot, where it remains.

RIGHT Wellington's committal in St Paul's Cathedral.

were properly repaired and garrisoned. He was at Elvas in mid-March, writing sharply to General Don Carlos de España, who had asked him for fifteen or twenty artificers, that he was at a loss to see how such men could not be found in Spain: it was a 'melancholy reflection' the state of an alliance in which 'every thing ... must be performed by British soldiers.'[40] But it was not all gloom: the Spanish Cortes created him Duke of Ciudad Rodrigo and a Grandee of Spain, and his own government raised him from viscount to earl. As one Wellesley rose, another fell. Richard, whose scandalous love life aroused great criticism, relinquished the foreign office, telling Wellington that Spencer Perceval's 'republic of a Cabinet' was 'but little suited to any man of taste or of large views'. But he botched an opportunity to bring down the government and perhaps emerge as prime minister. When Perceval was assassinated by a merchant ruined by the war shortly afterwards, there was no job for Richard. Liverpool became prime minister, with Castlereagh remaining at the foreign office, and Lord Bathurst taking over as war minister. William might have held office but declined to, arguing that it would damage relations between him and Richard. The outcome might have been worse, with the opposition in power and peace with Napoleon, but Wellington felt that the government was now likely to be less resolute in its prosecution of the war, and perhaps more vulnerable to bad news from the front.

In mid-March 1812, Wellington's thoughts turned more to fortifications than to politics. It was always clear that Badajoz would prove harder to take than Ciudad Rodrigo. The town was protected on one side by the Guadiana and on the other by the flooded Rivillas brook, and its fortifications were powerful squat modern bastions, with only the old Moorish castle at the north-east corner offering an easy target to artillery – though the flooded brook prevented guns from getting to close range. The governor, Major General Armand Phillipon, was experienced and determined, and his garrison of 4,000 men was actively supported by many towns-people. At dusk on 17 March, in filthy weather, Wellington's work-ing parties began their trenches opposite the south-east front of Badajoz, but French artillery did serious damage to the trenches the next day. That night the French mounted a determined sortie which did more damage and wounded Colonel Fletcher, Welling-ton's chief engineer. The outlying Fort Picurina was stormed on the 24th, enabling breaching batteries to get in close and batter the bastions of Santa Maria and Trinidad, and on 6 April, Wellington was told that three practicable breaches had been made. He would have liked more time to widen them further, but although Sir Thomas Graham seemed able to contain Soult in the south, in the north Marmont was on the move again, and Wellington feared for the safety of Ciudad Rodrigo. He ordered an assault that very night.

The Light and 4th Divisions were to attack the main breaches, Picton's 3rd Division was to scale the castle walls, and Leith's 5th Division would assault the intact walls in the north-west. When the attack began at 10pm, the garrison was well prepared. Debris which might have given cover to the attackers had been cleared away; spiked planks had been laid on the rubble slope of the breaches themselves; and sword-blades hammered into stout tim-bers barred the tops. Fused shells and grenades were to hand, and infantrymen in the front line were to be passed loaded muskets by their comrades behind. Even getting to the foot of the breaches was not easy, for there was a steep drop into the ditch which killed some of the men who fell from the ladders they used to descend; others drowned in the water. Lieutenant Harry Smith of the 95th recalled that the first shot:

brought down such a hail of fire as I shall never forget, nor ever saw before or since. It was most murderous. We flew down the ladders and rushed at the breach, but we were broken, and carried no weight with us, though every soldier was a hero ... A Rifleman stood amongst the sword blades on the top of one of the cheveaux de frises. We made a glorious rush to follow, but, alas! in vain. He was knocked over. My old captain, O'Hare, who commanded the storming party, was killed. All were awfully wounded except, I do believe, myself and little Freer of the 43rd. I had some seconds at the revetment of the bastion near the breach, and my red-coat pockets were literally filled with chips of stones splintered by musket balls. Those not knocked down were driven back by this hail of mortality to the ladders.[41]

More than forty separate attacks made no progress, and French soldiers at the top of the breaches taunted their assailants, asking them if they did not want to enter Badajoz.

Picton's men did no better at the castle. They had to carry their heavy and roughly-made ladders for half a mile and then plant them against walls thirty feet high, while the defenders fired down, and scattered shells and blazing carcasses, wicker containers filled with oil-soaked rubbish, which gave them light to shoot by. Young George Hennell was serving as a gentleman volunteer in the 94th, and had never been in action before. As his company crept up the slippery slope on hands and knees, a single shot from a 24-pdr hit twelve men, who 'sank together with a groan that would have shook to the soul the nerves of the oldest soldier ...' When he reached the foot of the wall 'the dead and wounded lay so thick that we were continually treading on them ... The men were not so eager to go up the ladders as I had expected they would be. They were as thick as possible in the ditch . . .'[42]

Wellington was on high ground east of the town, receiving reports that were increasingly gloomy. His chief medical officer, Dr James McGrigor, was looking at him when he heard that all assaults had failed with heavy loss:

> At this moment, I cast my eyes on the countenance of Lord Wellington lit up by the glare of the torch . . . I shall never forget it to the last moment of my existence . . . The jaw had fallen, the face was of unusual length, while the torchlight gave to his countenance a lurid aspect; but still the expression of the face was firm.[43]

Wellington, taking McGrigor for a staff officer, asked him to order Picton to make a last try at the castle and then, realising his mistake, sent an aide instead. We cannot be sure that this desperate request spurred the 3rd Division into new activity, because repeated efforts were already being made to get ladders up against the wall. Picton had been wounded, and Major General James Kempt took over, but it was probably Lieutenant Colonel Henry Ridge of the 5th who was the first to make his way up a ladder and gain the ramparts. He was shot dead moments later, but enough of his men followed him to fan out along the walls and drive back the defenders. Lieutenant MacPherson of the 45th, breathing with some difficulty because a musket-ball, providentially deflected by Spanish dollars in his pocket, had broken two ribs, rushed up to the tower, tore down the French flag and ran up his own scarlet jacket. At about this time Leith's men, who had attacked late, forced their way in at the north-west as the defence weakened. Phillipon made a last attempt at counter-attacking, and then escaped across the bridge to Fort San Cristobal where he surrendered the next morning.

Badajoz was a terrible place that night. Edward Costello of the 95th remembered: 'The shouts and oaths of drunken soldiers in quest of more liquor, the reports of fire-arms and the crashing in of doors, together with the appalling shrieks of hapless women, might have induced anybody to believe himself in the regions of the damned.[44] Private John Spencer Cooper of the 7th Fusiliers admitted that: 'All orders ceased. Plunder was the order of the night. Some got loaded with plate etc; then beastly drunk; and lastly, were robbed by others. This lasted until the second day after.'[45] Lieutenant William Grattan was equally shocked by men who would fall:

> upon the already too deeply injured females, and tear from them the trinkets that adorned their necks, finger or ears! And finally, they would strip them of their wearing apparel ... many men were flogged, but although the contrary has been said, none were hanged – yet hundreds deserved it.[46]

The heavy casualties incurred in the storm – the allies lost nearly 5,000 men in the siege, and the Light and 4th Divisions, 2,500 in the breaches – partly explain, though they do not condone, what happened at Badajoz. There are still unhappy memories in the town in part the result of atrocities committed when Franco's north African troops took the place in the Civil War, and the Royal Regiment of Fusiliers was recently denied permission to erect a memorial to its role in the storm. The breaches have been repaired and the bastions grin out across park and suburb, but the castle, still scarred by cannon fire, has a gloomy air and is not the place to linger after dark. I was glad to get away from Badajoz.

Wellington informed Liverpool that the storm of Badajoz 'affords as strong an instance of the gallantry of our troops as had

Wellington in the breach at Badajoz. The artist has used some licence, showing dignified French prisoners under guard in the breach and minimising the effect of close-range fire on the bodies lying in it. But he gives a good feel for the rubble-strewn slope that constituted the breach, and the *cheveaux de frise* (beams studded with sword-blades) that helped defend it can be seen clearly.

ever been displayed. But I greatly hope that I shall never again be the instrument of putting them to such a test'. He was profoundly shaken by the carnage in the breaches, where Grattan thought that 'it was not possible to look at those brave men, all of them dead or frightfully maimed, without recollecting what they had been just a few short hours before . . .'[47] Wellington broke down in tears, and when Picton stumped along on his wounded leg: 'I bit my lips, and did everything I could to stop myself for I was ashamed he should see it, but I could not, and he so little entered into my feelings that he said "Good God, what is the matter?"'[48]

The scenes in the town were scarcely less shocking. Wellington remembered entering a cellar where soldiers were lying so drunk that wine was actually flowing from their mouths, and he was nearly hit by a soldier firing in the air. A General Order of 7 April 1812 announced that it was time that the looting ceased, and a gallows was erected in the square to drive the point home. An aide-de-camp wrote that Wellington was so angry that he could hardly bring himself to thank the troops.

While Wellington was preparing to move from Badajoz, half a continent away, Napoleon was about to depart for his fatal campaign against Russia. And, yet again, there were links between the emperor's ambitions and affairs in the Peninsula. Before departing, he ordered Marmont to mount another offensive into Portugal, and forbade him to cooperate with Soult in the south. Although there were over 230,000 French soldiers in Spain, they were split up between five armies, and the need to mount operations against guerrillas and Spanish regular forces would have made it hard for them to co-operate against Wellington's much smaller army – he had some 60,000 regulars – even had they been directed to do so. But with the unmartial King Joseph in overall command, his elbow jogged by dispatches from Paris that might take a month to arrive, there was little to stop the marshals from feuding, nor much chance to impose a coherent strategy.

Wellington was unsure whether to attack Marmont or Soult, but knew that he needed to re-provision Ciudad Rodrigo before doing anything else. He set in motion a variety of diversions that would hinder any French attempts at concentration, and a well-handled raid by Hill captured the Tagus crossing at Almaraz – where the French had replaced the damaged masonry bridge with a pontoon bridge – severing communications between Marmont and Soult. Wellington then set off for Salamanca, entering this most beautiful university city on 17 June 1812 to rapturous enthusiasm, and taking its forts ten days later. There he heard news of Major General

John Slade's defeat in a little cavalry action at Maguilla, rightly called 'the most discreditable cavalry fight of the war' by Ian Fletcher, which prompted him to write to Rowland Hill his much-quoted censure of the mad-brained tricks of cavalry officers.[49]

He then marched out to manoeuvre against Marmont, who was trying to force him back on Ciudad Rodrigo, and for the next few days both armies moved parallel with one another, like swordsmen watching for an opportunity. 'Marmont will certainly not risk an action unless he should have an advantage,' Wellington told Sir Thomas Graham, 'and I shall certainly not risk one unless I should have an advantage; and matters therefore do not appear to be brought to that criterion very soon.'[50] At dawn on 22 July, there was no reason to think that the day would not be like any other and the two armies, about 50,000 men apiece, marched across open country in the great loop of the River Tormes, west of Salamanca.

It had been a trying time for Wellington. The days were scorching, and the dust made men look like sweeps, but the nights were so cold that troops even dug up coffins to use as firewood; Wellington declared that he had never been colder in his life. He was short of sleep – he spent less than forty-eight hours in bed in a fortnight – and catnapped when he could, sometimes lying in the grass with a newspaper over his face. His practice of delivering orders in person and 'superintend[ing] every operation of the Troops' meant that he was frequently at risk, and that July, he and his staff were cut off by French cavalry. An observer saw Wellington and Beresford galloping out of the mêlée with drawn swords, the former looking 'more than half pleased'. Despite the stress of campaigning, at forty-three he was:

> in the prime of life, a well made man five foot ten inches
> in height, with broad shoulders and well-developed chest.

Of the cruiser, rather than the battleship build, the grey-
hound, rather than the mastiff breed, he seemed all made
for speed and action, yet as strong as steel, and capable
of great endurance.[51]

He boasted that he had inherited 'the family eye of a hawk'. Gleig
thought that his eyes were 'dark violet blue, or grey' and observed
that 'even to the last he could distinguish objects at an immense
distance'.[52]

The battlefield of Salamanca remains one of the most evocative
of this or any war. It is unspoiled by development, and the plain
– not unlike a treeless Salisbury Plain on a much greater scale –
is still dominated by the two flat-topped hills known as the Greater
and Lesser Arapile, with the honey-coloured buildings of Salamanca on the horizon. The plain is by no means flat, however,
and ridges roll across it, most notably west and north-east of the
Lesser Arapile. Early on the 22 July, there was some fighting around
the ruined chapel just west of Calvarrasa de Arriba, important
because whoever held it could see something of what went on
behind this latter ridge. Shortly afterwards the British occupied
the Lesser Arapile and the French the Greater, repulsing Portuguese troops who lunged for it. As the morning went on, both
armies marched south-west, with most of Wellington's men out
of sight of the French behind the long ridge north-east of the Lesser
Arapile. An exception was Ned Pakenham, who had replaced the
wounded Picton at the head of the 3rd Division, and was heading
for Aldea Tejada on Wellington's extreme western flank.

Wellington spent the morning on the Lesser Arapile or the
ridge to its west, above the little village of Los Arapiles. He could
see that the French, as usual, were marching faster than his own
men. Francis Seymour Larpent, Wellington's censorious judge
advocate-general, had his own views on this:

In marching, our men have no chance against the French.
The latter beat them hollow; principally, I believe, owing
to their being a more intelligent set of beings, seeing
consequences more, and feeling them. This makes them
sober and orderly whenever it becomes material, and
on a pinch their exertions and unrivalled activity are
astonishing. Our men get sulky and desperate, drink
excessively, and become daily more weak and unable to
proceed, principally from their own conduct . . . In every
respect, except courage, they are very inferior soldiers to
the French and Germans . . .[53]

Suspecting that Marmont might turn his right, Wellington
brought up troops from behind the long ridge and formed a line
running through Los Arapiles, and for a time it looked as if
Marmont, whose skirmishers pushed into the southern edge of
the village, would indeed attack. But then it became clear that the
French, strung out across the plain in division-sized blocks, were
still moving westwards. At about midday Wellington, stumping
about a farmyard in Los Arapiles, munching a chicken leg and
snatching glances at the French through his telescope, suddenly
exclaimed: 'By God, that will do!' He flung the chicken leg in the
air, sprang into the saddle and cantered up the hill behind for a
better look. Then he turned to General Miguel de Alava, his
Spanish liaison officer. '*Mon cher Alava,*' he said, '*Marmont est
perdu.*' And with that he galloped westwards, outdistancing his
staff, to find Ned Pakenham. 'Ned, d'ye see those fellows on the
hill,' he asked, pointing at the leading French division. 'Throw
your division into column, have at them and drive them to the
devil.' 'I will, my Lord,' relied Pakenham 'if you will give me your
hand.' Wellington was not a demonstrative man, but shook hands
with his brother-in-law with evident emotion.[54]

As Pakenham's men advanced to the attack, not coming into view until they were about 500 yards from the French, Wellington hurtled back the way he had come, issuing orders for an attack that would begin as soon as the 3rd Division struck. What followed was a succession of hammer-blows, falling on the flanks of over-extended French divisions, which were never able to concentrate to meet the threat. As the three infantry divisions on his right surged forward, Wellington's cavalry, under Lieutenant General Sir Stapleton Cotton, crashed into the French. The heavy dragoons under Major General John Gaspard Le Marchant broke one French division and badly damaged another, but Le Marchant was killed, shot through the spine in the very moment of victory. 'By God, Cotton,' shouted Wellington, 'I never saw anything more beautiful in my life. The day is yours.'

Marmont had been wounded at the start of the action by a shell fired by a British howitzer (in later life some insensitive soul introduced him to the sergeant who had pointed the piece). Command passed to General Bonnet, who was also hit, and then to General Clausel. The latter reacted brilliantly to the destruction of his left wing by sending two strong divisions against Wellington's centre. This counter-attack went in just after the repulse of an allied attack on the Greater Arapile, and had it been launched against a commander of average capacity, it might very well have succeeded. But Wellington had the strong line of his 6th Division ready to meet the French, and a familiar story was played out as columns met line between the Arapiles. Clausel managed to block the road to Alba de Tormes with Ferrey's intact division, which fought gallantly as night came on, folding only after its commander had been cut in two by a round-shot. Marmont had lost at least 14,000 men and 20 guns, and the allies less than half as many men. The scale of the defeat might have been even greater, but

Carlos de España had withdrawn the garrison from the bridge at Alba de Tormes, which allowed the French to cross the river safely. 'If I had known there was no garrison at Alba,' Wellington observed, 'I should have marched there, and probably had the whole.'[55]

Salamanca gives the lie to the suggestion that Wellington was simply a great defensive general. Maximilien Foy, who commanded a French division that day, thought that the battle:

> raises Lord Wellington's reputation almost to the level of Marlborough. Hitherto we have been aware of his prudence, his eye for choosing a position, and his skill in utilising it. At Salamanca he has shown himself a great and able master of manoeuvres. He kept his dispositions concealed for almost the whole day: he waited till we were committed to our movements before he developed his own: he played a safe game: he fought in the oblique order – it was a battle in the style of Frederick the Great.[56]

Salamanca opened the road to Madrid, which the allies entered on 12 August 1812. Substantial quantities of arms and ammunition were captured, and Wellington became embroiled in lengthy discussions as to the best use to which these could be put. News from other parts of Spain was generally good, especially in the south, where Soult had at last given up the long siege of Cádiz. The Spanish appointed Wellesley *generalissimo* of all their forces, and on 22 September, he heard from Henry (himself now a Knight of the Bath) that the Prince Regent made him a marquess, and parliament voted him £100,000 towards the cost of a future residence. He would have preferred ready money, for he had been complaining to Bathurst that his daily allowance of ten guineas, reduced by income tax and other deductions to about eight, simply failed to meet the demands placed on him, and he would be 'ruined' unless it was increased.[57] And he was not hugely gratified by his promotion in the peerage, complaining: 'What the devil is the use of making me a marquess?'

The cumulative strain was biting deep into him and the Goya crayon sketch of Wellington, drawn from life in Madrid that summer, shows haunted eyes set in a worn face. His correspondence also reveals a man battered by a sea of troubles. His army continued to commit 'enormous outrages' which were likely to forfeit Spanish sympathy. The Spanish themselves were brave but hopelessly unmilitary and corrupt. His own government did not understand the war, and Horse Guards had no idea of the difficulties the army laboured under – on 13 September he pointed out that nobody in his army had been paid since late April – and the incompetent and the inadequate were foisted upon him. When one of the latter, Lieutenant General Sir William Erskine, threw himself through a window, it transpired that 'he had been two years confined, and that he should not have been sent out here as chief officer of the cavalry – it was too great a risk'.[58] On looking at a list of senior officers being sent out to join him, Wellington jested darkly that he did not know what effect their names would have upon the enemy, but they certainly frightened him.

All this reinforced his tendency to trust almost nobody and to do everything himself, producing the symptoms of what we would now term a control freak. His chief medical officer, James McGrigor, was one of the most efficient and farsighted military doctors of his age, and Wellington not only secured him a knighthood after the Peninsula, but also helped him obtain the Order of the Bath when, belatedly, medical officers were made eligible for it. But when, after Salamanca, McGrigor used his initiative to establish a line of evacuation that differed from (and was a good deal better than) that prescribed by Wellington, he was given a fierce roasting. 'I shall be glad to know who is to command the army, you or I?' thundered Wellington. 'As long as you live, sir, never do so again; never do anything without my orders.'[59]

Captain Norman Ramsay, Royal Horse Artillery, had distinguished himself at Fuentes de Oñoro, leading his troop to safety through a thick cloud of French cavalry. After the battle of Vitoria in 1813, although Wellington instructed him not to move his troop until he personally told him to, Ramsay moved on the orders of a staff officer. But Wellington meant just what he said, and put Ramsay under arrest, where he remained for three weeks. The incident rankled, and contributed to the Royal Artillery's belief that Wellington had a low regard for the arm. Ramsay and Wellington did not speak again, and the gunner was killed at Waterloo. But long-term hostility was rare, for Wellington often followed a wigging with cordiality. The evening that McGrigor received his great rebuke, he found himself seated at Wellington's side for a genial dinner.

There was not much geniality in Wellington that autumn, however, for, as McGrigor observed, 'this was the period of his life when fortune seemed to turn her back on him'. He decided to push Clausel towards the French border, but the northern town of Burgos, capital of Old Castile and recently refortified on Napoleon's orders, stood in his way. Wellington was ill-prepared for a siege, with only three heavy guns – Thunder, Lightning and Nelson (which had lost one of its trunnions) and little enough ammunition even for them. The French field army declined to attack his covering force and bring on a general engagement. He took some outlying defences but had lost over 2,000 men to 623 French by the time he decided to break up the siege on 21 October 1812.

Amongst the casualties was Major the Hon. Edward Somers

Cocks, eldest son of John, Lord Somers, killed by a point-blank musket shot while leading the light companies of the Highland Brigade in an assault on the main wall, retaken by the French in a sortie. Many officers agreed with John Mills that his loss was 'irreparable'. He had commanded a troop of the 16th Light Dragoons with outstanding success for two years before becoming a major in the 79th Highlanders. One of his brother officers in the 16th, Lieutenant William Tomkinson, told how: 'The men in his troop ... were very fond of him, and would hollo, when in a charge, "Follow the captain, stick close to the captain" ... he had always been so lucky in the heat of fire that I fancied he would be preserved to the army.'[60] He was a particular favourite of Wellington's: brave, well-connected and devoted to his profession. He had spent some time as one of his 'directed telescopes', an 'out-post officer' charged with long-range reconnaissance and confidential missions.

His loss shook Wellington to the very core. When he heard of it, he entered the room of Colonel Frederick Ponsonby, one of his staff, paced about and then said 'Cocks was killed last night' but could not utter another word. They buried him in the 79th's camp, in the presence of the officers of the 16th Light Dragoons and the 79th. Wellington attended with all his staff, but was so over-wrought that nobody dared speak to him. 'He is regretted by the whole army,' wrote Tomkinson, 'and in those regiments in which he has been no man can lament a brother more than they do him.'[61] Wellington told Lord Somers that had he lived, the young man would have been 'one of the greatest ornaments of his profession ... an honour to his family, and an advantage to his country.'[62]

Having failed to take Burgos, Wellington was obliged to retreat in appalling weather, with strong French forces at hand, and described it as 'the worst scrape I ever was in'. On 23 October, the French cavalry jabbed hard at his rearguard, beating two British cavalry brigades and being checked only by a brigade of KGL infantry, which formed squares that stood like rocks beneath the torrent. The route lay through a wine-producing region, and the army made the most of it. 'I remember seeing a soldier fully accoutred with his knapsack on in a large tank,' recalled William Wheeler, 'he had either fell in or been pushed in by his comrades, there he lay dead. I saw a dragoon fire his pistol into a large vat containing several thousands of gallons, in a few minutes we were up to our knees in wine fighting like tigers for it.'[63]

An officer saw Wellington near Salamanca on 15 November 1812: 'he wore an oil-skin cloak, and looked extremely ill, which was not to be wondered at considering the anxiety of mind and fatigue of body he was enduring'.[64] Yet he still had the ability to inspire. Assistant Surgeon George Burrows remembered that:

> The spirit of enthusiasm was raised to the highest pitch, by the electric effect of the words 'here he comes', which spread from mouth to mouth with the rapidity of lightning. The noble commander passed our columns in review, as usual unaccompanied by any mark of distinction or splendour; his long horse cloak concealed his under garment; his cocked hat soaked and disfigured with the rain.[65]

But Burrows was writing for publication, and in 1814, when Wellington was a national hero. The failure at Burgos and retreat to Portugal shocked many who, like Ensign Mills, were writing private letters.

> Our want of success at Burgos and the subsequent retreat ... has turned the tide of affairs here and Spain I think is lost. If ever a man ruined himself the Marquis has

done it; for the last two months he has acted like a madman. The reputation he has acquired will not bear him out – such is the opinion here.[66]

To his credit, Wellington never sought to shift the blame. At the time, he told Liverpool that 'The Government had nothing to say to the siege. It was entirely my own act.' And years later he told friends that:

> It was all my own fault; I had got, with small means, into the forts near Salamanca. The Castle [in Burgos] was not unlike a hill-fort in India, and I had got into a good many of those. I could not get into this, I very nearly did but it was defended by a very clever fellow . . .'[67]

By late November Wellington was at Freneida, south-west of Rodrigo, quartered in the mayor's house in a small square over-shadowed by the church. There is a little courtyard at the back, now firmly gated against the quiet street, but once the haunt of aides-de-camp and orderly dragoons, and a terrace looking across the square. Wellington was in a foul temper when he arrived. James McGrigor found him:

> in a miserable small room leaning over the fire. He was attentively reading some printed paper. He begged me to be seated. I could see that the paper he was reading was Cobbett's Register [a radical newspaper] . . . After reading it for a few minutes he threw it in the fire, and anxiously enquired what reports I had of the sick and wounded. He was in a very bad humour; he adverted in bitter language to the disorder of the retreat.[68]

Wellington immediately wrote a stern circular to divisional and brigade commanders, complaining that 'irregularities and outrages' of all descriptions were committed with impunity because of 'the habitual inattention of the officers of the regiments to their duty, as prescribed by the standing regulations of the service, and the orders of this army'. Generals and field officers were to insist that captains and subalterns understood and performed their duties: that was the only way in which 'the discipline and efficiency of the army can be maintained during the next campaign'.[69]

The order was deeply resented. William Tomkinson thought it 'an imprudent letter', and John Mills asked his mother 'what encouragement has a man to do his duty?' John Kincaid of the 95th agreed that 'not only censure, but condign punishment' was merited for some of the disorder, and had Wellington hanged soldiers (and commissaries too) and cashiered officers, nobody would have blamed him. But:

> In our brigade I can safely say that the order in question excited more of sorrow than of anger; we thought that, had it been *particular*, it would have been just; but as it was *general*, that it was inconsiderate; and we, therefore, regretted that he who had been, and still was, the god of our idolatry, should thereby have laid himself open to the attacks of the ill-natured.'[70]

Officers quickly sent copies home, and the order was printed in newspapers, provoking muttering at Wellington's severity and embarrassing the government. There is no doubt that the order was unfair; if men stole food, it was because the commissariat had broken down and they could either pillage or starve. As Ian Fletcher observes, drink was another matter, but even here some veterans argued that it was only looted wine that kept men going.[71] But all this was overshadowed by news of a far more important retreat. Napoleon had stayed too long in Moscow, and suffered appalling losses as he fell back. In Spain, however, 'the South was free, and Andalusia sang in the sunlight. Twelve hundred miles away the *Grande Armée* was dead.'[72]

That winter, as his army recuperated in north-eastern Portugal, Wellington settled into the routine of life in winter quarters. At Freneida there was an air of practical informality. Commissary August Schaumann noted that:

> There was no throng of scented staff officers with plumed hats, orders and stars, no main guard, no crowd of con-tractors, actors, valets, mistresses, equipages, horses, forage and baggage wagons, as there is at a French or Russian headquarters. Just a few aides-de-camp, who went about the streets alone and in their overcoats, a few guides, and a small staff guard; that was all.[73]

When the army was on the move during a campaign, Wellington usually slept in a small tent enclosed in a large marquee, which also served as sitting- and dining-room. Staff officers had a tent apiece. Wellington's cook, James Thornton, took over the kitchen in places like Freneida, but in the field he cooked under a tarpaulin draped over poles, with his fire surrounded by an earth bank scooped with niches to hold the saucepans. Meat was suspended on a pole over the fire. When it rained hard, as it often did, there was nothing to eat but bread and cold meat. General Miguel de Alava declared that he was tired of enquiring what time the army was to move and what was for dinner and being answered: 'Day-light. Cold meat.' Wellington thought that Thornton was no genius. 'Cole gives the best dinners in the army,' he wrote. 'Hill the next best; mine are no great things.'[74] This was partly because Wellington had no real interest in food, once telling Cambacérès

'I don't much care what I eat', while Creevey remembered a very poor meal which 'made no impression on the Duke, who seemed quite as pleased and well satisfied as if he had been in a palace'.[75]

Captain Thomas Henry Browne, a junior staff officer, was more sanguine. He thought Wellington's cook 'a good one & the wine principally furnished by the Guerrillas excellent'.[76] Wellington normally dined with twelve to sixteen people at his table, always including some officers of the two principal staff branches, those of the adjutant-general and quartermaster-general, some of the medical and commissariat staff, and commanding officers of nearby regiments. Generals visiting on business were invited to dinner and pressed to stay in quarters kept available for them. Although Wellington drank little by the standards of the age – half a bottle to a bottle with dinner – Browne tells us that, 'there was an abundance of wine at his table & guests might take just as much as they pleased'. Dinner was at five, and was famously informal. George Gleig, Wellington's future biographer, dined with him as an infantry subaltern, and found:

> The conversation ... most interesting and lively. The Duke himself spoke out on all subjects with an absence of reserve which sometimes surprised his guests ... He was rich in anecdote, most of them taking a ludicrous turn, and without any apparent effort he put the company very much at their ease ...[77]

At about 8.30, Wellington would summon coffee, and rise as soon as he had drunk it, which was the signal for all present to withdraw, although the young and bold found somewhere comfortable 'to smoak cigars [Wellington did not allow smoking at his table] & drink grog till bed-time ...' He wrote or read for about half an hour, and then retired.

At Freneida, some distance from the French outposts, Wellington felt able to undress and go to bed in his nightshirt. On campaign, however, he used to change his linen and boots, and lie down on an iron-framed collapsible bed that was carried on a mule. He kept two dragoons, with horses saddled, at his door, so that if any important information came in, he could ride off at a moment's notice with this small escort. Browne admitted that 'it has occasionally happened that when his staff awoke in the morning they learnt that their chief had been on horse-back and with the picquets of the army hours before'.[78]

Even if the army was not on the move, Wellington rose early; he could not bear lying awake in bed. He had a heavy growth of beard, often shaved twice a day, and hated to be disturbed when shaving. Lord Aylmer interrupted this 'sacred rite with which no emotion was allowed to interfere' to tell him that Massena had fallen back from the lines of Torres Vedras. 'Ay, I thought they meant to be off,' he replied, lifting his razor for a moment. 'Very well', and the shave went on.[79] He dressed simply, with a blue or grey frock coat, cut slightly shorter than was fashionable, white or blue-grey breeches, and the eponymous boots, shorter and looser than modern riding boots, with the scalloped top typical of the fashionable 'Hessian' boot of the period. Larpent thought that:

> like every great man, present or past, almost without exception, he is vain . . . He is remarkably neat and most particular in his dress . . . He cuts the skirts of his coat shorter to make them look smarter: only a short time since, going to him on business, I found him discussing the cut of his half-boots and suggesting alterations to his servant. [80]

Outside he wore a cocked hat, with an oilskin cover in bad weather. To deal with summer rain, he wore a short blue cloak (some called it his boat cloak) with a white lining. He also had a white winter cloak – Gleig thought that it was 'so that he might be more easily recognised from afar'. He wore it in the Pyrenees in the wet winter of 1814, and one officer, watching him writing out orders while sitting on a stone, said: 'Do you see that old White Friar sitting there? I wonder how many men he is marking off to be sent into the next world.'[81] In the Peninsula and at Waterloo he usually carried the same sword, an elegant Indo-Persian weapon now in Apsley House. His immaculate appearance was the source of one of his nicknames, 'The Beau'. Kincaid recalled that Dan Mackinnon of the Coldstream Guards (such a great practical joker that the famous clown Grimaldi said that if Mackinnon donned the clown's costume, he would totally eclipse him) rode up to a group of staff officers and asked them if they had seen Beau Douro that morning. Wellington, catnapping on the ground under his cloak, sat up and said: 'Well, by —, I never knew I was a beau before!'[82]

Wellington dealt with a prodigious amount of correspondence. He tried to answer letters as they arrived and his workload was absurdly centralised by modern standards. Officers wishing to go on leave were obliged to apply to him in writing or in person, and were usually informed that their personal circumstances were insufficiently pressing for them to take leave: Wellington took none himself. The dejected and the dissatisfied wrote to complain. A cashiered dragoon officer was told that he was mistaken to think that 'any thing which happened to you in this country was occasioned by any feeling of irritation on my part, or any thing but a desire to uphold the discipline and subordination of the army'. The man owed his downfall to 'great and persevering indiscretion and the misapplication of very great talents', and it was impossible for him to be restored to his rank in the service. Wellington begged him 'with your talents and prospects in other professions', to reconsider the wisdom of joining as a gentleman volunteer in the hope of making his way.[83] He took his duties as colonel of the 33rd very seriously, telling its commanding officer in October 1812 that no changes should be made to uniform unless they were required by regulations: 'Every thing is now, I believe, as I found it 20 years ago; and if once we begin to alter, we shall have nothing fixed, as there are no bounds to fancy.'[84]

He had usually completed a great deal of correspondence by the time he saw his senior staff at about 9am. There were two principal staff officers, the quartermaster-general, for much of the period Major General George Murray, and the adjutant-general, Major General the Hon. Charles Stewart, Castlereagh's half-brother. The former was responsible for movements, camps and bivouacs, and the latter for personnel issues such as appointments, transfers and the promulgation of regulations. Neither was a chief of staff in the modern sense, although Murray, a very competent staff officer, came closest to it. Stewart, presuming, perhaps, on his half-brother's importance to Wellington, went so far as to cross him, maintaining that the examination of prisoners of war was not his responsibility. 'I was obliged to say', recalled Wellington,

> that, if he did not at once confess his error, and promise to obey orders frankly and cordially, I would dismiss him instanter and send him back to England under arrest. After a good deal of persuasion he burst out crying, begged my pardon, and hoped that I would forgive his intemperance.[85]

Heads of department, like Fletcher, the chief engineer, Dickson, commander Royal Artillery, and McGrigor of the medical department were expected to brief their commander briskly and without consulting their papers. 'He was very fidgety,' recalled McGrigor, 'and evidently displeased when I referred to my notes.'[86] Although both Fletcher and Dickson were knighted, Wellington was often critical of the artillery, largely, thought Larpent, 'because their officers are rather heavy and slow'.[87]

There was nothing heavy or slow about Wellington's personal staff officers. It was said that 'in looking for able young men for his personal staff he preferred ability with a title to ability without', partly a reflection of his conviction that the army as a whole should be officered by gentlemen.[88] Lord FitzRoy Somerset (the future Lord Raglan, and as such British commander-in-chief in the Crimea) was appointed an aide-de-camp through the Duke of Richmond's influence in 1808. At Roliça Wellington, who had known him from childhood, asked: 'Well, Lord FitzRoy, how do you feel under fire?' and was pleased by the answer 'Better, sir, than I expected.'[89] Lord FitzRoy was appointed Wellington's military secretary, responsible for his confidential correspondence, as a 22-year-old captain in 1808, and the two men remained closely associated until Wellington's death. Wellington thought that Fitz-Roy had no particular talents, but always told the truth and could be relied upon to carry out his orders quickly and exactly.

Also on the staff were the Prince of Orange, prince of the Netherlands and a colonel in the British army; the Marquess of Worcester, later seventh Duke of Beaufort, who had been involved with Harriette Wilson; Captain the Hon. Alexander Gordon, the Earl of Aberdeen's brother; Lord Burghersh, only son of the Earl of Westmoreland; and Lord March, son of the Duke of Richmond. But connections would not save an incompetent youngster. Wellington's nephew William, son of William Wellesley-Pole, showed himself 'lamentably idle and ignorant' and was sent home after 'doing things he has no right to do'.[90] Wellington also had particular friends on the general staff and in the army more widely. Ned Pakenham, assistant adjutant-general until he took over the 3rd Division and was wounded at Badajoz, and Galbraith Lowry Cole, Kitty's old suitor, now commanding the 4th Division, were treated with extraordinary confidence.

Wellington was certainly neither the first nor the last general to surround himself with young men whose military careers depended on him. There was nothing homoerotic about the relationship, though he was certainly very close to them. We have already seen him distraught at the death of Cocks, and when Lord March was severely wounded, Wellington, one of his own legs badly bruised, rode several miles to see him and emerged from his room, hobbling on two sticks, with tears rolling down his cheeks. He was sometimes closer to men who, like McGrigor, Larpent or his favourite chaplain Samuel Briscall, were in the army but not of it, than he was to the mass of his officers. His personal orderly, a gruff old German trooper called Beckerman, was a particular favourite. He was utterly reliable but not cringingly deferential (many more recent commanders have enjoyed similar relationships with their drivers). In all this we see a man who needed affection but disliked large-scale public adulation, and who managed to create, in his busy headquarters, that happy family life that had eluded him elsewhere.

There were women in his life, although it is a measure of his discretion that hard evidence is difficult to find. He disapproved of Richard's scandalous behaviour, and in 1810 had told Henry: 'I wish that Wellesley was castrated; or that he would like other people attend to his business and perform too.' Lady Sarah Napier might have been repeating gossip passed on by her soldier sons (or relaying a Whig canard) when she wrote after Talavera that

Wellington 'publickly keeps a mistress at head-quarters'. Larpent later hinted that he was having an affair with his landlady in Toulouse, and there is a 'brief but affectionate' note from a Spanish lady amongst his papers. He once granted an officer leave to spend forty-eight hours in Lisbon on the grounds that that was as long as any reasonable man might wish to stay in bed with the same woman, and it may be that he was as brisk with his amours as with much else. But Elizabeth Longford's point is crucial: 'his private life created no scandals of the dimension that did so much damage to Richard's career'.[91]

We are on safer ground where other relaxations are concerned. Most great generals have their safety-valves – absorbing occupations that enable them to forget the cares of office, if only for the moment. For Joffre in the First World War it was a good lunch, eaten in reverent silence; for Alan Brooke in the Second, it was birdwatching. For Wellington, it was foxhunting, although he was a thruster who hunted to ride, not an aficionado who rode to hunt and enjoyed watching hounds work. No sooner had he arrived at headquarters than Larpent wrote:

> We have three odd sorts of packs of hounds here, and the men hunt desperately: firstly, Lord Wellington's, or, as he is called here, the Peer's; there are fox-hounds, about sixteen couple; they have only killed one fox this year, and that was what is called mobbed. These hounds for want of a huntsman straggle about, and run very ill, and the foxes run off to their holes on the Coa ... Lord Wellington has a good stud of about eight hunters; he rides hard, and only wants a good gallop, but I understand knows nothing of the sport, although very fond of it in his own way.[92]

Thomas Browne was pleased to see that:

He had at Head Quarters a pack of hounds from England & hunted two or three times a week with such Officers of Head Quarters as chose to join in the chase. There were not many, as few could afford to have English horses, & our Spanish or Portuguese steeds were not equal to the work. There was no want of foxes, but it was a difficult and rocky country to ride over. He went out shooting every now & then, but did not appear fond of it, as he was a very indifferent shot.[93]

Hunting improved when Tom Crane, late of the Coldstream Guards, came out as huntsman. Lady Salisbury sent Wellington the sky-blue coat of the Hatfield Hunt, and suitably attired he rode to hounds:

> no longer the Commander of the Forces, the General-in-Chief of three nations, the representative of three sovereigns, but a gay, merry country gentleman, who rode at everything, and laughed as loud when he fell himself as he did when he witnessed the fall of a brother sportsman.

George Murray told Larpent that 'on hunting days he could get almost anything done, for Lord Wellington stands whip in hand ready to start, and soon dispatches all business . . .' Some generals took the opportunity 'to get him to answer things in a hasty way . . . which they acted upon', so he would not do business with them on hunting days. '"Oh d—n them," said he, "I won't speak to them again when we are hunting."'

Wellington also enjoyed a good party, and bent the same ferocious energy to partying that he did to everything else. On 13 March 1813, he gave a ball at Ciudad Rodrigo, at which he invested Lowry Cole with the Order of the Bath. Larpent wrote that:

He stayed at business at Freneida until half past three, and then rode full seventeen miles to Rodrigo in two hours to dinner, dressed in all his orders etc., was in high glee, danced himself, stayed supper, and at half past three in the morning went back to Freneida by moonlight and arrived before day-break at six, so that by twelve he was again ready for business, and I saw him amongst others upon a Court-martial when I returned at two . . .[94]

But for all this, there was no doubting that Wellington was the pivot on which the army turned. He was secretive even with his closest confidants, and remained steadfastly opposed to the notion of a second-in-command, although one was generally foisted on him by the government – first Lieutenant General Sir Brent Spencer, then Lieutenant General Lord Paget (who had the ill luck to be captured soon after coming out in 1812), and lastly Lieutenant General Sir Thomas Graham. As he told Beresford, who he regarded as de facto second-in-command because of his broad understanding of operations, 'there is nobody in a modern army who must not see that there is no duty for the second in command to perform, and that this office is useless. It can at the same time be inconvenient, as it gives the holder pretensions which cannot be gratified except at the public inconvenience.'[95]

Wellington was convinced that the campaign of 1813 would be decisive, and there were essential preliminaries to be completed before he could embark upon it. The first was the honing of his own army, achieved in winter quarters. Discipline was re-established and useful changes made to equipment: the infantry was given light tin cooking-pots instead of heavy iron camp-kettles, and tents that housed about twenty-five men apiece. All this helped restored morale, bruised by the retreat from Burgos. 'We were not pleased with Lord Wellington at the beginning of the winter,' admitted

Captain William Bragge. 'He has now given the infantry tents. Therefore he is again a fine Fellow.'[96]

It was also essential to negotiate with the Spanish to ascertain the real limits of his authority as commander-in-chief of their army. In December Wellington travelled to Cádiz to meet the Cortes – the journey took him eleven days – and although he did not accomplish all he hoped for, as an alarmist campaign in the Spanish press had caused concern, he was content with the agreement. The experience helped colour his political views, and he wrote to Lord Bathurst on 27 January that: 'I wish that some of our reformers would go to Cadiz and see the benefits of a sovereign popular assembly ... and of a written constitution ... In truth there is no authority in the state, apart from the libellous newspapers ...'[97] He also organised diversionary operations, like one mounted by Major General Sir John Murray from Alicante: there were still 200,000 French soldiers south of the Pyrenees, and he had to ensure that they could not concentrate against him.

On 22 May 1813, he crossed the frontier into Spain, turning his horse as he did so and doffing his hat with the words: 'Farewell, Portugal! I shall never see you again.' His intelligence network, now working better than ever before, speedily told him that the main French army, under Joseph and Jourdan, had relinquished Madrid and was marching north in an effort to join Clausel, now commanding French forces in the north-west. Wellington was anxious to catch Joseph before the meeting could take place, and set off in hot pursuit. This time he moved faster than his enemies. Joseph's army, 'encumbered with a King, a Court, large portions of a Civil Service ...' had such an abundance of camp-followers that one disenchanted general described it as 'a walking bordello'. On his way through Salamanca, Wellington attended mass, his 'very light-grey pelisse coat, single-breasted, without a sash' in sharp contrast to the glittering Spanish generals in his suite. It was the same at Zamora, where they could not understand that 'the man sitting there so meekly in a grey coat' was the famous Lord Wellington.[98] Soon he was at Burgos, of evil memory, but a series of mighty explosions announced that the French, as Harry Smith put it, 'had blown Burgos to where we wished it' and did not intend to make a stand.

Wellington caught them at last at Vitoria, in the valley of the River Zadorra, on 21 June. Although the French were well-placed to meet an attack from the west – Wellington's line of approach – he divided his army into four large columns and ordered two of them to attack from the west, pinning the French to their positions, while the others struck through the hills to the north, feeling for the French flank. The French fought well to begin with, and inflicted 5,000 casualties on the allies, but Wellington's army was at the peak of its form and would not be denied. The 3rd Division, back under Picton's command, played an especially distinguished part, led forward by Picton himself with cries of 'Come on, ye rascals! Come on, ye fighting villains!' As the flanking attacks bit home, the French collapsed, abandoning the whole of their baggage and all but two of their guns.

The large-scale looting that followed temporarily cost Wellington more men than the 7,000 lost by the French, and he fulminated predictably against poor discipline and lack of attention to duty. His letter to Bathurst complained that the battle had 'totally annihilated all order and discipline'. 'This is the consequence of the state of discipline of the British army,' he concluded. 'We may gain the greatest victories; but we shall do no good, until we shall so far alter our system, as to force all ranks to perform their duty.'[99] This time he had a point, for this was not the necessity-driven theft of the sort that had disfigured the retreat from Burgos, but larceny on a gigantic scale in which officers participated enthusiastically, and which brought the pursuit to a halt. William Tomkinson described an Aladdin's cave of 'carriages, wagons, mules, monkeys, parrots . . .' and admitted that his regiment's commissary took £600 in cash.[100] The 15th Light Dragoons carried off King Joseph's silver chamber-pot, earning the nickname 'The Emperor's Chambermaids.' Captain Browne, having escaped from brief captivity, found a friendly sergeant who stuffed his pockets with £210 of captured money, saying 'at all events your Honour if you have got a hard thump today you have got your pockets well lined with Doubloons'.[101] Wellington himself had the paintings of the Spanish royal collection packed and sent to England for safe-keeping. In March 1814, he told Henry Wellesley that he was anxious to return them, but was invited by King Ferdinand to retain them as they had 'come into your possession in a manner as just as they are honourable'.[102] Marshal Jourdan's baton was found in the baggage, and Wellington sent this trophy to the Prince Regent. Amongst the prisoners was Madame Gazan, wife of a general on Joseph's staff. When asked if another unfortunate lady was also a general's wife, she replied: '*Ah, pour cela – non, elle est seulement sa femme de campagne.*'[103]

Although Vitoria was a less desperate battle than Talavera or Albuera, it was of far greater strategic significance: a *Te Deum* was sung in St Petersburg, and Beethoven composed 'Wellington's Victory' in its honour. The French grip on Spain was definitively broken, and all Napoleon's generals could now do was to hold the Pyrenees and their approaches in an effort to prevent an invasion of southern France. However, Marshal Soult, who replaced Joseph and Jourdan in mid-July, skilfully reorganised his army and mounted a counter-offensive. He cut up British detachments at Roncesvalles and Maya, but was checked by Wellington himself at Sorauren, just north of Pamplona, on 28 and 30 July. 'The 28th was fair bludgeon-work . . .,' Wellington told his brother William. 'I escaped unhurt as usual, and I begin to believe that the finger of God is upon me.'[104]

San Sebastián, keystone of the frontier, was blockaded by the allies in late June and bombarded in July 1813. It was attacked on the 25th after two practicable breaches had been established, but the assault was beaten off with heavy losses. Wellington concluded 'that it would be necessary to increase the facilities of the attack before it should be repeated . . . and desired that the siege should for the moment be converted into a blockade'.[105] It was not until late August that he was ready to proceed. Bombardment was renewed on the 26th, and five days later the place was assaulted in daylight so that the attackers could profit from the low tide. The garrison resisted desperately, compelling Graham, in command of the attack, to pause and recommence artillery fire, but by nightfall the town, now largely in flames, was in allied hands. The capture of San Sebastián was marred by the depressingly familiar pillage that followed it, and anti-British feeling was aroused by rumours that Wellington had fired the town deliberately, to punish it for its pre-war trade with the French. Had he wished to do so, he could have mortared the place at no risk to his army, but that was not an argument that commended itself to the wilder sections of the Spanish press.

Operations on the north-east coast of Spain were not going well, with the allies held in check by Marshal Suchet near Barcelona. Wellington considered intervening in that sector, but concluded that he was better placed to enter France from the north-west. News from elsewhere in Europe was encouraging, with early reports suggesting that Napoleon was in real trouble deep in Germany. With San Sebastián taken, he proposed to cross the River Bidossoa and then force the passes of the Pyrenees beyond it.

On 7 October Wellington crossed the Bidossoa, giving Ensign Howell Rees Gronow of the 1ˢᵗ Foot Guards his first view of 'the immortal Wellington':

> He was very stern and grave looking; he was in deep meditation, so long as I kept him in view, and spoke to no one. His features were bold, and I saw much decision of character in his expression. He rode a knowing-looking thoroughbred horse, and wore a gray overcoat, Hessian boots, and a large cocked hat.[106]

Wellington was now a field marshal. He had been promoted full general in 1812, although the new rank only applied in the Peninsula, but his success at Vitoria encouraged the Prince Regent to write (Elizabeth Longford points out that the language is as fine as the writing is faint) from Carlton House on 3 July that:

> Your glorious conduct is beyond all human praise, and far beyond my reward. I know no language the world affords worthy to express it . . . You have sent me, among the trophies of your unrivalled fame, the staff of a French Marshal, and I send you in return that of England.[107]

Alas, it was not that simple, for there was no regulation field-marshal's baton in the British army of the age, and the prince, that 'fountain of taste' had helped design one. The Duke of York, never slow to tarnish the gilt, also sent a letter of congratulation, observing that the promotion had been mooted after Salamanca but was turned down because of the 'spirit of jealousy' it would have inspired.

The French defended the Bidossoa from stout field fortifications, but Wellington broke their line at Vera. The fall of Pamplona on 31 October released more troops, and with their aid he then unhinged Soult's defence with battles on the Nivelle, the Nive and

St Pierre, and was able to threaten Bayonne. On 1 November, he issued a proclamation to the French population, warning it to take no part in the operations but stressing that he had ordered that no harm would be done to civilians. However, it was soon evident that while British and Portuguese soldiers were conducting themselves so well that 'the inhabitants are living very comfortably and quietly with our soldiers cantoned in their houses', the Spanish were another matter altogether. They fiercely resented what the French had done to their country, and in consequence 'plundered a good deal, and did a good deal of mischief . . .'[108] This persuaded Wellington to send some of his Spanish troops back to Spain, which reduced the size of the force available to meet Soult when campaigning resumed in 1814, but also reduced the risk of large-scale French popular resistance to his invasion.

Wellington spent the winter of 1813 at St Jean de Luz, where his headquarters settled down to the familiar between-campaign routine. Larpent wrote that 'everyone works hard, and does his business: the substance and not the form is attended to.' The young gentlemen of the staff were in sparkling form. George Gleig described how:

> They had many school-boy tricks; among others, that of giving nick-names, at which nobody took offence. 'Where is Slender Billy?' said Lord FitzRoy Somerset, looking round the table, and apparently missing somebody. 'Here I am, FitzRoy,' replied the Prince of Orange, 'what do you want?'[109]

Several Bourbon sympathisers appeared, amongst them the Duc d'Angoulême, nephew of Louis XVIII, legitimate king of France. Visitors to headquarters had long been nicknamed tigers, and the duke, 'a short, rather mean-looking man, with a strongly-marked

Bourbon cast of countenance, and endless grimaces . . .' became known as 'The Royal Tiger.'[110] The duke might have become even more tigerish had he known that Wellington was urging Bathurst that it would be better to impose a moderate peace on Napoleon than to unseat him in favour of a Bourbon restoration, because: 'If Buonaparte becomes moderate, he is probably as good a sovereign as we can desire in France.' Larpent noted that Wellington's appetite for work seemed to have slackened slightly, and he enjoyed some hunting, appearing 'just like a genuine country squire and fox-hunter', and habitually spending two hours each afternoon in 'a common blue frock [coat] . . . and with a round hat on his head' walking up and down the quay. The mayor gave a ball, but it was pronounced a failure, largely because there were 200 splendidly-attired gentlemen but very few ladies who could or would dance. Gronow thought that this was because most 'were too patriotic to appear'.[111]

There had been something of a change in the character of Wellington's generalship. He himself thought that 'there seems to be a new spirit among the officers . . . to keep the troops in order', and he reciprocated by showing greater trust. When he was preparing his attack on the Nivelle, he kept Charles Alten of the Light Division and his brigadiers, John Colborne and James Kempt, sitting beside him on the summit of the Grande Rhune mountain while he explained how he would 'beat the French out, and with great ease', from their position. The explanation concluded, Colborne rose to depart, but Wellington told them all to stay where they were while he dictated his orders to George Murray. There was more than a glimmer of Nelson's 'band of brothers'.[112] When Rowland Hill beat the French in a hard-fought action at St Pierre, Wellington rode up and congratulated him with the words: 'My dear Hill, the day's your own!' Jac Weller suggests that Wellington's new disposition to trust his subordinates reflected his desire to ensure that Britain had generals with experience of independent command. But it is at least as likely that he now recognised that there were indeed generals who were up to the task: the hour had brought forth its men. And he was now prepared to let the Spaniards win victories where they could. On 31 August, he had declined to reinforce a Spanish force under determined attack on the heights of San Marcial above San Sebastián, telling its commander that 'if I send the English troops you ask for they will win the battle; but as the French are already in retreat you may as well win it for yourselves'.[113] And win it they did.

As soon as the weather enabled him to move, Wellington sent Hill and a strong force to lure Soult away from the River Adour at Bayonne. Hill did his job well, cutting off St Jean Pied-de-Port and going on to approach Orthez. On the left, meanwhile, a huge pontoon bridge was brought up by the navy into the bay of St Jean de Luz. As soon as the boistrous weather abated, Lieutenant General Sir John Hope seized a bridgehead over the Adour, and on 24 February 1814 bridging began. Hope was soon secure enough on the far bank to commence the siege of Bayonne. With 17,000 of Soult's men penned up in the city, Wellington moved parallel with Hill to attack the French at Orthez, where he beat Soult on 27 February 1814. Wellington, well forward on horseback as usual, laughed when Alava cried out that he had a 'knock' on his backside. The next moment Wellington himself was hit by a musketball which drove his sword-hilt hard against his thigh, breaking the skin and causing a contusion which had him limping for several days. Alava said that the duke had brought it on himself by laughing at his misfortune.

Orthez cost Soult 4,000 men to Wellington's 2,000, and one of his new conscript divisions had left a rich haul of prisoners. However, he remained a doughty adversary, and there was a real danger that Suchet would march north from Catalonia to join him. Wellington's intelligence system, so reliable in the Peninsula, had now outrun its sources, and news from further north was confusing. Napoleon, badly defeated at Leipzig in October 1813, was enjoying something of a revival in a lightning campaign against the Russian, Prussian and Austrian army advancing into Champagne. Wellington decided to take Toulouse, which was believed to be strongly royalist in sentiment.

Early in April 1814, he rode down to the River Garonne with only two of his staff, and a French sentry fired at him unsuccessfully. There was a well-established understanding that pickets did not fire upon one another, and the man's officer, scandalised, came forward to apologise, saying that the fellow was a new recruit. Wellington had a conversation with the officer, stealing a good look at the river-line as he did so. Then he raised his anonymous cocked hat, and rode off. On 10 April, his army launched attacks from the south, west and north, but Soult wisely decided not to allow himself to be shut up in the city as the pincers closed around it, and slipped away to the east after inflicting 4,500 casualties in return for over a thousand fewer.

Toulouse was indeed delighted to welcome Wellington, and he entered the city on 12 April to find Napoleon's statue lying smashed on the ground and workmen chipping imperial iconography from public buildings. He was to give a dinner at the prefecture that evening, and was dressing when Colonel Frederick Ponsonby galloped in from Bordeaux with extraordinary news: Napoleon had abdicated. 'You don't say so, upon my honour! Hurrah!' Wellington, still in his shirtsleeves spun round on his heel, snapping his fingers like a schoolboy.'[114] Official confirmation arrived during dinner. Napoleon had abdicated on 6 April 1814, and had been given a pension and the tiny Mediterranean island of Elba. Louis XVIII had been restored. Wellington at once called for champagne and proposed a toast to the French king. Alava then proposed 'El Liberador de España!' Immediately everyone was on his feet, acclaiming Wellington in French, Spanish, Portugese and German. 'And this was followed,' writes Larpent,

> not by a regular three times three, but by a cheering in all confusion for nearly ten minutes! Lord Wellington bowed, confused, and immediately called for coffee.[115]

FIVE

TWO RESTORATIONS AND A BATTLE

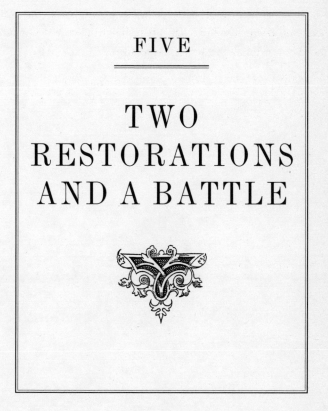

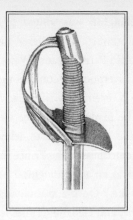

WELLINGTON WENT to the theatre in Toulouse on the night of 12 April 1814 with the white cockade of the Bourbons on his cocked hat. The play was 'Richard Coeur de Lion', but the audience's mind was elsewhere, for 'a person in black, attended by many candles, having a paper in his hand' made his way into a nearby box and read out the terms of the new constitution. Europe had been at war for most of Wellington's adult life. Looking back at the period from our vantage point nearly two centuries on, with two dreadful wars within living memory, it is easy to forget the destruction caused by the Revolutionary and Napoleonic Wars. Alan Schom lays much of the blame at Napoleon's door, declaring that 'The memory of Genghis Khan paled in comparison', and estimating war deaths at three million.[1] This is probably too low a figure, for France alone had lost 860,000 soldiers killed, half of them below the age of 28.[2] Most British contemporaries welcomed the peace and were determined that it should be preserved. But quite how this should be accomplished, and how domestic politics should reflect the new change in emphasis, were different matters altogether.

On 21 April Wellington was visited by Castlereagh's half-brother, Sir Charles Stewart, who offered him the appointment of British ambassador in Paris. Because Wellington's brothers had fallen out with Lord Liverpool, he could not join the government, and he accepted the Paris embassy with alacrity. Stewart also told him that he was to be made a duke. The elevation was gazetted on 3 May, and on the 9th, he wrote to acknowledge Liverpool's kindness and his indebtedness to the Prince Regent. A month later he told Henry almost as an afterthought: 'I believe I forgot to tell you I was made a Duke.'[3] On the journey to Paris he deferred to the Duc d'Angoulême, and General Clausel, calling on his former adversary, was surprised to find that the field marshal opened his own door: there was not an aide-de-camp in sight. He entered Paris on 4 May, riding a white horse but wearing plain clothes – blue frock-coat and top-hat – for he came as an ambassador, not a conqueror. 'I felt for my own part,' recalled the radical John Cam Hobhouse, 'an insatiable desire to see him, and ran many chances of being kicked and trampled down to get near our great man.'[4] The Comtesse de Boigne saw him enter a ballroom 'with his two nieces [daughters of his brother William] hanging on his arm. There were no eyes for anyone else.'[5]

He was not in Paris for long, for Castlereagh asked him to visit Madrid, 'in order to try whether I cannot prevail upon all parties to be more moderate, and to adopt a constitution more likely to be practicable . . .'[6] Wellington submitted a long memorandum to the restored King Ferdinand, and gave practical advice on the reconstitution of the Spanish army. He was not optimistic that his efforts would bear much fruit, however, for the king's reactionary advisers were in firm control, and Ferdinand himself told the duke that the only acts of the Cortes of which he approved were those making Wellington commander-in-chief and giving him an estate.

His pessimism was well founded, and there was a revolt against the capricious monarch in 1820. Ferdinand was restored, ironically with French military assistance but he died in 1833 leaving a legacy of division and bitterness that resulted in a long period of civil war.

On his way back from Madrid, Wellington stopped at Bordeaux, the main port of embarkation for his Peninsular army. The enthusiasm for peace was not shared by many of those whose business was war. John Kincaid declared that they had been 'born in war, reared in war, war was our trade, and what soldiers had to do in peace was a problem yet to be solved among us'.[7] Officers faced the prospect of being shunted off on half-pay and soldiers discharged to an uncertain future. There were ironies even here. Ned Pakenham, who was quite content to face the hazards of peace, was selected to command an army sent to the southern United States, soon to become a theatre of the misnamed War of 1812. John Spencer Cooper, eager to return home to Barnard Castle with his brother, only needed his colonel's signature on his discharge papers, but could not get it before his ship also sailed for America.

On 14 June Wellington published his last words to his army:

GENERAL ORDER

1. The Commander of the Forces, being upon the point of returning to England, again takes this opportunity of congratulating the army upon the recent events which have restored peace to their country and the world.

2. The share which the British army has had in producing these events, and the high character with which the army will quit this country, must be equally satisfactory to every individual belonging to it, as it is to the

Commander of the Forces; and he trusts that the troops will continue the same good conduct to the last.

3. The Commander of the Forces once again requests the army to accept his thanks.

4. Although circumstances may alter the relations in which he has stood towards them, so much to his satisfaction, he assures them that he shall never cease to feel the warmest interest in their welfare and honour, and that he will at all times be happy to be of service to those whose conduct, discipline and gallantry, their country is so much indebted.[8]

This tribute came from the heart, but it was not well received by all. Some put it in the context of previous dispatches which thanked too few. 'A man gets no thanks for getting his head broke now-a-days,' wrote Captain Arthur Kennedy of the 18th Hussars after Vitoria. 'This has been amply verified with us, never did a Regiment lose so many officers with so little thanks from the Head Butcher, as literally he is . . .'[9] Lieutenant William Grattan complained of the way that 'the never-to-be-forgotten services of that wonderful army were treated by the Government and the Duke of Wellington'.[10] Soldiers who had married local women had to leave their wives behind them, and the expected rewards of cash or promotion were often not forthcoming from a government striving to retrench, and an army beginning to contract. There was little Wellington could do about much of this. He had tried to get a majority for Harry Smith, but had been told that there were too many senior officers in his way. 'A pity, by G-d,' said the duke. 'Colborne and the Brigade are so anxious about it, and he deserves anything.'[11]

For the rest of his life he was the target 'of begging-letters and hats touched by eager fingers as his horse went by'.[12] He certainly did not please everybody. The former Captain George Elers, who had served with him in India and left the army in 1812, was disgusted to find that the duke would not provide him with a job in 1828. He was not even interested in receiving a gift: 'the Duke of Wellington presents his compliments to Mr Elers, and is much obliged to him for his letter of this day. The Duke has no occasion for a Newfoundland Dog, and will not deprive Mr Elers of him.'[13] The disgusted Elers asked rhetorically 'Can He have a Heart?' He did indeed have a heart, but he had a head too, and it was never easy to reconcile the honouring of obligation with the exercise of unreasonable patronage. Yet he often tried far harder on their behalf than the disappointed ever knew. When two generals wrote to complain that they had not been knighted after the victory, he told Lord Bathurst that although it was now too late for anything to be done for them, in justice he would forward their letters, and declared that 'if I had been desired to recommend those ... on whom it was intended to confer this honour, I should certainly have mentioned their names in preference to those of many, on whom I see it has been conferred'.[14]

Wellington travelled to Paris for another burst of lionising, and then sailed from Calais in the sloop *Rosario*, reaching Dover on 23 June. He was welcomed by frantic crowds, and cheered all the way to London. When his carriage reached Westminster Bridge there was a determined attempt to take the horses out of the traces so that the crowd could pull him home – now 4 Hamilton Place, Piccadilly. But he was too quick for them and galloped on alone. He had not seen Kitty for five years. They had corresponded (she thoughtfully knitted him a blanket in 1809 and made a quilt the following year), but he was so concerned about her ability to bear even slightly bad news that he made no mention of the wound he incurred at Orthez. Her eyesight had grown much worse, and she read and drew with her eyes inches from the work. To avoid apparently cutting acquaintances in a crowd because she could not recognise them, she habitually went about with her eyes screwed up and cast down; it was not an engaging trait. And she was no judge of clothes, with an affection for muslin dresses that matched neither her years nor her station. Wellington's sons, the eldest now Lord Douro, were schoolboys aged six and seven. They had grown up without him, and like so many men who were themselves starved of affection as children, Wellington found it hard to lavish what he himself had lacked. Even now he did not remain at home for long, but slipped away to visit his mother in Upper Brook Street.

On 28 June, Wellington took his seat in the House of Lords as baron, viscount, earl, marquess and duke, wearing a field marshal's uniform beneath his ducal robes, and hearing the Lord Chancellor applaud the fact that he had received 'all the dignities in the Peerage of this realm which the crown can confer' in little more than four years.[15] The House of Commons paid its own tribute on 1 July, and the City's Court of Common Council – which had petitioned to have him tried for Cintra – gave a banquet in his honour. So too, in his own happily inimitable style, did the Prince Regent. When the prince proposed his health, Wellington rose to reply and began: 'I want words to express . . .' 'My dear fellow,' interrupted the prince, 'we know your *actions* and we will excuse your *words*, so sit down.' The duke did so at once, with all the delight of a schoolboy given an unexpected holiday.[16]

His own holiday was coming to an end, and he set off for the continent in early August, shortly after giving away his niece, Emily Wellesley-Pole, at her wedding to FitzRoy Somerset. HMS *Griffon* took him to Bergen-op-Zoom, and he travelled on via

Antwerp to Brussels, to see the Prince of Orange, Slender Billy of Peninsula days, whose father was king of the Netherlands. He accompanied the prince around the frontier fortresses, noting as he did so 'good positions for an army', one of them at 'the entrance to the *forêt* de Soignies by the high road which leads to Brussels from Binch, Charleroi, and Namur'.[17] He arrived in Paris on the 22 August, and moved into 39 rue du Faubourg St Honoré, built in 1720 and owned by Napoleon's youngest sister Pauline, Princess Borghese. Charles Stewart's agents had just bought it from her, fully furnished, for what Wellington thought a 'remarkably cheap' price; he would happily have paid £2,000 a year to rent it, and told the Foreign Office that he was content to have that sum stopped from his salary. It is still the British Embassy, and Duff Cooper, ambassador there in 1944–7, called it: 'The perfect example of what a rich gentleman's house should be. Neither palatial nor imposing, but commodious and convenient, central and quiet . . .'[18]

Napoleon thought Wellington's appointment an unwise one, as he would be facing those he had humbled, and his presence in Paris was certainly one of the many 'piquant contrasts' of that first restoration, with bewigged *émigré* dukes going to mass with scarred marshals, and Swiss sentries at the Tuileries presenting arms to crippled veterans who turned back a coat lapel to reveal the Legion of Honour. Wellington met Marshal Ney out hunting soon after his arrival – though there was wide agreement amongst the young men at the embassy that French hunting was staid stuff, with few chances of 'an English run'. Soult and Wellington recognised one another well enough, for Wellington had scrutinised Soult through his telescope on the ridge at Sorauren, and Soult had peered at Wellington in their coach when they were both on their way home in April. In December he met Massena at a party. The two men quizzed one another through lorgnettes as they might have done before a battle, and Massena was first to advance, saying: 'My lord, you owe me a dinner – for you positively made me starve.' 'You should give it to me, Marshal,' replied the duke, 'for you prevented me from sleeping.'[19] He saw a good deal of the royal family, and endured Louis' spectacular greed. The corpulent monarch (Wellington described him as 'a walking sore') would tip a whole serving-dish of strawberries onto his plate without offering them to anybody else.

Wellington was a welcome figure at the city's many salons, attending the Duchesse d'Angoulême's parties at the Pavillon de Flore, and enjoying afternoons with Mme de Staël, 'a most agreeable women', provided you kept her off politics. Not all his lady friends were above reproach. Pretty little Aglaé Ney, the marshal's wife, was having an affair with a young Englishman, Michael Bruce, and Giuseppina Grassini, the opera singer once known as 'La Chanteuse de l'Empereur' had been Napoleon's mistress. She may well have been Wellington's too, and Lady Bessborough, staying in Paris that autumn, found his attentions to the singer rather too obvious. He certainly kept her portrait in his room, but then again, as Christopher Hibbert dryly observes, he kept pictures of Pauline Borghese and Pius VII there too. He also saw a very great deal of the tragic actress Marguerite Josephine Weimer, such a splendidly caparisoned lady that Napoleon had stuffed the not inconsiderable sum of 40,000 francs between her breasts after their first night together. She boasted that both the duke and emperor had been her lovers: 'Mais M. le duc était de beaucoup le plus fort.'[20] And then there was Harriette Wilson, kissed 'by main force' in the Bois de Boulogne and rattling on ambiguously and unreliably about the duke's practice of visiting noble ladies à cheval.

But it was not all strawberries and beautiful women. The British government was keen to persuade France to put an end to the slave trade in her colonies, and the issue was one that engaged Wellington's emotions as well as his professional attention. The abolitionist Thomas Clarkson visited Paris and was delighted to discover that the duke 'had made himself master of the subject'. Wellington assured William Wilberforce, who had done so much to get slavery abolished in Britain in 1807, that he would pursue his task 'with all the zeal of which I am capable'.[21] Despite encouraging signs in early skirmishes, he could not carry the position, partly because the Chamber of Peers (created, in the new French constitution, on the model of the House of Lords) contained many men whose fortunes had been made in the trade.

Yet Wellington's position was just as uncomfortable as Napoleon had suggested. The Bourbons had indeed learnt nothing and forgotten nothing. 'They imposed upon us,' wrote Philippe de Ségur, nobleman but Napoleonic officer, 'the flag under which they had fought us.' Seasoned veterans were sent off on half-pay while former *émigrés* took command. Families ruined by the revolution hoped for more than the restored monarchy could deliver, and Bonapartists compared *le tondu* (back at the peak of his form for that last campaign of 1814) with their gouty king. 'We who were lately masters of Europe,' wrote General Foy sadly, 'to what servitude are we reduced? ... O Napoleon, where are you?'[22] France had evidently not settled to the hands of its new rulers, and Wellington was persistently warned of attempts to kill or abduct him. In October, the British prime minister begged him to leave Paris as soon as possible. It would not, however, be essential to move him without good cause, so as not to 'betray any alarm on our part as to the prospect of internal convulsion in France'.[23] He was asked if he would rather go to Vienna, to assist Castlereagh in the negotiations concerning the framing of a post-war settlement, or take command in North America. Wellington replied that he would rather stay on in Paris for the time being, but Liverpool replied that 'we shall not feel easy till we hear of your having landed at Dover, or at all events, of your being out of French territory,' so on 16 November the duke agreed that he would go, although he saw no need for haste.[24]

A peace treaty was signed between Britain and America on 24 December 1814, blasting one excuse for his removal, but Castlereagh was now required back in England, and so Wellington was sent to Vienna as British representative. News of the peace travelled too slowly to reach America before Ned Pakenham had attacked the Americans at New Orleans. Before leaving England, he had been advised that as commander-in-chief, he would not need to hazard his person as he had when a divisional commander; he replied that he knew this well, but would not hesitate to lead if he had to. When the attack bogged down in the face of heavy fire from well-entrenched defenders, some of the attacking infantry broke, and Pakenham rode forward to rally them, shouting: 'For shame! Recollect that you are British soldiers.' He was shot through the spine and killed. Wellington was both sad at Ned's death and angry at Ned's naval colleague, whom he blamed for the failure.

> We have but one consolation, that he fell as he lived, in the honourable discharge of his duty, and distinguished as a soldier & as a man.
>
> I cannot but regret that he was ever employed on such a service or with such a colleague.
>
> The expedition to New Orleans originated with that colleague, & plunder was its object ... The Americans were prepared with an army in a fortified position which

still would have been carried, if the duties of others, that is of the Admiral, had been as well performed as that of him whom we lament.[25]

But providence performed it otherwise & we must submit . . .

Ned's death struck another blow at Wellington's own marriage. Elizabeth Longford suggests that the facial likeness between Ned and Kitty was so strong that Wellington may have seen in his brother-in-law the looks that he once found so attractive in his wife, and Ned's regard for his sister and hero-worship of Wellington may have helped preserve the peace between the soaring duke and his awkward, short-sighted duchess.[26]

It is no surprise that Kitty stayed behind in Paris with the Somersets when Wellington set off for Vienna on 24 January 1815. He travelled at top speed, stopping for only four hours a night, and arrived in the depths of an Austrian winter – the overheated rooms soon gave him a cold. It was not a time for quick decisions. When Wellington asked his colleagues what they had done towards achieving a settlement for Europe, Prince Metternich, the Austrian representative, replied: 'Nothing; absolutely nothing.' He soon immersed himself in the politics of peace-making, trying to find some way of reconciling the aims of the Russian-inspired Holy Alliance of Prussia, Austria and Russia, with Britain's need to collaborate with France in order to secure a lasting peace. And there were enough ladies about to raise the enticing prospect of liaisons: Castlereagh's half-brother Charles, now raised to the peerage, was ambassador at Vienna, and was the lover of one of the Duke of Courland's pretty daughters; another announced her devotion to Wellington. But on the morning of 7 March 1815, he was just getting ready to go hunting when he heard momentous news: Napoleon had escaped from Elba. It quickly became clear that he had landed in France, and that the army was going over to him en masse – on 20 March Napoleon was carried shoulder-high into the Tuileries.

On 12 March, Wellington told Castlereagh that the allies planned to assemble three large armies: one, wholly Austrian, in nothern Italy; another, with Austrians, Bavarians, Badeners and Württembergers, on the upper Rhine; and a third, largely Prussian, on the lower Rhine, whence it would join British and Hanoverian troops in the Netherlands. The Russians, moving to the theatre of war more slowly, would constitute a reserve. Tsar Alexander hoped to 'manage the concern' in a council consisting of himself, the king of Prussia and the Austrian Prince Schwarzenberg. He had asked Wellington to join him, but the duke thought that 'as I should have neither character nor occupation in such a situation, I should prefer to carry a musket'.[27] Wellington was invited to remain British plenipotentiary in Vienna or to become commander-in-chief of British forces in the Netherlands, and not surprisingly chose the latter. Before he left Vienna, Tsar Alexander laid his hand on his shoulder and said: 'It is for you to save the world again.'

Wellington arrived in Brussels on 4 April 1815 and found himself facing difficulties on every front. The dismal performance of King Louis and his supporters induced him to seek what he called a 'third term', to give the French a choice between the legitimate (but unappetising) Bourbons and the illegitimate (but appealing) Bonaparte. He thought that there might be some hope with a junior branch of the Bourbons in the person of the Duc d'Orleans (who did indeed become king as Louis-Philippe in 1830), but Castlereagh told him that dynastic changes were not among the government's objectives. And although he got on well with Slender Billy (known less flatteringly as the Young Frog), his relationship with the prince's father, King William I of the Netherlands (the Old Frog), was less comfortable. In part this reflected the fact that the king's own position was insecure. His realm combined Holland with large parts of the former Spanish and Austrian Netherlands, and there were already signs of the schism that would later separate the southern provinces, the future Belgium, from Holland. Many of his officers and men had fought for Napoleon, and their loyalty could not be taken for granted. But although Wellington was very careful not to offend his allies – when Madame Catallani sang at a concert at the end of April he stared down his officers when they called for an encore of 'Rule Britannia' – he was concerned that the garrisons of the frontier fortresses might go over to the French. On 3 May, he was appointed a field marshal in the Netherlands army and commander-in-chief of its forces in the theatre of war, superseding the Prince of Orange who, by way of compensation, was to be given command of a corps in the allied army.

For an allied army it was to be, with British, KGL and Hanoverian units combined within British divisions and Netherlands troops in their own divisions but interleaved into the fabric of the army. In arranging his force, Wellington deployed those talents rough-hewn in India and polished in Spain, using veterans to stiffen youngsters, and the robust to buttress the less reliable. Sir John Fortescue catches the real cleverness of the structure:

> In every British Division except the First, foreigners were blended with Redcoats. Alten's and Clinton's had each one brigade of British, one of the [King's German] Legion, and one of Hanoverians; Picton's and Colville's had each two brigades of British and one of Hanoverians. Even so, however, the subtlety of mixture is as yet not wholly expressed. In Cooke's division of Guards the three

young battalions were stiffened by an old one from the Peninsula. In Alten's, where all the British were young, the battalions of the Legion were veterans and the Hanoverians were regulars; in Colville's, where the British were both old and young, the Hanoverians were both regulars and militia; in Clinton's, where the British as well as the troops of the Legion were old, the Hanoverians were all militia.[28]

The fact that all this laminating was necessary testifies to the nature of Wellington's army. Some British historians have joined their contemporary countrymen in expressing a uniformly low opinion of the Netherlands troops. However, it is beyond question that many fought bravely at Waterloo, and, but for the common sense of a Netherlands general, there might have been no battle there at all. It is more honest to observe that across the board, Wellington's army was of patchy quality, with Peninsula veterans alongside battalions filled out with new recruits. He later affirmed that if he had had his old Peninsula army, he would have attacked Napoleon at Waterloo and beaten him in about three hours. This may be hyperbole, but it reflects his conviction that, in April 1815, he had what he called 'an infamous army, very weak and ill-equipped, and a very inexperienced staff'.

Many old hands were unavailable. His former quartermaster-general, George Murray, was in Canada; Ned Pakenham was dead; Larpent was in Vienna, and Sir James McGrigor (as he now was) could not be spared from his medical responsibilities in London. In France in 1814, Sir Thomas Picton had come to him to admit that: 'I am grown so nervous, that when there is any service to be done, it works upon my mind so that it is impossible for me to sleep at nights. I cannot possibly stand it, and I shall be forced to retire.' But he let neither resentment at not having been made a peer, nor a premonition of death, hold him back when offered command of the 5th Division. Sir Stapleton Cotton, who had done so well at Salamanca, had now become Lord Combermere and would have been a good choice for command of the cavalry, but Lord Uxbridge (once Lord Paget) had been promised the job.

Major General Sir Hudson Lowe, of whom Horse Guards had a very high opinion, was sent out as quartermaster-general. Wellington thought him 'a damned fool'. He persisted in telling the duke the Prussians were better than the British so much that 'I was obliged to tell him that I had commanded a much larger force in the field than any Prussian general.'[29] Even this did not work, and Wellington was obliged to ask the government to replace him. His successor was Colonel Sir William De Lancey, who had served under George Murray in the Peninsula and mastered the Wellingtonian style of correspondence. On one occasion he regretted that the commander-in-chief could not reply to an officer's letter because it was illegible, and so the man's colonel was told that 'his Lordship requests that you will recommend to Captain Campbell to pay a little more attention to his writing as it is impossible in many cases to allot the necessary time to trace the Characters in his letters without neglecting other public business'.[30] Sir Edward Barnes, another Peninsula veteran, was adjutant-general.

Unusually, the duke divided his army up into three corps, the first under the Prince of Orange and the second under Rowland (now Lord) Hill, each containing two British and two Netherlands divisions. Wellington himself commanded the reserve, with two British divisions, a divisional-sized 'corps' of Brunswickers under the Duke of Brunswick, and a small Nassau contingent. He had a grand total of just over 92,000 men and 192 guns by the time Waterloo was fought.

Whatever its strengths and weaknesses, Wellington did at least command the allied army forming up in the Netherlands in the late spring 1815. He did not command the nearest coalition contingent, on whose effective co-operation the conduct of the campaign would depend. The Prussian army in the Netherlands numbered nearly 121,000 men and 312 guns by the time the campaign opened. Its commander, Marshal Gebhard von Blücher, Prince of Wahlstadt, was a sprightly 73-year-old who had first been commissioned into the Swedish army a lifetime ago and entered Prussian service after being taken prisoner. A doughty adversary of Napoleon, he had had horses shot beneath him at Jena in 1806 and Lutzen in 1813, and had helped crush Napoleon's last brilliant flicker in 1814. His headquarters were at Namur, and his four corps were stationed around it, with two posted forward close to the French border at Charleroi and Ciney. His chief of staff, the brave and experienced August Wilhelm von Gneisenau, was something of an anglophobe, possibly because he had served alongside the British army in North America during the Revolutionary War, when it was not at its best.

The campaign was to turn on the relationship between Wellington and Blücher. They had met in Paris the previous year, and quickly established a sound working relationship. Most anglophone historians had long regarded the collaboration between Wellington and Blücher as an honest and fruitful one. However, the publication, in 1998 and 1999, of Peter Hofschröer's two carefully-researched books on Waterloo raised issues that had long troubled German historians and cannot be lightly brushed aside by any modern biographer.[31] Making extensive use of German sources, Hofschröer accuses Wellington of duplicity during the Waterloo campaign, and terms the battle 'the German victory'. The debate has generated more heat than light, and has not been helped by the fact that while Hofschröer's attack on Wellington appears in popular books, John Hussey's reasoned rebuttal of some specific accusations are in the less widely circulated pages of the academic journal, *War in History*.[32] And the clash is not simply national, for it is not hard to discern in the dispute something of the 'tall poppy syndrome' which makes Britain uncomfortable with her heroes, living and dead. One British reviewer looked forward to 'the Oxford-accented screams' that Hofschröer would cause.

Three general points deserve mention. First, military history tends to fall prey to monolinguality. For example, British histories of the 1916 Battle of the Somme often pay as little attention to the Germans, who the British fought against, as they do to the French, who fought alongside them, and in the process suffered about one-third of the allied casualties.

Secondly, the campaign to defeat Napoleon during the Hundred Days was always an allied struggle – not a British, Prussian or a German one. The great majority of allied troops in the theatre spoke German as their first language, and their enormous contribution to victory cannot be denied. But nor should it be taken out of context, and if the Prussians were able to set the seal on victory at Waterloo, it was only because Wellington's army, with its British, Netherlands, Hanoverian and Brunswick contingents, had set the conditions for that victory before they arrived.

Thirdly, any commander of a national contingent within a wider coalition force in any century must answer to two masters. On the one hand, he has a responsibility to, and loyalties within, the alliance. On the other, he derives his authority from his own government, and will be aware that there will be times when his national duty will override his responsibilities to the alliance. Wellington believed that his prime duty was to defeat the French in collaboration with his allies, and his first general memorandum on the campaign and his subsequent letters before the opening of hostilities make this clear. The allied object was to 'defeat the army, and destroy the power of one individual', and this could be accomplished by a concentric advance in the direction of Paris with 'the largest body of men that can be assembled'.[33] On 8 May, he told Charles Stewart that 'Blücher and I are so well united, and so strong' that he thought it unlikely they would be attacked.[34] As Paris was their objective, he believed that he and Blücher would meet 'the greatest force and the greatest military difficulties', and their thrust should accordingly not be launched until offensives elsewhere could keep the French in play.

However, there was another agenda. Wellington was fighting expeditionary warfare; his continental allies were not. Just as his army in the Peninsula had relied on its base at Lisbon, defended by the lines of Torres Vedras, so his army in the Netherlands relied on the ports of Antwerp and Ostend. These were indispensable for the continued arrival of troops and supplies, and, if the campaign turned badly against him, they offered him the chance of preserving at least part of his army by evacuation. Antwerp lay due north of Brussels and Ostend north-west, offering alternative lines of retreat. His concern about the reliability of Netherlands troops meant that these ports had substantial British garrisons, and he had ordered work to be carried out on their fortifications. All this was entirely in keeping with his well-established notion of a plan of campaign which, as he himself put it, resembled a rope head-collar rather than a finely-made set of harness: if it broke, he simply tied a knot.

He would take measured risks, but not gamble, for what would he have gambled with? While this was not his old Peninsula army, as he constantly pointed out, it contained the core of the British regular army. If lost, these troops could not readily be replaced in a country that relied on voluntary enlistment. Although the Liverpool government, to which the duke was very close, might conceivably have survived his defeat, it could not have done so had this been accompanied by the destruction of his army. Moreover, the army was more than an instrument of foreign policy; in the absence of a police force, it provided the government's most reliable defence against internal disorder. There had been serious riots against the Corn Laws, which kept the price of bread at an artificially high level, and the situation in Ireland was causing concern. Wellington had good reasons, political and military, for ensuring that he had a plan available if coalition war went as sour in 1815 as it had in 1793 or 1809.

It was not in Wellington's interest, however, to declare his concern for preserving his army in the event of a catastrophe. Throughout his time in Brussels he took pains to radiate confidence, taking Lady Jane Lennox off to watch a cricket-match at Enghien, giving and attending parties – there were the usual complaints that he asked all the 'Ladies of Loose Character' to his own – and talking up his prospects of victory. When Thomas Creevey asked him, as they walked in a Brussels park, whether he was confident, he replied: 'By God, I think Blücher and myself can do the thing.' He then pointed at a British private, gawping at the statues, and added. 'No, I think Blücher and I can do the business. There,' pointing at the soldier, 'it all depends on that article there whether we do the business or not. Give me enough of it and I am sure.'[35]

Privately he felt less confident. On 8 June he warned the Duchess of Richmond, comfortably established in Brussels, not to organise a picnic down by the frontier: 'You'd better not go. Say nothing about it, but let the project drop.'[36] After the campaign had opened he urged Charles Stewart, now also in Brussels: 'Pray keep the English quiet if you can. Let them all prepare to move, but neither be in a hurry nor a fright, as all will turn out well.'[37] The same letter enclosed one to the Duc de Berri, who commanded the French Royalist troops, suggesting that he move King Louis from Ghent to Antwerp. He also dashed off a note to Lady Frances Wedderburn-Webster (with whom he had enjoyed a tender assignation in a wooded glade, where campaign planning may not have featured in the conversation), that 'you ought to make your preparations, as should [her father] Lord Mountnorris, to remove from Bruxelles to Antwerp in case such a measure should be necessary . . . I will give you the earliest intimation of any danger that may come to my knowledge: at present I know of none.'[38] He ordered the governor of Antwerp to consider the place in a state of siege, opening the sluices to flood the protective ditches, but to admit any refugees from Brussels. Colonel De Lancey, as close to the duke as anybody, was concerned enough to send his young wife off to Antwerp. She left as Wellington's troops were marching up, and her description catches the dreadful poignancy of the moment:

> It was a clear refreshing morning; the scene was very solemn, and melancholy, the fifes playing alone, and the regiments one after another marched past, and I saw them melt away through the great gate at the end of the square.[39]

If one of the duke's objectives was to maintain confidence in Brussels, another was to ensure harmonious relations with the Prussians. While his own lines of communication lay north and north-west, those of the Prussians lay to the east, almost at right-angles to a French thrust. The closer to Wellington Blücher came, the greater the risk to his own communications, and Napoleon was too experienced a general not to exploit this. It was in Wellington's

interests to ensure that Blücher trusted him, co-operating effectively even if his communications were threatened – and disclosing
contingency plans for the defence of Antwerp and Ostend would
scarcely be calculated to boost Blücher's confidence. There is no
evidence that a withdrawal on his lines of communication was
ever Wellington's preferred option, and even his hurried letters,
dashed off in the small hours of 18 June, when the campaign was
not going well, still spoke of withdrawal as something he hoped
to avoid. Contingencies existed, and Wellington would have been
gambling had they not. If he did not discuss them with Blücher,
it is because he feared that by doing so, he might have induced
that old warrior to suspect that they weighed more heavily on his
mind than they did.

Lastly, Peter Hofschröer complains that Wellington's duplicity
is emphasised by his efforts to suppress Clausewitz's history of
the campaign, which would have given the German view. Wellington was frank enough on the score:

> If it is to be history, it must be the truth, and the whole
> truth, or it will do more harm than good ... But if a
> true history is written, what will become of the reputation
> of half those who have acquired reputation, and who
> deserve it for their gallantry, but who if their mistakes
> and causal misconduct were made public, would not be
> so well thought of?[40]

He was no more in favour of a history of Waterloo than he had
been of a history of Talavera. It is impossible to assess the degree
to which this reflected a desire to preserve his own reputation
but, given his experience with the press, he would have been less
than human were this not, at least in part, the case. He was
certainly capable of changing his view of events with the passage

of time. For instance, when he first heard news of Napoleon's escape from Elba, he suspected that he would head for Italy, but later maintained that he always knew that he would go to Paris. Although he famously admitted that Napoleon stole a march on him at the beginning of the Waterloo campaign, he grew to dislike suggestions that he had been surprised. By the end of the battle, he was heard hoping that night or the Prussians would come, but when Sir Thomas Lawrence painted him in 1824 with a watch in his hand he objected: 'That will never do. I was *not* waiting for the arrival of the Prussians at Waterloo. Put a telescope in my hand if you please.'

Wellington and Blücher met at Tirlemont on 3 May, but it is hard to be certain of precisely what was agreed. They certainly decided that the old Roman road from Bavay (just west of Maubeuge) to Maastricht would form the 'strategic line of demarkation' with Wellington to the west and Blücher to the east. They probably agreed that if the French advanced through Charleroi or Mons to threaten the two armies at their point of junction, the Prussians would concentrate at Sombreffe and the allies at Nivelles. Liaison staff were exchanged, Colonel Henry Hardinge (of Albuera fame) representing Wellington at Blücher's headquarters and Major General Baron Friedrich Karl Ferdinand von Müffling accompanying Wellington.

Both sides strove to gain intelligence, but this was not easy because, as Wellington put it when writing to the Prince of Orange on 11 May, they were 'neither at war nor at peace, unable on that account to patrole up to the enemy and ascertain his position by view'.[41] Lieutenant Colonel Colquhoun Grant, one of Wellington's intelligence officers from the Peninsula (known as Grant El Bueno to distinguish him from a less popular homonym, who commanded a cavalry brigade) ran an intelligence network inside

France, and Major General Sir William Dörnberg, with his cavalry brigade forward at Mons, collected reports and forwarded them to headquarters. Unfortunately Dörnberg was unaware of Grant's mission or the weight Wellington attached to the information he provided, and on 14 June he failed to forward a message from Grant which would have given Wellington news of the time and place of French concentration.

The picture that emerged was, not surprisingly, an incomplete one. Wellington knew that Napoleon was raising troops better than he had expected, and was (unusually) visibly downcast when he heard of an enthusiastic *Champ de Mai* review in Paris. By the beginning of the campaign Napoleon had assembled around 124,000 men and 344 guns, divided into the Imperial Guard and five corps. The emperor commanded in person, with Marshal Soult as his chief of staff. This was not Soult's natural *métier*, for he was more of a field commander, but Marshal Berthier, for so long the emperor's trusted amanuensis, had not joined Napoleon; having sworn allegiance to King Louis, he died after falling from a window on 1 June. Like Wellington's, Napoleon's army was heterogeneous, with veterans rubbing shoulders with untried conscripts, and enthusiastic Bonapartists marching alongside resentful royalists. It lacked the innate cohesion and staying power of the armies that Napoleon had once commanded.

Napoleon himself was arguably not at his best, although historians are unable to agree quite what was wrong with him. Some have suggested a tumour on the pituitary gland, others a bladder infection, and still others a painful bout of prolapsed haemorrhoids. However, an aide-de-camp later paid tribute to his 'energy, authority [and] . . . capacity as a leader of men' during the campaign, and Andrew Roberts surmises that most explanations of failing health 'hint at apologists' *ex post facto* rationalisations for his defeat, employed largely to keep their hero's military reputation intact.'[42] Yet there were to be unaccountable fits of torpor, notably on the morning of 17 June, and his orders to Marshal Grouchy, detached with a large force to keep the Prussians from joining the British, are a masterpiece of unclarity. It is difficult to be sure whether there was a physiological cause for these lapses or whether Napoleon was simply off a game he had played so well for so long. The distinguished Napoleonic scholar David Chandler sees him as 'obstinate, arrogant and overconfident', and although he too believes that 'the decline in his mental and physical powers have been overrated,' he continues 'there are yet some undeniable indications of deterioration in his overall ability.'[43]

Wellington had little regard for Napoleon as a man, regarding him as a mountebank who had risen through sheer opportunism, but had immense respect for his military ability. In 1814 someone had pointed out that Wellington was never opposed to Napoleon in person, and he replied: 'No, and I am very glad I never was. I would at any time rather have heard that a reinforcement of forty thousand men had joined the French army than he had arrived to take command.'[44] The duke had studied Napoleon's masterly 1814 campaign, when he had kept defeat at bay by jabbing hard at each allied opponent in turn, like an agile fencer lunging at clumsy opponents. At the Congress of Vienna he had discussed Napoleon with the Bavarian Field Marshal Wrede, who had served under Napoleon from 1805 to 1814 and who been told by *le tondu* himself that he never had a plan of campaign. Wellington believed himself to be up against a man who was as much of a master opportunist in the military sphere as he was in his political life, and who had to be treated very seriously.

Yet it is evident that, for all his defensive precautions, just before the campaign opened, he had no real inkling that he was about to be attacked. He gave Lieutenant General Sir Galbraith Lowry Cole, Kitty's old suitor and now a divisional commander, permission to get married in England on 15 June. On 13 June, he wrote to Thomas Graham, his old Peninsula comrade-in-arms, now Lord Lynedoch, that:

> There is nothing new here. We have reports of Buona-parte's joining the army and attacking us; but I have accounts from Paris of the 10th, on which day he was still there; and I judge from his speech to the Legislature that his departure was not likely to be imminent. I think we are now too strong for him here.[45]

Yet this strength was dangerously dissipated. In May, Wellington had warned that 'we should not extend ourselves further than is absolutely necessary to facilitate the subsistence of the troops'.[46] It was partly to ensure adequate food for men and fodder for horses that his force was widely spread, with 1st Corps forward on his left, with its headquarters at Braine le Comte, the 2nd Corps forward on his right, with its headquarters at Ath, and the duke's own reserve back around Brussels. This deployment also gave him a chance of meeting any of Napoleon's three most likely offensive options: a thrust through Tournai, aimed at cutting British communications; a jab to Brussels via Bavay and Mons, the most direct route; or a stab through Charleroi at the junction between the allies and the Prussians.

On Thursday 15 June 1815 Wellington rose early. He spent the day hard at work, *inter alia* writing to Sir Henry Clinton about renumbering the British divisions, and penning a long letter, in French, to the Tsar of Russia. According to FitzRoy Somerset he was having dinner at about five o'clock when he received a message from the Prince of Orange, saying 'that the French had attacked the Prussian advanced posts on the Sambre'. When he received the first message, Wellington told De Lancey to order the units under his immediate command, the reserve, to assemble at the headquarters of their respective divisions and to be ready to move at short notice. FitzRoy Somerset, who had gone back to his own quarters, returned to headquarters as soon as he heard what was happening, and:

> found the Duke in the Park giving necessary orders to those around him. He wished everything to be in readiness to move on an instant; but was waiting for further information before he made a decided movement with any part of his army, it being of the utmost consequence first to ascertain the point to which Bonaparte directed his operations.[47]

At about 10pm Somerset remarked: 'No doubt we shall be able to manage those fellows [the French].' Wellington replied that 'there was little doubt about it provided he did not make a false movement'.[48]

Two salient points emerge. The first is that at the very least, in Wellington's own words, 'there was certainly something out of order in the communication between the two armies in the middle of June'.[49] Communications between the allied and Prussian armies were not helped by the fact that French was their common language, which meant that all messages had to be translated, and by practical difficulties in carrying messages and ensuring that they reached the right person. Peter Hofschröer is amongst those detecting conspiracy rather than cock-up, arguing that news of the attack on the Prussians reached Wellington very much earlier, but he did nothing in response, letting down his allies and putting the campaign in doubt, then twisting the evidence to conceal the fact. Wellington's supporters maintain that 'Wellington's whole life and character argue against it. Besides, it is not logical; he would have reacted immediately if he had known that the French had begun an attack anywhere.'[50]

Readers with a deep interest in this issue should compare Hofschröer and Hussey, and they will see just how hard it is to reconcile accounts. But if the duke did wilfully suppress news of a Prussian message reaching him in the morning, it was a conspiracy which must have included not only FitzRoy Somerset, but also Madeleine De Lancey, who reported her husband's sudden and extraordinary agitation late that afternoon, and his warning that he would be working all night. It must also have swept up Major General Sir Hussey Vivian, who recalled that he heard the news after he had dined with Lord Anglesey, as well as an unnamed officer of Picton's division, who wrote that he was having dinner with several other officers at about 3pm when the news came in, and saw Prussian messengers at about 6pm. There is no doubt that both Blücher and Lieutenant General von Zieten, commanding his II corps, sent Wellington messages, but the balance of probabilities (and it can be no more than that), suggests that Wellington did not receive them till mid-afternoon, shortly after he had received word of the French advance from the Prince of Orange.

Secondly, when Wellington warned FitzRoy Somerset of the risk of making a false movement, he meant exactly that. He needed to be sure of the real direction of the French advance, for if he concentrated to meet a feint, he would be off-balance, unable to meet the real attack. Yet if premature concentration was dangerous, late reaction was scarcely less so, and Wellington's primary problem on the 15th and 16th was to ensure that he swung his bat to meet the oncoming ball neither too early nor too late.

Even now Wellington was in worse trouble than he knew. Lead-

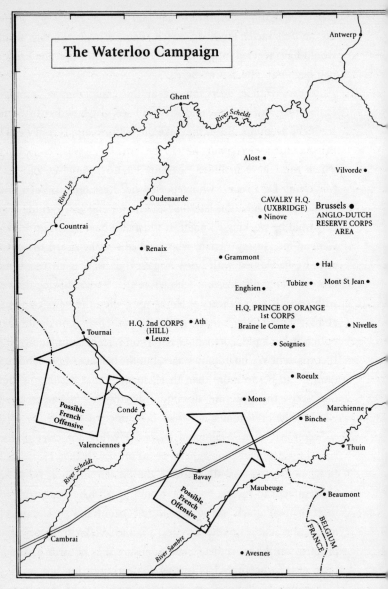

The Waterloo Campaign

Antwerp •

Ghent •

River Scheldt

River Lys

Alost •

Vilvorde •

Oudenaarde •

CAVALRY H.Q.
(UXBRIDGE)
• Ninove

Brussels •
ANGLO-DUTCH
RESERVE CORPS
AREA

• Countrai

• Renaix

• Grammont

• Hal

Enghien •

Tubize •

Mont St Jean •

H.Q. 2nd CORPS
(HILL) • Ath
• Leuze

H.Q. PRINCE OF ORANGE
1st CORPS

Braine le Comte •

• Nivelles

• Tournai

• Soignies

• Roeulx

**Possible
French
Offensive**

Condé •

• Mons

Marchienne •

• Binche

Valenciennes •

**Possible
French
Offensive**

River Scheldt

Bavay •

• Maubeuge

• Thuin

• Beaumont

Cambrai •

River Sambre

• Avesnes

BELGIUM
FRANCE

The Waterloo Campaign

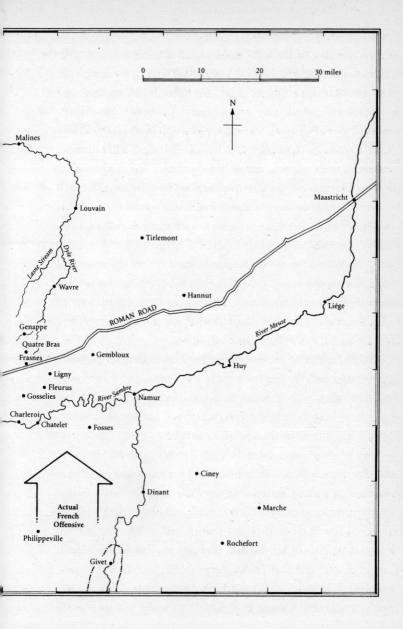

0   10   20   30 miles

N

Malines

Louvain

Tirlemont

Maastricht

Lasne Stream

Dyle River

Wavre

Hannut

Liége

ROMAN ROAD

Genappe

River Meuse

Quatre Bras

Frasnes

Gembloux

Huy

Ligny

Fleurus

Gosselies

River Sambre

Namur

Charleroi

Chatelet

Fosses

Ciney

Actual
French
Offensive

Dinant

Marche

Philippeville

Rochefort

Givet

ing elements of Napoleon's army had crossed the frontier at 3.30 on the morning of the 15th. Napoleon too had his share of difficulties: a messenger to General Vandamme lay in a ditch all night with a broken leg sustained when his horse rolled on him, and a traffic-jam ensued; also a pro-royalist divisional commander deserted to the Prussians, taking the plans with him. Yet by midday Napoleon's troops had taken Charleroi in the face of stiff resistance and were soon pouring across the Sambre. That afternoon he ordered Marshal Ney to take two corps and a substantial force of cavalry to push the enemy down the Brussels road as far as the crossroads at Quatre Bras. This was more easily said than done, for Ney was unsure precisely where the corps were and was not privy to Napoleon's ideas. Napoleon gave the newly-promoted Marshal Grouchy command of his right wing, telling him to push the Prussians on to Sombreffe. Blücher began to concentrate to meet the attack, telling Wellington what was afoot and expecting that he would, as they had agreed at Tirlemont, move to join him.

Unfortunately, as we have seen, his first dispatches probably arrived late, and Wellington went to the Duchess of Richmond's ball that night, with his army at a high degree of readiness, but not yet moving to meet the French because, as he told Müffling, he was still unsure of their precise direction.

That evening word came in from Dörnberg that there were now few French troops in front of him, for most seemed to have swung off towards Charleroi. At 10pm the duke sent off a second set of orders, modifying his first instructions but still not allowing for a concentration further east than Nivelles. What he did not know, as he dressed for the ball, probably shaving for the second time that day, was that Prince Bernhard of Saxe-Weimar, commanding a brigade of Perponcher's Netherlands Division, was heavily engaged at Quatre Bras. The fact that he was there at all spoke much for the 'intelligent disobedience' of Major General Baron Constant Rebecq, Orange's chief of staff, who had ordered a concentration there rather than at Nivelles.

Wellington was never one to turn down a good party, but there was more than mere hedonism to his attendance to the Duchess of Richmond's ball, held in a coachbuilder's large workshop in the rue de la Blanchisserie. It was important to preserve calm in the city, and a sudden cancellation of the ball, or the disappearance of many of its leading guests, would give precisely the wrong impression. Moreover, most of his senior officers would be there, and it would be no bad thing to have them close at hand if news arrived. Some would have cause to regret the decision, as they found themselves going off to war in silk stockings and dancing-pumps. Wellington arrived at about 10.30pm and seemed at the peak of his form, although those who knew him well could see tension behind the mask. Lady Hamilton-Dalrymple, who sat beside him on a sofa, thought that: 'Although the Duke affected great gaiety and cheerfulness, it struck me that I had never seen him have such an expression of care and anxiety on his countenance.'[51] Some officers had begun to slip away before supper, although the duke himself went in, with Lady Charlotte Greville on his arm.

It was probably well past midnight when the Prince of Orange, who had just received word of the action at Quatre Bras, appeared and whispered something in his ear. Wellington said that he had no fresh orders to give, but suggested that the Prince should go to bed. He then announced his own intention to retire, but quietly asked the Duke of Richmond if he had a good map. Richmond took him off to his dressing-room, where Wellington closed the door and declared: 'Napoleon has humbugged me, (by G-d), he has gained twenty-four hours march on me.' His host asked him what he planned to do. 'I have ordered the army to concentrate at Quatre Bras,' he said, 'but we shall not stop him there, so I must fight him here' and he traced the Waterloo position with his thumbnail on the map.[52] There are two problems with this account, one of the best-known Wellington anecdotes. Its source is secondhand, although its author, Captain George Bowles of the Coldstream Guards, emphasised that the conversation between Richmond and Wellington was repeated to him, two minutes after it occurred, by the former. The second is that Wellington had not yet issued orders for a concentration at Quatre Bras, and would no doubt have been much happier if he had. It was approaching two in the morning, and he now had the firmest indication yet that the greatest commander of his generation had broken the hinge between him and the Prussians, and was making straight for Brussels.

Wellington was probably not in bed until after two on the morning of the 16th, but rose at five-thirty, breakfasted on tea and toast, wrote some letters and left the city on horseback at about seven. His reserve was already on the move southwards, headed by the 5th Division, and citizens and visitors alike had already been awoken by the fifes and pipes. A lady's maid saw him ride out, and told her mistress: 'There he goes, God bless him, and he will not come back till he is King of France.' It is twenty-two miles to Quatre Bras, and he reached the crossroads by about 10am, which is brisk riding. He found Prince Bernhard's men still in possession, and there seemed no sign of an imminent attack. He had a few words with the Prince of Orange, and then wrote a letter to Blücher, giving the position of his army, and declaring that 'I await news from Your Highness and the arrival of troops to decide my operations for the day.' It concluded that 'Nothing has appeared near Binche, nor on your right.'

This letter is no less controversial than the dispatches of the 15th. It places most of Wellington's divisions further south-east than was in fact the case. He apparently relied on an inaccurate disposition supplied by De Lancey, and both this, and the letter arising from it, form part of the accusation of duplicity. But again the case is not clear-cut. By this stage Wellington was planning to fight at Quatre Bras, and his reserve was coming forward to support the Netherlanders: if the letter was an inaccurate representation of fact, it said much for his intent. Wellington followed the letter by riding across to see Blücher himself, taking the Roman road that crosses the main Brussels *chaussée* at Quatre Bras. The two commanders met at Bussy windmill near the village of Brye and exchanged information. Blücher now had three of his corps concentrated in front of Sombreffe around the village of Ligny, and could see that he would shortly be attacked. Most of those present recorded the conversation somewhat differently, but the upshot was clear: Wellington was to send substantial reinforcements to the Prussians that afternoon, though he added the rider 'provided I am not attacked'. It is significant that Müffling, a Prussian officer, recorded this caveat in his own account of the meeting. In later life, Wellington claimed that he thought at the time that 'if I were in Blücher's place ... I should withdraw all the columns I saw scattered about the front, and get more of the troops under the shelter of the rising ground', and Henry Hardinge recalled him saying that 'if they fight here they will be damnably mauled'.[53]

And so they were. That afternoon Napoleon's right wing attacked the Prussians at Ligny and beat them after a very bitter battle. Blücher, leading a cavalry charge in the gloaming at the end of the battle, was unhorsed and ridden over, but a devoted aide-de-camp, Count Nostitz, managed to get him away safely. His army was split, and in his absence Gneisenau, influenced by Wellington's failure to support the Prussians that day, decided that the army should fall back on its line of communications, swinging away from Wellington. He told the king of Prussia that: 'On the 16th of June in the morning the Duke of Wellington promised to be at Quatre Bras at 10am with 20,000 men . . . on the strength of these promises and arrangements we decided to fight the battle . . .'[54] Given the fact that the Brye meeting did not take place until after 10.00 the factual foundation for this assertion is wobbly, but it does testify to the fact that honest men can have different views of traumatic events. Blücher eventually rejoined Gneisenau in a farmhouse, with wounded lying around and stragglers passing the door. The old field marshal insisted that the army should keep in touch with Wellington, and Major General Karl von Grolmann, the quartermaster-general, observed that a retreat on Wavre would enable it to do so and also to preserve its lines of communication if all else failed. Orders went out for a concentration on Wavre: the Prussians were still in the game.

Blücher was determined not to break his word: but had Wellington broken his? He returned to Quatre Bras to find that the situation had changed. Wellington was badly outnumbered – Ney had about 42,000 men, and Wellington only about 6,000 when the action began – but the long shadow of the Peninsula fell across the battlefield. French commanders knew how fond Wellington was of reverse slopes, and one of Ney's subordinates was so forceful in his warnings that the attack was delayed by perhaps two hours. Ney's men had begun to work their way forward, and Perponcher's were being forced to give ground when Wellington returned. But Picton's battalions were starting to come up, and the duke spent much of the day at the crossroads, sending units forward as they arrived, and checking the French attack. However, his situation looked unpromising: French skirmishers pecked away at his infantry, standing in the tall rye on the long slope south of the crossroads, and French artillery quickly asserted its superiority.

The battle became a race between Picton's men, marching up the *chaussée*, battalion after battalion, in weather so hot that a soldier in the 95th Rifles 'went raving mad, from excessive heat . . . cut a few extraordinary capers, and died in the course of a few minutes', and Ney's attackers, feeling their way with more caution. The Brunswick contingent arrived, and the Duke of Brunswick bravely led his cavalry in two charges, but was mortally wounded as he did so. Wellington, mounted on Copenhagen, was caught up in a swirl of charging horsemen as the French followed up the retreating Brunswickers and had to ride for his life. The nearest battalion was the 92nd Highlanders, and as he approached, with French *chasseurs* close behind, he yelled: 'Lie down, 92nd!' He jumped into their square, and the rolling volleys sent the French horsemen away with many an empty saddle.

But the next charge, this time by two regiments of lancers, was far more damaging, in part because of the cover provided by the standing crops, and in part because of confusion over the colour of the lancers' uniforms – some British units had already fired on Netherlands cavalry in error that day. The 42nd Highlanders were caught with their square only half-formed, but, fighting mad, closed the square by main force and killed the horsemen inside. As the afternoon went on, a pattern became established of French charges swirling up the slope and eddying away, giving French gunners the opportunity to pound a line, which grew thinner. Some of the infantry who had arrived early were now running short of ammunition, and by late afternoon things were desperate. However, Colin Halkett's brigade of Sir Charles Alten's 3rd British Division arrived in the nick of time, with a Hanoverian brigade close behind, and Wellington sent them forward to buttress his position. Halkett's battalions were ordered from square into line by the Prince of Orange, who could see no cavalry at that moment and thought that firepower was what was required. Halkett complied under protest, and was almost immediately charged by French *cuirassiers* who broke one of his battalions, the 69th, and forced the 73rd to take cover in a wood, and although the 33rd formed their square in time, when it did so, it was cruelly mauled by French artillery.

Yet again defeat stared Wellington in the face, but yet again fresh troops arrived, this time Cooke's 1st British Division, with a battalion of 1st Guards leading the way. They went into action west of the road, and made remorseless progress through the wood which then stood there. On the other side of the *chaussée*, the 92nd had been in action all afternoon, but its commanding officer, the distinguished Peninsula veteran Lieutenant Colonel John Cameron of Fassiefern, was so eager to get to grips with the French infantry now coming up the slope that Wellington had to shout: 'Take your time, Cameron, you'll get your fill of it before night.' When the moment came Wellington ordered 'Now, 92nd, you must charge those two columns of infantry.' The attack was successful – a two-storey redbrick house stormed by the Highlanders still stands beside the road – but Cameron was killed. By the time nightfall put an end to the fighting, Wellington was in possession of all the ground he had held at the start of the day, and had inflicted just over 4,000 casualties at the price of about the same. But in one respect the battle's cost had been even higher. He had not been able to support the Prussians. It is clear that his failure to do so reflected his own urgent operational necessity, but that was not a reason easily grasped by a bitter Gneisenau, sitting on a pickle-barrel in a crowded farmhouse a dozen miles away.

We cannot be sure quite how much Wellington knew of what happened at Ligny. The two battlefields are three miles apart, and it is impossible, these days, to see one from the other. He maintained that he could see the battle – possibly by galloping westwards for a short distance – and he received several reports from Hardinge, one of them dictated after Hardinge lost a hand late in the afternoon. The duke left Quatre Bras at around 10pm, and rode back northwards three miles to Genappe, where he ate some supper and slept at the inn *Au Roi d'Espagne*. He was up again at 3am and returned to Quatre Bras, where he ordered his men to cook a meal. The morning was 'cold, and rather inclined to rain', and the duke joined the 92nd, saying 'Ninety-second, I will be obliged to you for a little fire.' They lit one by the door of a small shelter, improvised from branches, near the crossroads, and Wellington spent much of the morning in it, or pacing about outside it, 'at the rate of three and a half to four miles in the hour'. He had sent out his senior aide-de-camp, Lieutenant Colonel the Hon. Sir Alexander Gordon, escorted by a troop of the 10th Hussars, to make contact with the Prussians, and Gordon had returned at about 7am with news that the Prussians were on their way back to Wavre. This induced Wellington to tell George Bowles, once again on hand where history was being made, that:

> Old Blücher has had a damned good licking and gone
> back to Wavre, eighteen miles. As he has gone back we
> must go too. I suppose in England they will say that we
> have been licked. I can't help it, but as they have gone
> back we must go too.[55]

At 9am a Prussian officer who spoke both English and French rode over from Wavre, briefed Wellington and answered some questions. Wellington told Müffling that 'he would accept a battle in the position of Mont Saint Jean. If the Field-Marshal were inclined to come to his assistance even with one corps only.' By 11am all the troops ordered to concentrate at Quatre Bras had arrived, and Wellington began to shift his army northwards, protected by a force left on the previous day's battlefield. At around midday the last battalions slipped away, and he remarked: 'Well, there's the last of the infantry gone, and I don't care now.'

Lord Uxbridge and the cavalry covered the retreat. The French were now close behind, and Captain Cavalié Mercer, whose troop of Royal Horse Artillery had been ordered to give the French a round from each gun as they crossed the crest, saw 'a single horseman', the emperor himself, at the head of the pursuers. A heavy thunderstorm helped the cavalry break clear, not without a brisk action between opposing horsemen in Genappe. Uxbridge was well pleased with the day's work, calling it 'the prettiest Field Day of Cavalry and Horse Artillery that I ever witnessed'.

Battlefields are named by the victor, and a well-founded suspicion that his countrymen would never get their tongues around Mont Saint Jean induced Wellington to call this one Waterloo. In fact the small town of that name stands well behind the ridge that rolls away from the farm complex of Mont Saint Jean. The ridge was much shallower than many of Wellington's Peninsula positions, and there were re-entrants that slashed up into it and offered reasonable approaches. Wellington's left was protected by the boggy valleys of the Dyle and the Lasne, but his right was more open. The substantial farm of Hougoumont lay in front of his right centre; a similar group of buildings, La Haye Sainte, stood beside the *chaussée* in his centre; and a larger grouping, around the hamlet of Smohain, was on his left. It was not an ideal position, but it was the best to be found south of Brussels. Wellington arranged his men in it as they arrived on the 17th,

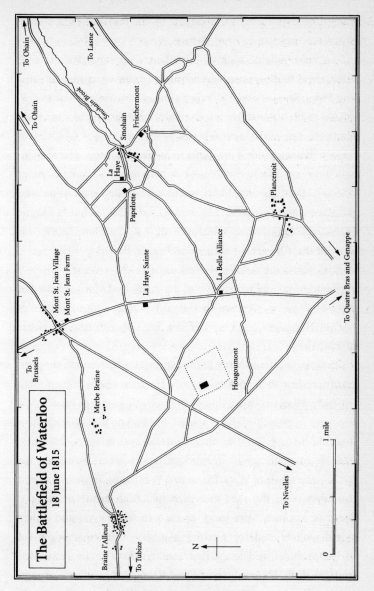

The Battlefield of Waterloo, 18 June 1815

though he found time for a catnap by the roadside with a copy of the *Sun* newspaper over his face.

The duke put the bulk of his infantry on the ridge's reverse slope where this was possible, and pushed picked garrisons forward into Hougoumont and La Haye Sainte, whose defence he saw as crucial to his success. He was careful to match men to their task, placing Lieutenant Colonel James Macdonell of the Coldstream Guards in command of the garrison of Hougoumont, defended by light companies from the footguards battalions and some German riflemen. Müffling asked him whether he really expected to hold the place with 1,500 men. 'Ah,' replied the duke. 'You don't know Macdonell. I've thrown Macdonell into it.' La Haye Sainte was held by the rifle-armed men of 2nd Light Battalion KGL, and a sandpit across the road contained some British riflemen of 1/95th. Wellington was still worried about his right, and sent a substantial force of about 15,000 men to Hal and Tubize, about eight miles west of Hougoumont. They did not fire a shot during the battle of Waterloo.

Wellington offered battle in the expectation of Prussian support, finally confirmed at 3pm on the 17th. He knew that a French force (in fact under Grouchy, though he did not know as much) had been sent in pursuit of the Prussians, but had no idea how effective it would be in preventing their junction with him the following day. He spent the night in headquarters, a plain two-storey inn in the main street of Waterloo, now a Wellington museum, spared the miseries of the rain that drenched both armies overnight. Some of his men were lucky enough to find cover, and others rigged shelters made of 'pitching blankets', with an arrangement of button-holes and loops that enabled them to be suspended from muskets. Those who could find strong drink did so. Corporal William Wheeler of the 51st, who thought that the weather was 'a

The 'grand old Duke of York' and his staff at Valenciennes in 1793, one of the few Allied victories in a disastrous campaign.

Fort St George, seat of British power in Madras, 1797. There was no proper harbour, and passengers landing were brought through the surf in small boats. Officers from the garrison were often on hand to assist good-looking ladies.

RIGHT Kitty, Viscountess Wellington, in 1811. Maria Edgeworth maintained that it was not a good likeness, for 'she has no face; it is all countenance.'

BELOW Robert Home's portrait of Wellesley as a major general in India in 1804, before the arrival of his knighthood. Another version has the star and ribbon of the Order of the Bath added.

A contemporary British print shows the embarkation of Junot's army at Lisbon after the Convention of Cintra, and captures the mood of the moment by depicting the defeated French laden with loot.

Wellesley and his staff atop the Medellín hill at Talavera, 1809.

British troops landing in Portugal, 1808. This print shows infantrymen, including highlanders, artillerymen, and some Light Dragoons in their crested 'Tarleton' helmets.

British troops drilling on cleared ground in front of one of the forts in the Lines of Torres Vedras.

Picton's 3rd Division storming the castle at Badajoz, 1812. This painting gives a fair idea of the problems involved in scaling the high walls. The French flag flying from the tower (top centre) was shortly replaced by a British officer's red jacket.

Marshal André Massena, Duc de Rivoli, Wellington's adversary in 1810-11.

Marshal Auguste Marmont, Duc de Ragusa, beaten at Salamanca in 1812.

A contemporary cartoon ridicules the troops involved in the 'Peterloo Massacre' of 1819. There is no doubt of the artist's sympathies: he has given the Yeomanry axes rather than swords, and their officer reminds his men (affluent part-time soldiers) that the more demonstrators they kill, the less poor-rates they will have to pay.

ABOVE Harriette Wilson, a society courtesan who maintained that she had a long relationship with Wellington.

LEFT Napoleon at the height of his powers: he was stouter and balder by 1815. Like Wellington he tended to dress down rather than up, with the undress uniform of the *chasseurs à pied* of his Imperial Guard as his favourite.

An unkind cartoon showing Roman Catholic priests using Wellington as a battering-ram. 'Now that we have got the right Tool,' says one, 'we shall soon get possession of all our Own Churches again.'

A crowd supporting pro-reform candidates in the run-up to the passing of the 1832 Reform Bill. What is striking is the respectable dress of those attending the demonstration.

A daguerreotype of Wellington in 1844, when he was 75 years old.

prelude to victory', for it had often rained before battles in Spain, had got hold of plenty of liquor and was 'wet and comfortable'.

Wellington had never had any time for seconds-in-command, and did not confide in Uxbridge, who would take over from him if he were killed or wounded. Uxbridge, quartered in Waterloo near the duke, walked across to Wellington's quarters in an effort to find out what his plans were. 'Who will attack the first to-morrow, I or Bonaparte?' asked the duke. 'Bonaparte,' replied Uxbridge. 'Well,' said Wellington, 'Bonaparte has not given me any idea of his projects: and as my plans will depend on his, how can you expect me to tell you what mine are?' Wellington sensed that this was close to a ritual humiliation, and quickly withdrew the sting: 'There is one thing certain, Uxbridge, that is, that whatever happens, you and I will do our duty.'

Although this is another shining example of the Wellingtonian aphorism, it underlines the extraordinary fragility of the duke's style of command. Uxbridge was an experienced and talented officer, and while he lacked Wellington's spark of genius, he was by no means an unsafe pair of hands. There were many things they might have talked through: the role of the force at Hal and Tubize; arrangements with the Prussians; or the supreme impor-tance of holding Hougoumont. Wellington had evidently made plans long before the first shot was fired at Waterloo, and by not opening his mind to Uxbridge, he was gravely compromising the latter's ability to take charge of the battle if the worst happened. But, as he had once put it in India, he had always 'walked by himself', and he was not about to change the lonely habit of a lifetime that rainy night in Belgium.

Wellington snatched a little sleep, but was awake between 2am and 3am on the 18 June 1815. He received another dispatch from Blücher, telling him that he would send Bülow's corps in his direction at daybreak, followed immediately by another corps, with his remaining two preparing to move. The fact that his men were tired and not all had yet joined him prevented him from starting more quickly. This dispatch crossed a message from Müffling to Blücher, reiterating Wellington's intention to offer battle if the Prussians supported him. Wellington wrote several letters, including those to Sir Charles Stewart and Lady Frances Wedderburn-Webster; Lieutenant Drewe of the 27th saw him at his window at 7am as the regiment went by, and the duke left for the battlefield on Copenhagen not long afterwards. He wore white breeches, a blue frock-coat, a black cocked hat, and put his short blue cloak on, by his own estimate, fifty times during the day as showers crossed the field. Lieutenant Gronow, who had gone out without official authorisation as Picton's aide-de-camp but had been advised to rejoin his regiment, which had been knocked about at Quatre Bras, was taking some French prisoners to Waterloo:

> We heard the trampling of horses' feet, and looking round we perceived a large cavalcade of officers coming at full speed. In a moment we recognised the Duke himself at their head. He was accompanied by the Duke of Richmond and his son, Lord William Lennox. The entire staff of the army was close at hand ... Felton Harvey, FitzRoy Somerset and Delancey were the last that appeared. They all seemed as gay and unconcerned as if they were riding to meet the hounds in some quiet English country.[56]

Wellington spent the morning making final checks. He first rode over to his right, where some nervous Nassauers fired on him. He dropped down to Hougoumont, where he had a word about the construction of firesteps inside the orchard walls, and then rode right across to his left about Smohain before returning to the centre, and was there when French guns opened fire at 11.30am.

This burning energy was in clear contrast to Napoleon's style that day. He had spent the night in a farmhouse on the Brussels road, and then rode forward to the inn 'La Belle Alliance', within sight of Wellington's position. He spent much of the day there, using gallopers to transmit his orders, and entrusting the conduct of the attack to Marshal Ney, deservedly known as 'bravest of the brave,' but never one for finesse. Not that there was much subtlety in Napoleon's plan. He intended to mount a diversionary attack on Hougoumont and then throw his main up the main road against Wellington's centre, which was to be hammered by his massed 12-pdr guns. Soult had warned him that the British infantry was the very devil if taken head on, but he snapped back: 'Because you have been beaten by Wellington you consider him a great general. And now I will tell you that he is a bad general, that the English are bad troops, and that this affair is nothing more serious than eating one's breakfast.'

The attack on Hougoumont was entrusted to Reille's corps, spearheaded by a division commanded by Napoleon's younger brother, Prince Jerome. Wellington, on the ridge behind, shifted Bull's battery of howitzers so that it could drop shells onto the attackers, pulled the Nassauers back from Hougoumont, and moved a steady brigade of KGL just behind the farm complex. The attack was beaten off but renewed, and now included part of Foy's division. This time the French smashed down the north gate and forced an entry, but Macdonell personally led the rush that closed the gate and killed all who had entered, apart (for there were flashes of decency even at such desperate moments) from a drummer boy. Wellington later maintained that the battle depended on the closing of those gates. He reinforced the garrison as need arose, content that he was applying economy of force, for the battle was sucking in far more Frenchmen than allies. And for the moment, because little was happening elsewhere on the field, he was able to devote himself to the battle for Hougoumont. He kept a pad of reusable sheets of goatskin for scribbling orders that were carried off by aides, and when the buildings caught fire, he sent a note to Macdonell:

> I see that the fire has communicated itself from the hay stack to the roof of the Château. You must however still keep your men in those parts to which the fire does not reach. Take care that no Men are lost by the falling in of the Roof or floors. After they will have fallen in, occupy the Ruined Walls inside of the Garden, particularly if it should be possible for the Enemy to pass through the Embers to the Inside of the House.[57]

Although Hougoumont was attacked repeatedly during the day, it was never taken. Perhaps 10,000 men from both armies fell around it, at least three-quarters of them French. Napoleon had failed to induce Wellington to weaken his centre, and failed to dispose of a position which was to cramp his attacks as the day wore on.

The second phase of the attack began at about 1.30pm, when d'Erlon's corps attacked astride the *chaussée*. Napoleon's grand battery, just west of the road, had been firing at Wellington's line for about two hours, but its effects were mixed because many allied troops were behind the crest of the ridge. However, a good deal of damage was done, some of it reflecting the sheer caprice inherent in war. A single shot took the head off the right-hand man in John Kincaid's battalion of rifles, just across the road from La Haye Sainte and in theory in front of the target area, while an officer of the Royal Scots Greys, well on the apparently 'safe' side of the crest, saw a shell obliterate a party of Highlanders carrying their wounded officer to the rear. Two of d'Erlon's divisions advanced in unusually configured columns, each composed of a battalion in line with others stacked behind it, in an effort to combine shock with firepower, with a thick cloud of skirmishers in front of them. Wellington had ordered his gunners to reserve their fire for the infantry and not expend ammunition on counter-battery work, and as the infantry came on, they were first raked by roundshot, whole files of men falling down as if tugged by a rope, and then, for the last 300 yards, hit by canister. But they kept going and forced back the first line of defenders, and the Netherlands units fought a good deal better here than anglophone historians often suggest. There was a savage firefight as British battalions came forward over the crest, and Picton, clad in his normal fighting rig of black frock-coat and round hat, was shot through the forehead as he led his men forward, cursing.

Wellington seems to have left Picton not long before and ridden westwards. The Prince of Orange had sent a Hanoverian battalion down to help the defenders of La Haye Sainte, but it was mauled by French cavalry hovering on the left of the main infantry attack. Wellington saw this, and ordered two nearby battalions into square to hold off the cavalry. Uxbridge, on the ridge not far behind, ordered his two cavalry brigades just behind the crest to charge. Lord Edward Somerset's Household Brigade (Life Guards and Royal Horse Guards) first rode down the French horsemen who had attacked the Hanoverians, and Sir William Ponsonby's Union Brigade, with its three regiments of heavy cavalry, charged the French infantry. The British horsemen, coming quickly up the reverse slope and over the crest, crashed into their opponents with little warning. One of their adversaries, Captain Duthilt of the 4th of the Line, admitted that:

Just as it is difficult for the best cavalry to break into infantry who are formed into squares and who defend themselves with coolness and daring, so it is true that once the ranks have been penetrated, then resistance is useless and nothing remains for the cavalry to do but to slaughter at almost no risk to themselves. This is what happened, in vain our poor fellows stood up and stretched out their arms; they could not reach far enough to bayonet these cavalrymen mounted on powerful horses, and the few shots fired in this chaotic melee were just as fatal to our own men as to the English.[58]

The two brigades, now somewhat intermingled, cut clean through the French infantry, capturing two eagles in the process. This was in itself no mean feat, for only two had been taken in battle in the Peninsula. Some of the horsemen got as far as the grand battery, sabred the gunners, and then attacked the drivers, who 'sat on their horses weeping aloud as we went amongst them; they were mere boys, we thought'. By this time, however, they were in disorder, their horses were blown, and the French cavalry counter-attack destroyed both brigades as a fighting force. Although the charge had accomplished its purpose, wrecking Napoleon's first major infantry attack, the cost was heavy, and needlessly so. Wellington may have remarked sarcastically to Uxbridge: 'Well, Paget, I hope you are satisfied with your cavalry now.' Gronow, a well-connected gossip but, as an infantry subaltern with pressing concerns of his own, not privy to the conversation, went further, declaring that: 'The Duke of Wellington was perfectly furious that this arm had been engaged without his orders and sent them to the rear ...'[59] Uxbridge was critical of his own performance, admitting later that:

I committed a great mistake in having led the attack. The carrière once begun, the leader is no better than any other man; whereas if I had placed myself at the head of the 2nd line, there is no saying what great advantages might not have accrued from it. I am the less pardonable in having deviated from a principle I had laid down for myself . . .[60]

Nevertheless, by early afternoon, Wellington had some cause for satisfaction. Hougoumont was holding well, and the threat to his centre had been checked for the time being, enabling him to send reinforcements down to La Haye Sainte and personally check the state of 1/95th, re-established in the sandpit, and in the process to tick off John Kincaid who, he thought, was deliberately making his horse cavort. He was reasonably confident that the French would not attack west of Hougoumont, but he kept the force at Hal and Tubize in case Napoleon was undertaking some sort of flanking manoeuvre – which, indeed, is precisely what some of his generals had urged him to do that morning. Another infantry attack on La Haye Sainte was beaten off with little difficulty, and while it was in progress, the grand battery was realigned, partly to take account of the damage inflicted by the cavalry.

The next challenge was posed by the French cavalry. Some 7,000 of them came on between Hougoumont and La Haye Sainte, regiments compressed by the lack of space, but advancing with utter determination. Sergeant Tom Morris of the 73rd Regiment was not alone in believing that 'Their appearance was of such a formidable nature that I thought we did not have the slightest chance against them.'[61] Wellington knew that the threat was more apparent than real, provided that his infantry stood fast and his gunners did as they had been told, firing till the last moment and then running into the infantry squares for safety. He told FitzRoy

Somerset that 'Napoleon was guilty of a great fault in not attacking us with infantry at the same time.'[62] The cavalry swirled around the squares but failed to break one. Wellington rode from square to square; sometimes he 'relied on his own dexterity as a horseman and the speed of his horse' and sometimes he took refuge inside a square as the horsemen surged around it. This was demonstrative leadership of the highest order: the duke's infantry could see him in their midst, and were not above making sharp observations. 'I recollect that when his Grace was in our square,' wrote Gronow, 'our soldiers were so mortified at seeing the French deliberately walking their horses between our regiment and those regiments to our left and right that they shouted. "Where are our cavalry? Why don't they come and pitch into those French fellows? . . ."'[63]

The attacks went on all afternoon. As the cavalry drifted back, the squares were raked by artillery fire, and this was the cruellest tribulation of Wellington's infantry that day. Tom Morris recalled that the horsemen attacking his square brought up some French gunners who turned an abandoned British piece onto them 'and fired into us with grape-shot, which proved very destructive, making complete lanes through us . . .' As the afternoon wore on things grew steadily worse:

> Our situation, now, was truly awful; our men were falling by dozens from enemy fire. About this time also a large shell fell just in front of us, and while the fuze was burning out we were wondering how many of us it would destroy. When it burst, about seventeen men were killed or wounded.[64]

'At four o'clock,' remembered Lieutenant Gronow,

> our square was a perfect hospital, being full of dead, dying and mutilated soldiers. The charges of cavalry were

in appearance very formidable, but in reality a great relief, as the artillery could no longer fire on us: the very earth shook with the enormous mass of men and horses. I shall never forget the strange noise our bullets made against the breastplates of Kellermann's and Mihaud's cuirassiers . . . who attacked us with great fury. I can only compare it, with a somewhat homely simile, to the noise of a violent hail-storm beating on panes of glass.[65]

The duke was inside the square at about this time, and Gronow thought him 'perfectly composed; but he looked very thoughtful and pale'. He asked an aide-de-camp what time it was, and when the aide replied twenty minutes past four, the duke, perhaps deliberately projecting a confidence he had good reason not to feel, said: 'The battle is mine, and if the Prussians arrive soon there will be an end of the war.'

Then, at about 4.30pm, Wellington heard cannon-fire from beyond his left flank, indicating that the Prussians were on their way, although he was not to know that Napoleon, desperate to finish Wellington before they could intervene, had sent Lobau's corps (over 10,000 men and 28 guns) to delay them. His line was still intact, but it was now badly battered, and he was concerned for the area north-east of Hougoumont, telling FitzRoy Somerset 'I'll be d—d if we shan't lose this ground if we don't take care.'[66] He moved Adam's brigade of British infantry up from reserve to secure it. A French combined arms attack, launched at perhaps 6pm, at last took La Haye Sainte, which was overwhelmed at around 6.30pm, only forty-three of its garrison escaping. Thick clouds of French infantry now pressed forward against Wellington's main line, in such numbers that Wellington's own skirmishers could not hold them. Wellington, just above Hougoumont at the time, sent 3/1st Guards and Adam's brigade to drive away the *tirailleurs* with volleys and controlled charges, and the position was again re-established in Wellington's right centre.

Around the crossroads, where the Brussels road breasts the ridge and an elm tree stood, marking the duke's position for part of the day, the situation was more perilous. The lie of the land meant that it was harder to shelter infantry behind the crest, and the damage done by French guns was truly appalling. The 27th, its position now marked by a dignified memorial just north-east of the crossroads, lost 400 men before it fired a shot, and when the survivors moved off at the end of the day the battalion's square was marked by the position of its dead. Major General Colin Halkett sent a message begging for relief, and 'asked that his brigade, which had lost two-thirds, should be relieved for a short time; but there was no reserve to take its place; and Wellington replied, "Tell him, what he asks is impossible: he and I, and every Englishman on the field, must die on the spot we now occupy."'[67]

Lieutenant General Sir Charles Alten, whose division held this sector, had been wounded, and one of his brigade commanders, Colonel Baron Ompteda, had been killed when the Prince of Orange launched him in a fruitless counter-attack on La Haye Sainte. Major General Count Kielmansegge, the senior surviving brigade commander, took over, and one of the divisional staff reported to Wellington that a gap was opening in his centre.

> This very startling information he received with a degree of coolness, and replied to it in an instant with such precision and energy, as to prove the most complete self-possession. He left the impression that he was perfectly calm during every phase, however serious, of the action. He felt confident of being able to guide the storm which raged around him: and from the determined manner in which he now spoke, it was evident that he

had resolved to defend to the last extremity every inch of the position which he then held. His Grace's answer to my representation was, 'I shall order the Brunswick troops in reserve behind Maitland ['s Guards Brigade] to the spot, and other troops besides. Go you and get all the German troops of the division to the spot that you can, and all the guns that you can find.[68]

Major General Sir Hussey Vivian's cavalry brigade was ordered across from the east – Vivian recalled that the Prussians had 'by that time formed to my left' – to help cover the centre. He arrived to find 'the ground actually covered with dead and dying, cannon shots and shells flying thicker than I ever heard musketry before, and our troops – some of them – giving way'.[69] Wellington himself galloped across to the threatened sector, rallied the Brunswickers as they recoiled from the horror confronting them, and steadied his whole line north of La Haye Sainte. The Prince of Orange, leading a counter-attack further to the west, was knocked from his horse by a musket-ball, and carried to the rear: the Lion Mound, which so disfigures the battlefield, marks the spot where he was hit. However, by around 7pm, the line in Wellington's centre was re-established.

The Prussians had been delayed by roads turned into quagmires by the appalling weather. Blücher pushed his men on with shouts of 'Forward, boys! . . . I have given my word to Wellington and you would not have me break it.' Part of his army struck the French towards the end of the afternoon, and became locked in battle with the troops sent by Napoleon to shore up his right flank while he dealt with Wellington. Zieten's corps, however, made straight for Wellington. The duke had sent Müffling across to his left to stage-manage the junction of the two armies. This proved a wise decision because an inexperienced aide-de-camp told

Ziethen that the British were falling back, and Müffling was quickly able to put things right. It would still take time for the Prussians to make their full weight felt, but Wellington faced the crisis of the battle knowing help was close at hand. He was by now almost alone, for his staff had been plucked away all day. Lieutenant Colonel Gordon lost his leg to a roundshot, and at about 3pm Sir William De Lancey was hit. Some said that he was fastening the duke's cloak to the front of his saddle, but Wellington thought that he was:

> speaking to me when he was struck. We were on a point of land that overlooked the plain. I had just been warned off by some soldiers ... when a ball came bounding along *en ricochet* as it is called, and striking him on the back, sent him many yards over the head of his horse. He fell on his face, and bounded upwards, and fell again. All the staff dismounted and ran to him, and when I came up he said, "Pray tell them to leave me and let me die in peace." I had him conveyed to the rear ...[70]

At about 7pm FitzRoy Somerset, riding alongside the duke, was hit in the right arm by a musket-ball fired from La Haye Sainte, and walked off to a field hospital where Dr John Gunning took off his arm above the elbow. Somewhat later, a grapeshot passed over Wellington's horse and hit Uxbridge in the knee. Uxbridge knew what this meant, and exclaimed: 'By God, sir, I've lost my leg!' 'By God, sir,' replied Wellington, 'so you have.'[71]

Uxbridge's leg was, however, still intact when Napoleon launched his last attack, sending five battalions of the Middle Guard, backed by three of the Old, against Wellington's right centre. Wellington was just behind Maitland's brigade, now lying down just behind the ridge, when one of the columns approached.

He shouted: 'Now, Maitland! Now is your time!' And then, unable to resist the temptation, he gave the fire order himself: 'Up Guards! Make ready! Fire!' Halkett's weak brigade joined in the firefight from the east, and Adam's fresher men played their part from the west. Colonel Sir John Colborne, acting on his own initiative, took 1/52nd out of the line and engaged the French from the flank. No troops, even veterans of the Imperial Guard, could stand such punishment, and the French broke and fell back. Still the crisis was not past, for Halkett's men also broke in the face of renewed artillery fire when they advanced to follow up the retreating guardsmen.

Wellington now threw the last ounce of himself into the battle, though his surviving staff begged him to take care. 'So I will,' he said, 'directly I see those fellows driven off.' Illuminated by a shaft of sunlight that broke through the clouds, he gestured with his hat to order a general advance. He yelled: 'Go on, Colborne! Go on. They won't stand. Don't give them time to rally.' John Kincaid, down by the sandpit with the 95th, heard a cheer spreading from the right, and: 'Lord Wellington galloped up on the instant, and the men began to cheer him, but he called out "No cheering, my lads, but forward, to complete your victory."'[72] He sent Vivian's cavalry forward, and then went on himself, despite warnings from an aide that 'we are getting into enclosed ground, and your life is too valuable to be thrown away'. 'Never mind,' he replied. 'Let them fire away. The battle's gained: My life's of no consequence now.'[73] At about 9pm, he met Blücher at *La Belle Alliance*, and they embraced on horseback. But the allies were still divided by language. 'Mein lieber kamarad,' said the old Prussian, 'quelle affaire'.

Blücher agreed that his army would carry on with the pursuit, and the duke rode back along the Brussels road to his headquarters in Waterloo, looking 'sombre and dejected . . . The few individuals who attended him wore, too, rather the aspect of a little funeral train rather than that of victors in one of the most important battles ever fought.'[74] After dismounting, he made the mistake of giving Copenhagen a pat, but the noble steed, who had had a day of it himself, lashed out and narrowly missed his master. He called on the wounded Gordon. 'Thank God you are safe,' whispered Gordon. 'I have no doubt, Gordon, that you will do well,' said the duke, and had him moved to his own bed. He ate supper at a table laid for too many who would never dine again, looking up anxiously every time the door opened. He drank a single glass of wine, toasting 'the Memory of the Peninsular War'. Then 'he held up both his hands in an imploring attitude', and said 'The hand of almighty God has been upon me this day', lay down on a pallet on the floor, and was asleep in an instant.

He was still asleep when Dr John Hume came in with the preliminary casualty list.

> As I entered, he sat up, his face covered with the dust and sweat of the previous day, and extended his hand to me, which I took and held in mine, whilst I told him of Gordon's death, and of such of the casualties as had come to my knowledge. He was much affected. I felt the tears dropping fast upon my hand. And looking towards him, saw them chasing one another in furrows over his dusty cheeks. He brushed them away suddenly with his left hand, and said to me in a voice tremulous with emotion, "Well, thank God, I don't know what it is to lose a battle; but certainly nothing can be more painful than to gain one with the loss of so many of one's friends." [75]

He rose at once, and began his formal dispatch to Earl Bathurst, which was speedily to arouse criticism because it was less generous with its praise than many wished. It did, however, 'attribute the successful result of this arduous day to the cordial and timely assistance' he received from the Prussians, affirming that their attack 'was a most decisive one'.[76] When, in later life, Wellington was asked if there was anything he could have done better, he replied: 'Yes, I should have given more praise.'[77] Yet it was his suggestion that all ranks who fought in the battle should be given a medal, and the Waterloo medal was to become the first generally issued to the British army.

I re-read Wellington's dispatch in the lee of the farm buildings at La Haye Sainte, and was struck, once again, by the sheer scale of Wellington's achievement. To write, largely from memory, a detailed account of the events of 15–18 June, with only a few hours' sleep and so many of his friends killed or wounded, was a prodigious accomplishment. He rode back to Brussels, where he wrote notes to the Earl of Aberdeen, commiserating on the death of his brother and adding, with his eye for detail, that Gordon had 'a black horse, given to him, I believe, by Lord Ashburnham, which I will keep till I hear from you what you wish should be done with it'. Another letter informed the Duke of Beaufort that his brother FitzRoy had lost his arm, but with luck would survive 'to join me again; and that he will long live to be, as he is likely to become, an honour to his country, as he is a satisfaction to his family and friends'.[78] Then he saw Creevey through his open window, and called him in. 'It has been a damned serious business,' he affirmed. 'Blücher and I have lost 30,000 [actually nearer 23,000] men. It has been a damned nice thing – the nearest run thing you ever saw in your life.' He used much the same words in a letter to Richard:

> It was the most desperate business I was ever in. I never took so much trouble about any battle, and was never

so near being beat. Our loss is immense, particularly in
that best of all Instruments, British Infantry. I never saw
the Infantry behave so well.[79]

Wellington believed that 'we have given Napoleon his death
blow', and he was right. As the allied armies advanced, Wellington
took care to emphasise that France was a friendly country: their
quarrel was with Napoleon and his adherents. Sergeant Edward
Costello of the 95th (soon to cement friendship between adversaries
by marrying a French wife), was so impressed that he inserted the
relevant General Order in his memoirs, but Captain Cavalié Mercer was not pleased that his former enemies 'shall be treated like
gentlemen, and not get the punishment which France, as a nation,
so richly deserves'.[80] An armistice was signed on 3 July, and the
allies entered Paris on the 7th, though without a parade, which
might have caused resentment. When Blücher declared his intention of blowing up the Pont de Iéna, named after the great Prussian
defeat of 1806, Wellington posted a single British sentry on the
structure, reasoning that the Prussians would not kill an allied
soldier. He pressed a policy of moderation on the allies as well as
on his own government, declaring that if Napoleon was to be
executed then the sovereigns 'should appoint an executioner which
should not be me'.

He found himself drenched by a torrent of honours: Louis XVII
gave him his own broad ribbon of the Order of the Holy Ghost,
and other sovereigns followed with orders and titles. He slipped
comfortably into the bright social life of the French capital, hotly
pursued by the pretty little Lady Shelley, and seeing so much of
Lady Frances Wedderburn-Webster that the St James's Chronicle
reported that her husband (himself no mean womaniser), was
divorcing her and seeking damages. Eventually the Wedderburn-

Websters successfully sued the newspaper, but the episode was unfortunate. However, Wellington was not deflected from his duty by a pretty face. When Aglaé Ney came to ask him to intervene on behalf of her husband, who was to be shot for treason, Wellington refused, arguing that he was a representative of the British government and a servant of the allies. Michel Ney went to his death in front of a wall at the Luxembourg gardens, and it was typical of his resolute courage that he gave the order to fire himself.

Appointed commander of the allied army of occupation, Wellington set up his headquarters in the Château de St Martin, near Cambrai, and divided his time between there and Paris. He produced the usual flood of orders, warning officers not to ride over crops when hunting, reminding them that no provocation justified their entering into a fist-fight (the sword was a gentleman's weapon), prescribing a new 'mode of changing the front of a column [to be] practised by the regiments of infantry', and reflecting on the relative ranks of civil and military officers. He took three visiting American ladies to the field of Waterloo, and was noticeably silent at dinner that evening. Yet his public life was less happy; reviled as *le tyran de Cambrai* by Bonapartists and extreme royalists alike, he was at constant risk of assassination, and one man who fired at him was not simply acquitted by a French jury but left 10,000 francs in Napoleon's will. As the army of occupation grew smaller and his own presence became no less irritating to the French, he knew that he could not stay on indefinitely, and in December 1818 he was offered the post of master-general of the ordnance, and a seat in the cabinet. He accepted, and, at the age of 49, embarked upon a political career.

Wellington was not sorry to have fought his last battle. He made no secret of the fact that Waterloo, that 'close-run thing', had been won by the narrowest of margins and perhaps that miscalculation which had allowed Napoleon to drive a wedge between him and Blücher had shaken him more deeply than he cared to admit. And, familiar though he was with battles, he had been shocked by the slaughter. 'Oh, do not congratulate me,' he begged his brother William's wife, putting his hands to his face to hide the tears, 'I have lost all my dearest friends.' He recovered his poise during his time in Paris, and put on weight too. But there were still times when the memory of Waterloo flooded back and unmanned him. Lady Shelley recalled him 'his eye glistening, and his voice broken', as he spoke of the battle:

> 'I hope to God,' he said one day, 'that I have fought my last battle. It is a bad thing to be always fighting. While in the thick of it, I am much too occupied to feel anything; but it is wretched just after. It is quite impossible to think of glory. Both mind and feelings are exhausted. I am wretched even at the moment of victory, and I always say that next to a battle lost, the greatest misery is a battle gained. Not only do you lose those dear friends with whom you have been living, but you are forced to leave the wounded behind you. To be sure one tries to do the best for them, but how little that is! At such moments every feeling in your breast is deadened. I am now just beginning to retain my natural spirits, but I never wish for any more fighting.'[81]

SIX

PILLAR
OF THE STATE

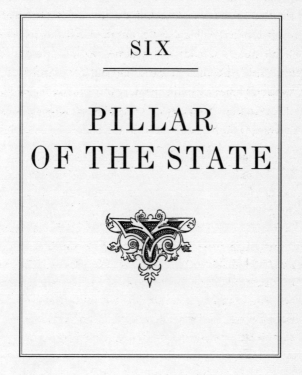

THIS TIME Wellington had a home to return to. His agent had been searching for a suitable country seat, and had eventually purchased Stratfield Saye, between Basingstoke and Reading, from Lord Rivers for £263,000, less than half the sum granted the duke for that purpose by parliament. The house was not well regarded and, at the time, the duke planned to demolish it and build a splendid new structure called Waterloo Place. Happily the scheme was never realised, and Stratfield Saye survives as one of the most pleasant stately homes of England, dignified without being grand, and accessible in a way that Blenheim Palace, built to celebrate the victories of the Duke of Marlborough, is not.

Before accepting office, Wellington had made it clear that he was not a party man. He happened to be 'sincerely attached' to the present Tory government, but believed that 'factious opposition to the government' was 'highly injurious to the interests of the country', and he would not indulge in it if his friends were to lose power.[1] As master-general he commanded the ordnance corps – officers and men of the Royal Artillery, officers of the Royal Engineers and other ranks of the Royal Corps of Sappers and

Miners. He also controlled the civilian ordnance department, responsible for stores and equipment for both army and navy and the maintenance of barracks at home and abroad. The master-general did not normally chair the board of ordnance, and much day-to-day work was pushed along by his secretary – from early 1819, FitzRoy Somerset. Wellington's cabinet seat, however, enabled him to advise the government on defence matters generally, and, in the absence of a police force, this included the preservation of civil order.

The times were violent. Britain's phenomenal industrial development and her take-over of markets once dominated by France had been accompanied by a rapid rise in population, from 15.74 million in 1801 to 24.15 by 1831. By 1801 about a third of this growing population lived in towns, and that proportion grew dramatically for the rest of Wellington's life. Just as the distribution of population changed, so too did its source of wealth, as industry came to dominate both trade and agriculture. Yet few – and all of them men – could vote and governments, both Whig and Tory, were composed of, and governed in the interests of, landowners. It was not surprising that the French Revolution had found answering echoes in Britain, and Tom Paine's radical *The Rights of Man*, published in 1791, demanding radical reform, had sold a staggering 200,000 copies. The excesses of the revolution had turned most Englishmen away from radicalism, but powerful undercurrents remained, and final victory over France, which added to social problems by throwing thousands of discharged soldiers onto the streets, saw a resurgence in demands for political reform. In 1819, a demonstration in Manchester, where the radical leader 'Orator' Hunt addressed a huge crowd, got out of hand, and cavalry charged the mob, causing many casualties.

Wellington was one of the thirteen ministers who signed a letter of congratulation to the magistrates who had directed the troops to restore order, believing that unless he did so, it would be hard to get local justices to do their duty. The following year a group of radicals, who met in a stable loft in Cato Street, planned to assassinate the entire cabinet while it was at dinner at Lord Harrowby's house in Grosvenor Square. Wellington proposed that the cabinet should dine as usual, but each minister should put a pair of pistols in his dispatch box, and soldiers should be posted nearby. Wiser counsels prevailed, however, and they dined elsewhere. The conspirators were arrested: two expressed particular hatred for Wellington, and one declared that he had intended to swear that the duke had begged for mercy on his knees. When the five ringleaders were executed, a sympathetic crowd attacked the hangman. Although the Cato Street Conspiracy was never really a threat to his life, Wellington had a narrower escape when a would-be murderer lay in wait for him in St James's Park, as he was walking home from the Ordnance Office to Apsley House, his London home. Happily, he fell in with FitzRoy Somerset, and the sight of the two men walking arm in arm was too much for the assassin, who made off.

George III, too deranged, for the past ten years, to have any impact on politics, died in January 1820, and the Prince Regent became George IV. Wellington had a poor opinion of him and his brothers. 'By God!' he told Creevey, 'You never saw a figure in all your life as he is! Then he speaks and swears so like old Falstaff, that damn me if I am not ashamed to walk into a room with him.' The royal dukes were 'the damnedest millstones about the necks of any government that can be imagined. They have insulted – *personally* insulted – two thirds of the gentlemen of England.'[2] But when the new king decided to rid himself of his consort, Caroline of Brunswick, on the grounds of her adultery.

Wellington, steadfast royalist that he was, felt obliged to support his monarch, although the king's private life, cushioned by a succession of pneumatic ladies, was hardly blameless. The queen returned to England in June 1820, and was rapturously received by the radicals, not because they had much confidence in her virtue, but because by supporting her they showed their hatred for the king and his ministers. Wellington was the government's go-between with her attorney-general, Henry Brougham, but the negotiations came to nothing and the government introduced a bill of 'Pains and Penalties' to deprive Caroline of her title and dissolve her marriage.

That summer, between the first and second readings of the bill, feelings ran high. Wellington feared that the army might side with the radicals: a battalion of 3rd Guards was heard shouting 'God Save the Queen!' He recommended the government 'to form either a police in London or a military corps, which should be of a different description from the regular military force, or both'.[3] The suggestion did not bear fruit for another eight years, when his political ally, Sir Robert Peel, was home secretary; had it done so earlier, then policemen might have been known, not as Bobbies or Peelers, but, perhaps, as Arties or Wellingtons. There was certainly need for them when the queen appeared for her trial before the House of Lords on 17 August 1820. Wellington was hissed so badly when entering Parliament Square that his horse shied. On another occasion, he was (so it was said), stopped by a gang of road-menders in Grosvenor Place who demanded that he should say 'God save the Queen.' 'Well, gentlemen,' he replied, 'since you will have it, God Save the Queen – and may all your wives be like her'.[4] There is no doubt that on 28 August 1820, he was attacked by a mob which tried to drag him from his horse, and he experienced, said The Times, 'considerable difficulty' before he broke away. Incidents like this heightened Wellington's distaste for the crowd. 'The mob are too contemptible to be thought about for a moment,' he told Lady Shelley, who had so admired him in Paris. 'About thirty of them ran away from me in the Park this morning, because I pulled up my horse when they were *hooting*! They thought I was going to fall upon them and give them what they deserved.'[5] The government carried the second reading by only the narrowest of margins, and Liverpool decided to drop the bill.

The crisis passed. The king, who had talked wildly about dismissing the government if it abandoned proceedings, had no real intention of doing so, and popular agitation abated. The Coronation, on 19 July 1821, went off reasonably well, with a furious queen locked out and the king shamelessly ogling Lady Coningham, unkindly nicknamed the vice-queen. But the king was still desperately anxious to be rid of the queen, and when, on Napoleon's death that year, he was told that his 'greatest enemy' was dead, he replied: 'Is she, by God!' Caroline did in fact die on 7 August 1821: her partisans diagnosed a broken heart.

The royal divorce, part tragedy and part farce, deepened Wellington's gloomy opinion of the state of the nation, with its untrustworthy monarch and fickle populace. Nor was there much comfort at home. One visitor to Stratfield Saye found the whole place an indication of 'the lack of sympathy between Duke and Duchess' whose bedrooms were as far apart as it was possible for them to be. Wellington told his close friend Harriet Arbuthnot that:

> He had repeatedly tried to live in a friendly manner with her . . . but it was impossible . . . She did not understand him, that she could not enter with him into the considerations of all the important concerns which are continually occupying his mind, and that he found he might as well talk to a child . . . his tastes were domestic, that nothing

wd make him so happy as to have a home where he
could find comfort; but that, so far from that, she made
his house so dull that nobody wd go to it.[6]

Mrs Arbuthnot eventually concluded that the duke was right,
and that Kitty was indeed 'totally unfit for her situation. She is
like the housekeeper and dresses herself exactly like a shepherdess,
with an old hat made by herself stuck on the back of her head,
and a dirty basket under her arm'. Although she did her best to
please him, her efforts were often almost comically misplaced:
when he complained about her greying hair, she not only bought
herself a wig but overdid the rouge. Her accounts were still in a
tangle, and she pressed the duke for her allowance of £500 a year
to be increased to £670. He would not hear of it. £500 was generous
for a lady of her rank, he asserted; only princesses had more.

And so the marriage spun further down its vicious circle. Wellington was sharp with his wife, and she responded by becoming
agitated. It was all the more painful because he could be utterly
charming to women who did not bore him: Lady Shelley had him
drawing a battle-plan of Orthez on the knee of his breeches, and
he was wonderful with her children and, indeed, with almost
everybody else's. But he was stiff with his own. His eldest son,
Douro recalled that 'he never even patted me on my shoulder
when I was a boy, because he hated my mother', but the boy grew
up to worship a man he both loved and feared. He was haunted
by the thought that he would one day inherit the title: 'Think
what it will be like when the Duke of Wellington is announced
and only I come in.'[7]

Some of Wellington's old habits died hard. At about this time
he had what Elizabeth Longford calls 'a passionate love affair' with
Lady Charlotte Greville, daughter of the Duke of Portland, and a

family scandal was averted only when she undertook to 'make the *immediate and unqualified relinquishment* of all intimacy & correspondence with the Duke of Wellington'.[8] He was very close to Harriet Arbuthnot, signing one of his letters 'Your most devoted and affectionate Slave', and joking that she was '*La Tyranna*' for he could do nothing without her consent. However, it was probably her mind and her capacity for friendship and discussion he valued, for she was 'a deeply conventional and faithful wife'.

Wellington hunted with his usual enthusiasm, and enjoyed shooting, although he was notoriously erratic. One of Lady Shelley's daughters was so frightened that her mother exclaimed: 'What's this, Fanny? Fear in the presence of the Lord of Waterloo? Stand close behind the Duke of Wellington, and he will protect you.' It was sound advice, because that was the safest place. He winged a dog and a keeper, and then hit an old lady doing her washing. 'I'm wounded, Milady', yelled his victim. 'My good woman,' replied Lady Shelley, 'this ought to be the proudest moment of your life. You have had the distinction of being shot by the great Duke of Wellington.'[9]

There was little comfort on the political front. Castlereagh was one of Wellington's oldest political allies, and without his support Wellington would not have been given command in Portugal in 1808 or been re-employed after Cintra. Although he had rendered his country extraordinary service by maintaining the coalition against Napoleon, as a skilled borough-monger, Castlereagh was deeply unpopular with the radicals. The fact that he was a steadfast supporter of Catholic emancipation alienated many of those who shared his opposition to political reform, and he was hated like few politicians before or since. In 1822, he began to display symptoms of derangement. Wellington listened to his ravings and told him: 'From what you have said, I am bound to warn you that you cannot be in your right mind.' Catlereagh covered his face and sobbed: 'Since *you* say so, it must be so.'[10] The duke warned Castlereagh's doctor, and all razors and pistols were removed, but Castlereagh kept a little knife in his pocketbook and used this to cut his carotid artery. An exultant mob cheered his coffin on its way into Westminster Abbey, and Lord Byron declaimed:

> So *He* has cut his throat at last! – He! Who?
> The man who cut his country's long ago.

There was doubt over who should take over as foreign secretary. The king favoured Wellington, but the preservation of the party's unity suggested George Canning, leader of its more liberal wing and Castlereagh's inveterate enemy, who was at that moment awaiting departure to India to take office as governor general. The king could not stand the man, for he had supported the queen and was a champion of Catholic emancipation, and Wellington had little use for him, but advised the king that the government could not do without him. So Canning was appointed, although the cabinet's hesitancy almost persuaded him to reject the job out of sheer pique. It was, he complained, as if he had been given a ticket to a fashionable club with the words 'Admit the Rogue' written on the back.

That year Wellington was to represent the British government at an international congress in Verona, prompted by the revolt in Spain and the imminence of French military intervention. However, before he departed, the duke, in his capacity as master-general of the ordnance, was attending the test-firing of some new howitzers, and a loud explosion left him with earache and a loud ringing in his left ear. His physician, Dr Hume, who had served under him in the Peninsula and at Waterloo, called in a specialist who treated the ear with a strong caustic solution, leaving his patient in agony. Dr Hume called next morning and found the duke unshaved and red-eyed, like someone 'who has recovered from a terrible debauch'. He never fully got over it. His balance was affected, and he was noticeably deaf. In later life he was a familiar figure in the Lords, with his hat pulled down low over his forehead, cupping a hand to his ear in an effort to follow the debate. It is a sad reflection on the medicine of age – Wellington had come through a score of battles with his hearing intact only to be deafened by a doctor.

He travelled first to Vienna, and complained that he felt very ill: 'sometimes I feel as if I was drunk & can't walk. I am very tired of being sick, never having been so before. Even the strength of my Iron constitution now tells against me.'[11] A newspaper reported 'a great alteration in his features, and a great change in his person', but when he arrived at Verona he proceeded confidently to implement Canning's policy of condemning French intervention in Spain, and, rather less happily, to support the liberation of Spanish colonies in South America. He found himself playing cards with Napoleon's widow, Marie-Louise, now Duchess of Parma, settling his debts in gold *napoléons*, and thought her son 'a fine lad, just like the archdukes.'[12]

The duke returned to England still feeling very seedy. In January 1823, he sent FitzRoy Somerset off to Madrid in a vain effort to persuade the patriots to amend the constitution, granting more power to King Ferdinand and averting a French invasion, but the mission was 'inevitably doomed and grossly unfair to him'.[13] The French invaded in February and restored Ferdinand to absolute power, and amongst the liberal refugees was Wellington's old friend Alava – probably the only man to have served, on different sides, at Trafalgar and Waterloo. Wellington installed him in a house on the estate at Stratfield Saye, and took him along to Coutt's bank, saying that as long as he had any money there, Alava was welcome to draw as much as he thought proper. But he was increasingly uneasy with Canning. He called him 'the gentleman', because he was suspicious of Canning's populist streak and desire to recognise South American revolutionaries (who looked, in their way, not unlike Irish ones), and was unsure whether Canning was a gentleman at all. The duke was defeated over the question of the South American republics, and at the end of 1824 the cabinet agreed to recognise them.

There was another upset in March 1825, when his younger son, Lord Charles Wellesley, was sent down from Oxford for a year for breaking out of college after a party in Lord Douro's rooms; both he and Douro were dispatched to Cambridge. And then, in the autumn, there was a sharp clash with Richard, now lord lieutenant of Ireland. They had fallen out during the Peninsular War when Richard's career had been crippled by his idleness and lechery, and, during the Hundred Days, the disappointed marquess had supported the Whig opposition's criticism of the campaign. Richard was a widower, for his French wife had died in 1816. He now proposed to marry Marianne Patterson, whom the duke greatly admired, and was accepted. Wellington was aghast that such a woman should marry 'a man totally ruined'. So too was Marianne's sister-in-law, Betsy Patterson-Bonaparte: 'I married [Jerome] the brother of Napoleon the conqueror of Europe,' she said, 'Mary has married the brother of Napoleon's conqueror.'[14] Things went from bad to worse when the duke was persuaded to offer help to Lord Wellesley, who had irritated the Protestants by banning the celebrations traditionally associated with William of Orange's birthday. Wellesley did not respond.

The duke was tired of the king, fed up with his family, and

irritated by painters who invented allegories he disapproved of and got his uniform wrong. Sir Thomas Lawrence, considered by the diarist Charles Greville, son of Wellington's lover, as the finest of living painters, failed on both counts: first with his waiting-for-the-Prussians Waterloo watch, and then with a sword which was so wrong that the duke ordered him not to leave the session until he had corrected his mistake.

When, at the end of 1825, Canning suggested that Wellington might go to St Petersburg to see the new tsar, he agreed to do so. Canning maintained that Wellington '*jumped* at the proposal', but there were those who suggested that Canning said this because he was glad to see the duke out of the city. Wellington took leave of his friends with unusual emotion; Alava had never seen him so moved. FitzRoy Somerset, who accompanied the duke to Russia, thought that at St Petersburg, the duke was treated 'like a prince' and was received by Nicholas I and his family 'in the most marked and flattering manner'.[15] The mission seemed a success, because Wellington was able to negotiate the secret Protocol of St Petersburg, by which Britain agreed to mediate between Russia and Turkey to achieve a measure of independence for Greece. They returned by way of Berlin, where they were received with 'marked kindness' by the Prussian royal family. There was less kindness at home. In April, a jealous Canning encouraged the opposition to describe Wellington's mission as a failure, and Lord Liverpool obstinately refused to make his brother Gerald a bishop because of his wife's adultery. There was more trouble with Douro, and the duke told Mrs Arbuthnot that he was 'very disappointed' in him. And there was death in the air: both Lord Liverpool and the Duke of York were ill.

The Duke of York had never liked Wellington. In 1821 he revealed to Charles Greville an 'extremely strong' prejudice against the man:

He does not deny his military talents, but thinks that he is false and ungrateful, that he never gave sufficient credit to his officers, and that he was unwilling to put forward men of talent who might be in a situation to claim some share of credit, the whole of which he was desirous of engrossing himself. He says that at Waterloo he got into a scrape and allowed himself to be surprised, and he attributes in great measure the success of that day to Lord Anglesey, who, he says, was hardly mentioned, and that in the coldest terms, in the Duke's dispatch.[16]

York died on 5 January 1827, and the king, often convinced that he had charged, disguised as Major General von Bock, at Salamanca, briefly entertained hopes of becoming commander-in-chief himself, but was politely dissuaded. Wellington was the obvious choice, and he became commander-in-chief that month, retaining, at the king's request, the post of master-general of the ordnance. 'Yes, yes,' he told Croker

> I am in my proper place, in a place to which I was destined by my trade. I am a soldier, and I am in my place at the head of the army, as the Chancellor, who is a lawyer, is in his place on the woolsack. We each of us have a trade, and are in our proper position when we are exercising it.[17]

But Liverpool, already very ill, suffered a severe stroke on 17 February and could no longer continue as prime minister. Wellington, commander-in-chief or not, was a strong candidate for the office. Both Canning and the duke were summoned by the king, and at a crucial stage in proceedings, the king sent Wellington off for a drive with the gossipy Princess Lieven. After he returned, Canning asked him if he was prepared to serve on in a new administration to ensure stability. The duke asked who was to be prime minister, and Canning replied with icy sarcasm that:

> I believe it to be so generally understood that the King usually entrusts the formation of an Administration to the individual whom it is His Majesty's gracious intention to place at the head of it, that it did not occur to me . . . to add that, in the present instance His Majesty does not intend to depart from the usual course of proceeding on such occasions.[18]

The furious duke resigned as commander-in-chief and master-general. Resigning the latter was natural enough, since it was a cabinet office, but the former was not, and cartoonists detected pique, showing Wellington, as Achilles, sulking in Apsley House: 'The Great Captain on the Stool of Repentance'. They had a point, for he had never been above sulking when rebuffed. However, although Canning managed to form an administration by bringing in some Whigs – for Wellington's close associates, marshalled by his lieutenant, Robert Peel, would not serve – nobody expected it to last. Yet the government fell in an unexpected way. Canning had contracted rheumatic fever at the Duke of Yorks' funeral in the icy St George's Chapel at Windsor, and he died that summer. The moderate Tory Frederick Robinson, not long ennobled as Viscount Goderich, became prime minister. He had failed to cover himself with glory during Canning's administration, and had been unable to steer reform of the Corn Laws through the Lords in the face of Tory opposition. Goderich's own time in office was blighted by the death of his young daughter, but his moderate administration, with the capable William Huskisson leading it in the Commons, deserved a better fate than it received.

Wellington had accepted the office of commander-in-chief

when the king offered it to him on Canning's death. He denied that he was a party leader, claiming, as he always had, that he should 'support the Government whenever their Measures were calculated to promote the Honour or interests of the Country'. However, Gleig was right to term him 'the acknowledged head of a great political party', for he was the hero of the ultra-Tories, and spent the summer recess in Tory strongholds in the north, on visits which 'though ostensibly those of private friendship were by others than himself converted into political demonstrations'.[19] The mood was mixed. Gentlemen who dined with him hung on to every word, and ladies 'as their custom was' flattered him at every opportunity. But he was less well received in humbler circles: the populace turned out to see him, but their welcome was cold. He was now a party politician, who seemed to advocate policies of which they disapproved.

The government was already in trouble when Admiral Sir Edward Codrington, liberally interpreting orders to apply 'a friendly demonstration of force' to the Turks in an effort to deliver Greece, sank a Turkish fleet in Navarino Bay on 20 October 1827. Whigs and radicals were delighted, and Wellington's Tory friends were shocked. Goderich lurched on until, on 8 January 1828, in tears once again, he resigned behind a borrowed royal handkerchief. Wellington was dressing at Apsley House the next morning when a note arrived from the Lord Chancellor, followed shortly afterwards by Lord Lyndhurst himself, who had come to take him to Windsor. He found the king sitting up in bed wearing a turban and a dirty silk jacket. 'Arthur,' he declared, 'the cabinet is defunct.' Wellington was invited to form a government on the clear understanding that Catholic emancipation should be no part of his programme. The duke asked for time to consult his friends, but asked the king if he had any particular objections, and discovered that only the Whig leader, Lord Grey, was unwelcome. Then he set off to consult Peel, who advised him to accept, although he warned that Catholic emancipation was bound to cause trouble, as were unreconciled Canning-ites.

When Wellington rode to his official residence, No 10 Downing Street, on Copenhagen, the charger he had ridden at Waterloo, he was making a political point. The king had assured him that he had no aversion to a strong government, and that was just what Wellington intended to provide. But he soon found himself mired in the treacle of patronage. Robert Peel was to be leader of the Commons, although Wellington was not pleased to be told by his somewhat chilly associate that he would have to give up being commander-in-chief. He reluctantly did so, advising the king to appoint Rowland Hill, who was so junior that there was briefly a plan to make him simply 'Senior General upon the Staff, performing the duties of Commander-in-Chief . . .' Charles Arbuthnot, husband of the devoted Harriet, was not offered a cabinet post, and for a time seemed inclined not to serve at all, but eventually rallied. There was no room for either Richard or William, giving the press a field day. Wellington had already been criticised for securing a peerage for Henry when Goderich was prime minister, and it was clear that, as far as family patronage was concerned, whatever he did was wrong for the press. He had a low opinion of journalists: 'What can we do with these sort of fellows? We have no power over them, God, for my part, I will have no communication with any of them.' Croker called to find him up to his knees in dispatch-boxes and letter bags. 'There is the business of the country,' he declared, 'which I have not time to look at – all my time being employed assuaging what gentlemen call their *feelings*.'[20]

Wellington held his first cabinet dinner at Apsley House on

22 January 1828. Everybody was scrupulously polite, but it was the politeness, as Lord Ellenborough put it, of people who had just fought a duel. The duke had never been comfortable with second-in-commands, and Peel, despite his many virtues, lacked Wellington's iron determination. But over the months that followed, this determination was much in evidence: when told by the Treasury that a change in accounting methods was impossible, he replied, 'Never mind: if *you* cannot accomplish it, I shall send you half a dozen pay-sergeants, who will.'[21] He displayed the same military briskness towards the cohesion of the party, and had no time for waverers. 'What is the meaning of a party,' he protested, having forgotten his personal objections to the very notion of party, 'if they don't follow their leaders? Damn 'em! Let 'em go!' He found the endless debate hard to tolerate. 'One man wants one thing and one another.' He said:

> they agree to what I say in the morning and then in the evening they start up with some crochet which deranges the whole plan. I have not been used to that in the early part of my life. I have been accustomed to carry on things in quite a different manner: I assembled my officers and laid down my plan, and it was carried into effect without more words.[22]

It was an uphill struggle. In March, the government very nearly split over a relaxation of the Corn Laws, with Huskisson, the colonial secretary, coming to the edge of resignation before a compromise measure, which was to please few when there were poor harvests for four years, was passed. Then Wellington fell out with Huskisson over the abolition of two of the most spectacularly rotten boroughs – so putrid that they smelt too strong even for his cabinet – Penrhyn and East Retford. Eventually the cabinet agreed that Penrhyn's members should go to Birmingham, and East Retford should be absorbed by the adjacent Bassetlaw. When the Lords obstructed the Penrhyn bill, Huskisson voted against the government over the absorption of East Retford. Early on the morning of 20 May 1828, he offered the duke his resignation, and although it was intended as a gesture, Wellington lost no time in accepting it. When some of Huskisson's Canning-ite associates tried to intervene, eventually sending an ambassador who said it was all a mistake, the duke declared that: 'There is no mistake, there can be no mistake, there shall be no mistake.' And with that, he strode out to take a turn down Birdcage Walk in case Huskisson came to call.

The duke's administration was weakened by Huskisson's disappearance, for the Canning-ites felt compelled to follow him. Wellington decided to appoint Vesey Fitzgerald, MP for Clare, to replace Charles Grant at the Board of Trade. At the time, ministers then had to face re-election before they could assume office, and Wellington counted on Fitzgerald's personal popularity as a good landlord and progressive Protestant who favoured Catholic relief. But he was opposed by Daniel O'Connell, founder of the Catholic Association. Although, as a Catholic, O'Connell could not sit in parliament if elected, there was nothing to prevent him from standing for election. He was duly elected, and the ensuing uproar ended with Wellington becoming convinced that: 'This state of things cannot be allowed to continue.' Catholic emancipation was the only answer. But he would need to take great care with the king. He warned him that rebellion was brewing in Ireland, and obtained permission 'to take into consideration the whole case of Ireland . . .' That summer of 1828, he was persuaded to go off to Cheltenham to take the waters, for the strain of office was visibly telling upon him. Peel warned him that the king, already inflamed by his brother Clarence's deposition as Lord High Admiral after a spat with Wellington, grew daily more Protestant.

Wellington took almost as much trouble marshalling his troops for Catholic emancipation as he had over preparing the lines of Torres Vedras. Peel was persuaded to remain in the cabinet, and the king was at last brought round after a series of long and usually one-sided conversations. 'I make it a rule never to interrupt him,' admitted the duke, 'and when in this way he tries to get rid of a subject in the way of business which he does not like, I let him talk himself out, and then quietly put before him the matter in question, so that he cannot escape from it'.[23] Wellington compared it to a battle, because the king resisted him yard by yard. Charles Greville, clerk to the Privy Council, reported on 5 March 1829 that 'Nothing could exceed the consternation which prevailed yesterday about this Catholic business.'[24] At the final audience Wellington was supported by Peel and Lyndhurst, but the king, steadily reinforced with brandy and water, struggled on – there was his coronation oath, and he must consult the bishops. The three politicians offered their resignations and set off for London. They arrived to find that the king had given way in a letter with the agonised postscript: 'God knows what pain it costs me to write these words. G.R.'

Gaining reluctant royal approval for emancipation was one thing, but getting the measure through parliament was quite another. The political cartoons of the period, in which the duke makes frequent appearances, testify to the strength of opinion on the subject: one shows the duke in league with the devil. Amongst the steadfast opponents of emancipation was George Finch-Hatton, ninth Earl of Winchilsea and fourth Earl of Nottingham, who spoke in the Lords 'as if he were shouting on a windy day upon Pendennen Heath' and was given to emphasising his points (as if further emphasis was required) by waving a large white handkerchief. He accused Wellington of 'an insidious design for the infringement of our liberties and the introduction of Popery into every department of the State'.[25] This was quite literally fighting talk. Although the duke disapproved of duelling, he felt that dispelling the prevailing 'atmosphere of calumny' would help his cause, and accordingly he demanded of the earl 'that satisfaction ... which a gentleman has a right to require, and which a gentleman never refuses to give'. The one-handed Sir Henry Hardinge, now secretary at war, was his second, and he asked Dr John Hume to bring a case of pistols to his house at 7.45 on the morning of Sunday 21 March 1829 for a meeting between 'persons of rank and consequence'.

When Hume arrived at Battersea Fields, he was surprised to see Wellington riding towards him. Anxious to waste no time, the duke told Hardinge to look sharp and step out the ground. Hardinge walked twelve paces, and pointed out where Winchilsea was to stand. 'Damn it,' called Wellington, 'Don't stick him up so near the ditch. If I hit him, he will tumble in.' Hume loaded both pistols (Hardinge could not manage it with his artificial hand), and Lord Falmouth, Winchilsea's second, was shaking with cold and excitement. The two men took their positions, and Hardinge gave the word to fire. Wellington, a poor shot with a pistol, had intended aiming at Winchilsea's legs, but seeing that his adversary kept his pistol arm at his side, he fired deliberately wide. Winchilsea fired in the air, and his second then read from a piece of paper. 'That won't do,' said the duke, 'it is no apology.' The magic word was added, and the duke bowed coldly, touched his hat, wished them 'Good morning, my Lords', and rode away. Wellington told Gleig that he had not fought because it was 'a private quarrel', but because it arose from 'a great public question'.[26]

It was still a remarkable thing to do. To duel was to attempt murder, and for the prime minister to break the law in such a way aroused great concern. The writer Jeremy Bentham ventured an epistle beginning 'Ill advised man', and received a brisk rejoinder: 'Compliments. The Duke has received his letter.' Charles Greville was more balanced. He thought that 'all blame Lord W.' and 'the letters on the Duke's part are very creditable, so free from arrogance or an assuming tone' but that 'the Duke should not have challenged him, he stands in too high a position, and ... should have treated him and his letter with the contempt they merited'.[27] However, the meeting had the desired effect on public opinion: the mob, hooting Wellington a week before, now took to cheering him. He treated the one with as little concern as the other.

Peel had introduced the emancipation bill into the Commons on 5 March 1829 with a four-hour speech, said to be far the best he ever made: 'very able, plain, clear and statesmanlike'.[28] The duke was not always a reliable speaker in parliament, sometimes hesitating, and sometimes saying more than his colleagues expected. But he opened the bill's second reading before the Lords, on 31 March, with utter confidence and sincerity. He spoke slowly and forcefully, without notes, and with his arms folded. He believed that Ireland was on the brink of civil war, and appealed to those peers who sought to put down the Catholic Association by force of arms:

> But, my Lords, even if I had been certain of such means
> of putting it down, I should have considered it my duty to
> avoid those means. I am one of those who have probably
> passed a longer period of my life engaged in war than
> most men, and principally in civil war; and I must say
> this, that if I could avoid by any sacrifice whatsoever,

even one month of civil war in the country to which I
was attached, I would sacrifice my life in order to do it.[29]

When it came to the vote, the bill was carried by 112 votes, a
greater majority than most expected. 'This tremendous defeat,'
thought Greville, 'will probably put an end to anything like serious
opposition: they will hardly rally again'.[30]

The unexpectedly large majority infuriated the king, who now
railed against a disgraced parliament and a revolutionary people.
This snapped Wellington's patience, and he told Mrs Arbuthnot
that the monarch was 'the worst man he ever fell in with in his
whole life, the most false, the most ill-natured, the most entirely
without one redeeming quality'.[31] Nonetheless, the king had no
option but to give the Royal Assent to the bill after it completed
its third reading on 10 April. It was a monumental achievement
on the duke's part, the brightest spot in his political career, but
he had widened splits within his own party, for amongst the Tory
peers who voted against him were some of his oldest political
friends. And Catholic emancipation was no longterm solution to
the problems of Ireland, which remained hampered by deep-seated
issues of land tenure and excessive dependence on a single crop
– the soon-to-be blighted potato.

Victory over Catholic emancipation raised Wellington to an
eminence he had not occupied since Waterloo. Greville observed
that he simply dictated to his cabinet, addressed the king in a style
used by no other minister, and treated him as an equal. Cartoonists
always found his unmistakable profile an easy target, and now he
was Jarvey the Coachman, 'The Man wot drives the Sovereign.'
Yet he remained personally unassuming. Howell Gronow tells
how, probably in 1814, Wellington was about to ascend the stairs
to the ballroom in the ultra-fashionable Almack's club. He was

wearing evening dress with black trousers, rather than the knee-breeches and silk stockings prescribed by 'the fair ladies who ruled this little dancing and gossiping world'. As he approached, 'the vigilant Mr Willis, guardian of the establishment, stepped forward and said "Your Grace cannot be admitted in trousers," whereupon the Duke, who had a great respect for orders and regulations, quietly walked away.'[32] At the height of his popularity over emancipation, he approached Hyde Park in his carriage on his way to Buckingham Palace, only to be told by the officer on guard at the gates that the Duke of Cumberland, as Gold Stick in Waiting, had given orders that no carriages should be allowed in the park. Wellington was a field marshal and prime minister, and the officer, quite understandably, said that he was sure that the prohibition was not meant to extend to him. The duke told him that he simply had to obey orders, and requested the carriage to go round the other way. Greville observed that while Wellington declared that the whole thing was a mistake, 'the Duke of Cumberland and the Duke of Wellington do not speak, and whenever they meet, which often happens in society, the former moves off'.[33]

There were other successes during his time as prime minister, notably the creation of the Metropolitan Police in the summer of 1829. However, most politicians believed that the administration could not survive for long without the Canning-ites, lost with Huskisson's resignation, and the Ultras, who had opposed emancipation. Indeed, had it not been for Wellington's famous luck, which kept the opposition in disarray, he might have been in greater difficulties sooner. Things were not well at Stratfield Saye, where he found house parties composed of strangers, and even Douro (now twenty-three and falling in love with rare facility), warned his mother about 'your dress being inconsistent with your station in the world'.[34] Wellington found a refuge that year when the king appointed him Lord Warden of the Cinque Ports, an office 'of great influence and power but without any salary'. It brought with it an official residence, Walmer Castle, mid-way between Dover and Deal. One of the coast defences erected by Henry VIII in the 1540s, with great squat round towers to mount what was then the new-fangled artillery, Walmer had comfortable, if often elliptically-walled rooms, and a bracing sea air. The duke loved it, and it was there that he 'found most time to indulge in his lifelong affection for children, one of his great charms'.[35] A boy who had to leave his pet toad behind when he was sent away to school received the duke's regular reports on the creature's well-being, and a child playing in the garden was greeted benevolently: 'You are a very nice little fellow, when you are old enough I will get you a commission in the Guards.' 'But I'm a girl, Mr Dook,' it replied.[36]

That autumn he wrote glumly of 'complaints from all quarters'. The fall of agricultural prices since Waterloo created a worsening depression in the countryside, and too much of the burgeoning population of the towns (many, like Manchester, Bradford and Birmingham, still unrepresented in parliament) survived on the narrowest of margins. He was also drawn into the debate on army reform. In April 1829, he wrote a lengthy paper setting out his own deeply held views on discipline, arguing that the British army, unlike continental forces raised by conscription, was:

> an exotic in England . . . disliked by the inhabitants, par-
> ticularly by the higher orders, who never allow one of
> their family to serve in it. Even the common people will
> make an exertion to fund means to purchase the dis-
> charge of a relation who may have enlisted . . .[37]

He believed that it required 'the gentleman officer' to provide gallant and selfless leadership, backed by professional non-commissioned officers, and 'that we should stand firm upon the establishment of our discipline, as it is'. He gave firm evidence to the Royal Commission on Military Punishments, arguing that drink was invariably 'the great parent of all crime in the British Army' and declaring that it was 'out of the question' that he could have preserved discipline in the forces he commanded without recourse to flogging.[38] Although flogging divided opinion within both army and society, the duke's argument struck a chord even with some private soldiers. John Spencer Cooper, for one, agreed with him.

> It is frequently stated that the Duke of Wellington was severe. In answer to this, I would say that he could not have been otherwise. His army was composed of the lowest orders. Many, if not the most of them, were ignorant, idle, and drunken.[39]

The duke's administration rumbled on into 1830, although he was increasingly sick of being at its head, and told Harriet Arbuthnot that he was considering standing aside in favour of Peel, soon to inherit his father's baronetcy and appear as Sir Robert. The king was visibly failing, and did nothing for his constitution by eating prodigious quantities of food and swigging laudanum for a bladder complaint. He died on 26 June, and Wellington, one of his executors, was at once involved in the delicate business of sorting out the late king's secret and illegal (though canonically valid) marriage to Maria Fitzherbert, whose portrait Wellington saw hanging round the dead king's neck beneath the nightshirt in which he had demanded to be buried. The modest Mrs Fitzherbert was paid off with £6,000 a year. Less easy was the scandal arising from the suggestion that a half-pay captain, Thomas Garth, the illegitimate son of Princess Sophia, the Duke of Cumberland's sister, had in fact been fathered upon her by Cumberland himself.

Welllington staved off Garth's attempt at blackmail: Garth disappeared to France, and the papers disappeared for ever. It is now clear, however, that a royal equerry, not Cumberland, was the author of the princess's misfortunes.

Although Charles Greville reported that 'the new King began very well', before long it was clear that William IV was going on rather badly. He had been a professional naval officer, and his salty manner of 'Getting a Grip' quickly caused unease. He shouted to the assembled generals and admirals to get in step at his brother's funeral, and bellowed 'this is a damned bad pen you have given me' when signing his first declaration.[40] He confirmed Wellington's government in office, but there had to be a general election with the change of monarch, and the opposition seized the opportunity to make parliamentary reform its major issue. The votes were nearly in when there was news of a revolution in Paris, where Charles X, son of Louis, Wellington's 'walking sore', had been brought down by the Paris mob and replaced by the same Duc d'Orléans Wellington had briefly considered as an alternative monarch during the Hundred Days of 1815. In Britain, radicals declared that if the French could have the parliament they wanted, so too could their own countrymen. In fact the Tories won the election, though against an ugly background of machine-breaking and rick-burning in a countryside worn to a thread by the depression.

In September, Wellington went up to Manchester for the opening of the Liverpool-Manchester railway, and doubtless to assess the climate in the industrial north and reinforce his own party's resources there before the new parliamentary session opened in early November. The duke duly enjoyed his first ride on a train, and near Liverpool, when the train stopped to take on water, he was introduced to his old rival Huskisson, the local MP. They had just shaken hands when another engine – George Stephenson's

Rocket – approached on the other track. Huskisson tried to get out of the way, but he was 'slow and heavy'. The engine knocked him down, and a wheel went over his leg. Although he was carried to a house nearby, there was no hope for him. Greville thought that 'he died the death of a great man, suffering torments, but always resigned, calm, collected . . .' The whole affair was profoundly shocking, with Huskisson 'crushed to death in sight of his wife and at the feet (as it were) of his great political rival . . .'[41] Wellington was upset, and was only persuaded to continue his journey when told that the mob might turn dangerous if he did not appear. It was clear that Huskisson's death would have a profound effect on politics, leaving his former followers 'at liberty to join either the Opposition or the Government'.

Wellington did his best to marshal his forces for the new session, but soon saw that if he included Whigs and Canning-ites he would lose Ultras, and vice-versa. 'I saw that it was a question of noses,' he told Lady Salisbury later, 'that as many as I gained on the one side I should lose on the other.' And he himself was firmly persuaded that reform was both unnecessary and 'injurious to . . . society . . .'[42] He had never been a man for wild charges, but launched one when the new session opened. The opposition leader Lord Grey spoke graciously and moderately, saying that he was not wedded to any particular reform measure, and Wellington, in reply, began as generously. Then the reins slipped through his fingers, and he was carried away:

> Under these circumstances I am not prepared to bring forward any measure of the description alluded to by the noble Lord. And I am not only not prepared to bring forward any measure of this nature, but I will at once declare that . . . I shall always feel it my duty to resist such measures when proposed by others.[43]

He sat down to a stunned silence, and muttered to Aberdeen, his foreign secretary, 'I have not said too much, have I?' The speech, setting his party against any measure of reform, shocked parliament and nation. Wellington immediately found himself receiving assassination threats from 'Captain Swing', spectral leader of rioting agricultural labourers, and well-wishers warned him that his life was at risk.

On 15 November the government was defeated in the Commons on a relatively minor matter, and that night Wellington, entertaining the Prince of Orange at a large dinner in Apsley House, was summoned downstairs to meet Peel and two other ministers who told him that he must resign. The cabinet went to St James's Palace the following morning, and the king received them 'with the greatest kindness, shed tears, but accepted their resignations without remonstrance'.[44]

The duke was out of office but not out of work. He was lord-lieutenant of Hampshire, where Captain Swing was hard at his smoky work, and set off 'for my County, to do what I can to restore order and peace,' adding that 'in Parliament, when I can, I will approve; when I cannot, I will dissent, but I will never agree to be the leader of a faction.'[45] He also turned his attention to the Tower of London, of which he had been made Constable in 1826, ordering that the noisome moat should be cleared of sewage and that the Tower's doctor should either do his job or resign. The yeoman warders were to be recruited from former NCOs, 'a respectable Class of Men', who richly deserved his patronage. There was the enduring backwash of another family scandal. His nephew William, sacked as an aide-de-camp in the Peninsula, was now, after marriage to an heiress, William Long-Wellesley, but having squandered his wife's fortune, he decamped with Mrs Helena Bligh who bore him a son and the shock of the news had killed off William's wife. The duke became guardian of William's children, but there were still more troubles, 'poignant commentary', as Elizabeth Longford puts it, 'on the fate of a loveless family with a drive towards self-extinction'.[46]

In the wider world, the duke was uneasy about being in opposition. However, when Lord John Russell rose in the House of Commons on 1 March 1831 and introduced the Reform Bill, he was clear in his mind: he could now see the enemy quite clearly. He declared that 'from the period of the adoption of that measure will date the downfall of the Constitution.' Although the bill was carried by the Commons with a majority of one, its fate looked uncertain in the committee stages, and Lord Grey urged the king to dissolve parliament to avoid the bill being defeated. At first William declined to act, but when he heard on 22 April that a Tory peer had tabled a motion that parliament should not be dissolved, he swept down to Westminster – the crown had to be brought from the Tower and his robes from a portrait painter's – and duly dissolved Parliament.

Wellington was not in the Lords to see the near-brawl that was afoot, with Lord Mansfield screaming abuse and Lord Londonderry brandishing a whip at Lord Richmond, when the king entered. Kitty was dying and now, with the pillars of the world he understood rocking around him, Wellington wanted to be at her bedside. We cannot tell whether her last illness was cholera or cancer, but its progress brought husband and wife together. Kitty, pale and frail on her bed amidst the trophies of the duke's glory, still rejoiced in the accomplishments of her hero. And as they held hands, she ran a finger up his sleeve to find if he was still wearing an amulet she had once given him. 'She found it,' Wellington told a friend, 'as she would have found it any time these past twenty years, had she cared to look for it.' How strange it was, he mused, that people could live together for half a lifetime and only understand one another at the end.[47]

News of the dissolution brought out an exultant mob that attacked the duke's home and smashed the windows – it 'did not care one pin for the poor Duchess being dead in the house' – and was driven off only when a servant fired blunderbusses over their heads. It deepened Wellington's distaste for the crowd, 'the mob run mad, and rotten to the core'. The reformers won a huge election victory, but Wellington was unabashed by parliamentary rout or public hostility. Now, even travelling down to Walmer was risky. George Gleig, behaving more like the subaltern he used to be than the reverend gentleman he had become, accompanied him on the journey and was glad to find:

> eight well-mounted men of Kent, who immediately broke into two parties, four riding about 100 yards in front of the carriage, while the others followed. They all carried heavy hunting whips, and were besides armed with pistols, as I found were likewise the duke and his servant. But no enemy appeared. The carriage swept up to the old castle gate, and the voluntary escort, having seen the Duke safe, dispersed without attracting attention.[48]

If he had lost the Commons, he could still find a majority in the Lords, who voted down a new bill in October. But far from settling the issue, this simply increased the frenzy, and Wellington's windows were smashed again. This time the duke was at home, working at his writing table, and one stone narrowly missed his head and broke a glass-fronted bookcase behind him. Elsewhere there was serious rioting: half the city centre of Bristol was burnt down, and hundreds died when troops eventually restored order. Wellington told FitzRoy Somerset, still soldiering on as military secretary

There was widespread rioting when the second Reform Bill was thrown out by the Lords. In Bristol, seen here, a combination of circumstances led to especially severe riots in which half the city centre was destroyed and hundreds of people were killed, many as they pillaged houses fired by the mob.

at Horse Guards, that weak leadership was the problem: 'Remember (and Bristol is an example) that an Army of Stags with a Lion at its head is better than an army of Lions with a Stag at its Head.'[49]

Undaunted by the defeat of the previous two measures, on 12 December Russell introduced a third Reform Bill into the Commons, only to see it too voted into oblivion by the Lords on 14 April 1832. Greville disapproved of the duke's continued resistance, but dined with him in May and recorded that:

> I never see and converse with him without reproaching myself for the sort of hostility I feel towards his political conduct, for there are a simplicity, a gaiety and a natural urbanity and good-humour in him, which are remarkably captivating in so great a man.[50]

The king still refused a mass creation of peers, which would have broken Wellington's strength in the Lords, and Grey and his colleagues accordingly resigned. Wellington, anxious to protect the king from a wholesale creation, tried to break the stalemate against a backcloth of what many felt to be imminent revolution. Endless discussions at Apsley House revealed that he could not find enough Tories who were prepared to join him in an administration committed to moderate reform, and on 15 May told the king that he could not form a government. The best that he could do was to call off his hounds in the Lords: Grey resumed office, and the Reform Bill became law on 7 June.

The Great Reform Act of 1832 now seems a very moderate measure: after it the 249 electors of Buckingham still returned as many MPs as the 4,172 electors of Leeds, and England, with 54 per cent of Britain's population, returned 71 per cent of the Commons.[51] However, the Whigs were disinclined to go much further, and the main impetus of reform passed from parliamentarians to radicals outside it, as the People's Charter demanded universal manhood suffrage, a secret ballot, equal electoral districts, the abolition of property qualifications for MPs, payment for MPs, and annual parliaments.

It took time for Wellington's role in the resistance to the 1832 act to be forgiven. On Waterloo Day that year, he found a mob waiting for him when he emerged from sitting to the painter Pistrucci at the Royal Mint. A magistrate offered his assistance, but the duke told him: 'You can do nothing. The only thing you can help me in is to tell me exactly the road I am to take to get to Lincoln's Inn; for the greatest danger would be in my missing my way and having to turn back on the mob.' He set off down Fenchurch Street with his groom. The mob tried to drag him from his horse, but two Chelsea Pensioners appeared ('that best of all instruments . . .') and he asked them to march at each stirrup and face outwards if he had to halt. In Holborn, a coal-cart appeared: 'Hillo!' said the duke, 'here's the artillery coming up; we must look out'. A brave gentleman drove his Tilbury close up behind to cover the rear, and delighted the duke by 'never looking to me for any notice'. He gained a little time by diverting through Lincoln's Inn, and by the time he reached clubland he had more supporters, and rode steadily on up Constitution Hill. The mob swarmed across the Park to hoot him as he clattered into Apsley House, its windows now iron-shuttered against the brickbats. He turned to Lord St Germans, who had accompanied him from Whitehall, and raised his hat: 'An odd day to choose. Good morning!'[52]

And yet, slave to duty, he could not stand aside from public life, and agreed to become chancellor of Oxford University. 'I am the Duke of Wellington,' he told Croker, and, *bon gré mal gré* must do as the Duke of Wellington doth.' He looked in on the House of Commons when the new parliament met in February 1833, and declared: 'I never saw so many shocking bad hats in my life.'[53] Greville agreed, for once, muttering about the 'pretensions, impertinence and self-sufficiency of some of the new members'.[54] The duke supported Grey's government because he saw it as the last line of defence against anarchy, but the worst seemed over, and he had his windows repaired in time for the Waterloo banquet that year. He lost Harriet Arbuthnot in August: the letter telling him of her death fell from his hands, and he flung himself on the sofa in a paroxysm of grief. But duty caught hold again, and he rode off to commiserate with her widower, for he had loved her too.

Yet he was not entirely finished with the flesh. Wellington was a devout but not ostentatiously religious man, and that year he was approached by a pretty orphan, Anna Maria Jenkins, who was determined to give him 'a new *birth* into righteousness'. When they met, there was an undeniable mutual attraction, with Miss Jenkins struck by the duke's 'beautiful silver head' and the duke, expecting something altogether more spinsterish, suddenly declaring 'Oh, *how* I *love* you! *How* I *love* you!' This was not quite the conversion that Miss Jenkins had in mind, but when asked if she was prepared to be a duchess, replied: 'If it be the will of God.' The relationship, always most decorous, went on in fits and starts, largely by post. There were occasional Wellingtonian outbursts, one in 1844 when, thinking that she was pressing him for money, the duke declared:

> I will give her any reasonable assistance she may require from me; when she will let me know in clear distinct Terms what is the Sum she requires.
>
> But I announce again; that I will never write upon any other Subject.[55]

But they remained friends, and eight years later she asked her doctor to post a letter on her side-table to the duke, only to be told gently that there was no duke to read it.

In the autumn of 1834, the Houses of Parliament burnt down and, as if taking this for a portent, the government, riven by internal dissent, fell. William IV summoned Wellington, who was at Stratfield Saye about to go hunting, no mean feat for a man aged 65, and invited him to form an administration. But Wellington had learnt his lesson – he suggested that the king should ask Peel. However, as Sir Robert was away in Italy ('just like him' muttered the duke), he undertook to set up the government and stand in as prime minister till Peel returned. The government did not survive for long, but it contributed to the restoration of the duke's authority. He was still capable of speaking well, and the young Disraeli admitted that 'there is a gruff, husky sort of downright Montaign-ish naiveté about him, which is quaint, unusual, and tells.'[56] And across the political divide, William Gladstone thought that 'The Duke of Wellington appears to speak little and never for speaking's sake, but only to convey an idea commonly worth conveying.'[57]

He was still busy, helping John Gurwood, a half-pay lieutenant colonel who had snatched his captaincy from the breach at Ciudad Rodrigo a lifetime ago, produce that edition of his papers which I have found so useful. And there were more painters to sit to, with B. R. Haydon catching the old eagle's profile looking out at the Lion Mound at Waterloo which had 'spoiled my battlefield'. And yet somehow, in peace as in war, he was always there at the crucial spot. When Mrs Fitzherbert died, he swept down with Lord Albemarle and burnt her papers. There was such a blaze that he suggested a pause in operations: 'I think, my lord, we had better hold our hand for a while, or we shall set the old woman's chimney on fire.'[58]

The ashes were scarcely cold in the grate when William IV died. Greville reported him 'desperately ill' in early June, and on the 18th, the king declared that 'I should like to live to see the sun of Waterloo set.'[59] The duke saw him that day, and although he attended the annual Waterloo banquet that night by the king's express command, it was with evident unhappiness. The king expired on the 20th, and the young Queen Victoria played her part so well that Wellington told Greville that if she had been his own daughter, he could not have wished to see her do better. But he was not easily admitted to the new royal circle, and at a banquet at Buckingham House in July he found himself the only Tory present, with a place-card describing him only as 'Chancellor of Oxford'. He kept it as a curiosity.

That summer he was not well. He swayed on his feet in the Lords, and the emphasis in his speeches was all wrong: then there were fits of giddiness. Miss Jenkins offered her services as a nurse, but the duke would not hear of it. That autumn he seemed a great deal better, however, and when Lord Hill died in December 1842, he was again appointed commander-in-chief. FitzRoy Somerset, still soldiering on as military secretary, found that his old master was as tireless as ever. A letter timed at 6pm told the unlucky Lord FitzRoy, who had clearly left 'early', that:

> I called at the office on my being up from the House of Lords ... Will you be so kind as to let me have at as early an hour as may be convenient tomorrow morning all the ... reports on the present operations. As I must read them all before I go to the Cabinet.[60]

However, Greville reported in 1847 that the duke was behaving increasingly irritably, and there were times when the duke's daughter-in-law, Lady Douro, had to smooth the path between Wellington and FitzRoy Somerset. The persistent unrest accompanying Chartist demonstrations induced Wellington to write to the Marquess of Anglesey, (once Paget, then Uxbridge, and now master-general of the ordnance) on a familiar theme: 'I am very sensible to the danger of our position ... My opinion is that we shall have to contend with mobs armed with pikes, and with Fire Arms of all descriptions.'[61]

He had now become firm friends with the 'Little Vixen'. He sat beside the queen at a banquet in August 1840 and was delighted to see that she drank wine repeatedly with him. She went to stay at Walmer Castle (where her carriage stuck in the tunnel-like entrance) and at Stratfield Saye. This closeness, for the queen had previously been entranced by the Whig Lord Melbourne, was a positive advantage to the Tory government returned in the 1841 election, and Wellington was leader of the Lords with a seat in the cabinet. When it seemed Peel would be unable to hold his administration together because of his wish to reform the Corn Laws, the queen told the duke that she had 'a STRONG *desire*' to see him remain as commander-in-chief, whatever happened. The queen, however, rejected Peel's resignation, and Sir Robert told his cabinet that he proposed to continue with or without their support. The duke declared that they should remain in office: 'It was not a question of measures,' he said, 'but of Government, of support for the queen.'[62] Good government was more important than the Corn Laws, and Wellington duly helped vote them into oblivion. As he walked from the House in the early hours of 28 May 1846, after the crucial vote, he found workmen crowding around the gate, eager to hear the news. They cheered him, and one shouted. 'God bless you, Duke!' Wellington's opinion of crowds was unaltered. 'For Heaven's sake, people,' he begged, 'let me get onto my horse.'

Although it was his last major political act, Wellington did not ride out of public life that morning, for he retained a profusion of offices and continued to take them all very seriously. When revolution seemed to threaten again in 1848, with a huge Chartist demonstration planned, he made careful preparations, assuring the queen that there was no danger provided he was allowed to continue with them. The rally duly took place on Kennington Common and was much smaller than had been expected: it proved to be the movement's last revival.

He had long lamented that all creatures, even a costermonger's donkey, got some rest, but the Duke of Wellington was to have none. The queen still asked his advice. When the giant glasshouse set up in Hyde Park for the Great Exhibition of 1851 was infested with sparrows, that gruff voice had a solution: 'Try sparrow-hawks, Ma'am.'[63] There were still enthusiastic children. 'How d'ye do,

Duke?' 'How d'ye do, Duke?' 'I want some tea, Duke' said one urchin. 'You shall have it,' said the great man, 'if you promise not to slop it over me, as you did yesterday.'[64] He was amazed 'with what a number of Insane persons I am in relation. Mad retired Officers, mad Women . . .' He told Prince Albert that he should succeed him at Horse Guards, although not at the moment, for he was only eighty-one. And there was always a sovereign in his waistcoat pocket for a man with a Peninsula or Waterloo medal.

On 13 September 1852, the duke rose at 5.30 to look at the garden, welcomed his son Charles, who arrived at Walmer with his wife and the duke's grandchildren, played with the children and ate venison for his dinner. He retired to his small bedroom in one of the great turrets, and lay down on his old camp bed. His valet, Kendall, woke him at 6.30 the following morning, but an hour later a maid reported that his grace was making a great deal of noise and must be ill. When Kendall entered, the duke, lying on his bed, asked him to summon an apothecary. Dr Hulke arrived at 9am, and his patient passed his hand across his chest and complained of 'some derangement'. Kendall asked him if he would like a little tea, and Wellington replied 'Yes, if you please.' Drinking it brought on a fit, and the duke was unconscious when Dr Hulke returned with his son: the two of them tried a mustard emetic and a feather to irritate the jaws, and Kendall and another servant applied poultices to the duke's body and legs. The local doctor arrived to help, but the duke did not regain consciousness. At 2pm, Kendall suggested that he should be lifted into his favourite wing chair, and he slipped away so quietly that Charles Wellesley would not believe he had gone until Dr Hulke's son held a mirror to his mouth. It came away bright.

SEVEN

ENVOI

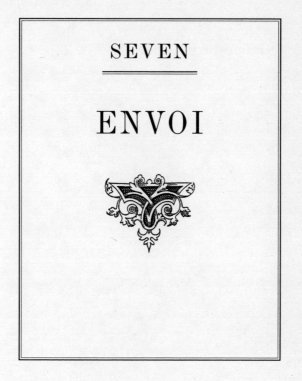

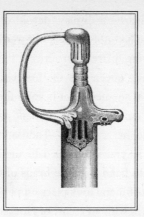

WELLINGTON WISHED to remain at Walmer, in the churchyard not far from the castle, for he had often told George Gleig: 'Where the tree falls, there let it lie.'[1] But he had become too much a part of the nation to be allowed quiet repose, and he was to be buried, with Nelson, in St Paul's Cathedral. No sooner was he dead than there was a brisk traffic in the morbid keepsakes so beloved of the Victorians. Lady Douro was given the false teeth he was wearing when he died, and a manservant, sending a lock of hair to a gentleman in Devon, regretted that there was very little but demand had been so great. Queen Victoria herself had a lock, soon to be enclosed in a gold bracelet, snipped from the duke's head by his valet Kendall moments before the coffin-lid was soldered down over the embalmed body. Local inhabitants filed past it on 9–10 November, 9,000 of them, queuing in a long silent line on the beach.

On 14 November, the duke was taken by train to London, and reached Chelsea Hospital at 3.00 on the morning of the 15th, where he lay in state in the black-draped Great Hall – once scene of the Cintra enquiry, and now the pensioners' dining-hall. His sons were at first appalled by a display 'devoid of taste and feeling', which they knew he had not wanted, but were soon persuaded of the wisdom of having 'placed ourselves at the disposition of the country'.[2] The young queen was the first visitor, but 'so deeply was she affected that she never got beyond the centre of the hall, where her feelings quite overcame her, and whence she was led, weeping bitterly, to her carriage'.[3] Thousands upon thousands followed her, and several were killed in the crush, their bodies passed from hand to hand over the heads of the living.

Wellington's state funeral took place on 18 November. His body had been transferred, with an escort of Household Cavalry, to his old office at Horse Guards, in what he would have recognised as Burgos weather, cold and rainy. The next morning troops lined the streets all the way to the cathedral, and more were formed up in St James's Park ready to follow the funeral car as it moved off to the thud of minute-guns. The car itself was widely deemed 'abominably ugly', though Prince Albert was delighted by its weighty allegory: 'no proof of his good taste', sniped Greville.[4] It was 21 feet long by 12 wide and weighed 18 tons, and its twelve horses were quickly overwhelmed by their task. When the wheels sank deep into the mud opposite the Duke of York's statue in Pall Mall, sixty police constables helped tug it clear. Well over a million people thronged the streets, 300,000 of them with seats in the stands. The car's mechanism worked when it had to be lowered to pass beneath Temple Bar, but the horses were utterly exhausted by the time they reached Ludgate Hill and sailors helped pull the car the last of the way. There was a hitch when the machinery which should have lowered the coffin onto the bier at the west door failed to work, and during the pause chilly gusts blew into the packed cathedral. But outside there was 'a respite, so to speak, in the war of nature', and Arthur Wellesley made his last journey in bright autumn sunlight. John

Colborne, now Field Marshal Lord Seaton, found the long and sonorous reading of the Duke's titles and the throwing of his broken staff of office into the vault to be 'inapplicable to the present age', but when the Death March played as the coffin was lowered (old Anglesey reached out and touched it), he was so much affected that he only just remained standing. Then the guns boomed out from the Tower; trumpets sounded at the West Door, and the troops marched back to barracks as the weather broke.

The nation was widowed. Queen Victoria lamented that 'we shall soon stand sadly alone; Aberdeen is almost the only personal friend of that kind that we have left. Melbourne, Peel, Liverpool – and now the Duke – *all* gone.'[5] Her husband felt 'as if in a tissue a particular thread which is worked into every pattern was suddenly withdrawn'.[6] Her niece, little Princess Feo, wondered 'what will become of the Aunt Victoria?' FitzRoy Somerset, who had known Wellington, warts and all, for more than half a century, was 'much affected' and talked of little else but the 'dear old Duke' when dining with the queen at Windsor.[7]

The Times thought that the duke had 'exhausted nature and exhausted glory', and that his career was 'one unclouded longest day'. Even the radical *Spectator* recognised that: 'As a Counsellor of his Sovereign, the great Duke is not to be replaced.'[8] Disraeli delivered a lavish funeral oration in the Commons, but was ridiculed when a newspaper pointed out that part of it was taken from Adolphe Thiers' panegyric on Marshal Gouvion St Cyr. Greville found the obituaries in the press 'admirable', although there were necessarily aspects on which they were silent: 'In his younger days he had been much addicted to gallantry ... and had been the successful lover of some women of fashion. Overall, thought Greville, his position was 'eminently singular and exceptional, something between the Royal Family and other subjects'.[9]

Wellington's death marked the passing of an age. He was born when the countryside dominated the town, industry bowed to agriculture, and Britain ruled North America. He was buried, amidst the smoke of busy railways and an accomplished industrial revolution, in a nation which ruled the centre of the greatest empire the world had ever seen, and had begun the long ascent to parliamentary democracy. He ranks, with the Duke of Marlborough, as one of the two greatest generals Britain has produced. It is no accident that both based their success on mastery of logistics, and both were principally commanders within coalitions, always obliged to blend the military with the political, as much strategists as tacticians.

Wellington's eye for the ground was legendary. When he and Croker were out in his carriage, they amused themselves by guessing what lay beyond the horizon, and the duke was generally right. He told Croker that he had spent most of his life guessing what lay on the other side of the hill, 'trying to make out from what I saw the shape of the country I did not see'.[10]

His military achievements were founded on eighteenth-century qualities of order, discipline, regularity, and a regard for place and precedent: here he was more Jomini with his linearity and slide-rule, than Clausewitz with his conviction that 'violence and passion' lay at the heart of war. 'Animosity amongst nations,' he declared, 'ought to cease when hostilities come to an end.'[11]

The eighteenth century also formed his political views: he was an oligarch, not a democrat. The French Revolution inspired his hatred of the mob, his experience in Spain reinforced it, and throughout his life he 'held popularity in great contempt'.[12] When a crowd cheered him outside Apsley House, he pointed ironically at the windows that a previous crowd had broken. The press was little better, and had, moreover, no legitimate interest in much of what it reported. When the queen visited his house in 1845 he denied reporters admission, telling them that 'he does not see what his house at Strathfieldsaye [sic] has to do with the public press'.[13]

Yet if he disdained the crowd, he respected individuals regardless of their station in life. It is often said that no man is a hero to his valet, but Wellington was: both Beckerman, his German soldier-servant, and Kendall, his valet, were devoted to him. He was never able to blind himself to the effect of his actions, political, military, or private, on others, and there was a sense of proportionality in all he did. When a gamekeeper was killed in a fight with poachers on his Hampshire estates, he gave up preserving game because it was not worth the risk to human life. It was, though, important that this station was preserved. At the height of the reform crisis in 1832, he warned Charles Arbuthnot that the 'lower orders' ... 'wanted to resort to our private houses, our entertainments; have the run of our kitchens and dance with our wives and daughters. Alternatively, they would invite us to their public houses, to live with them.'[14] But *déclassé* gentlemen were as bad as uppity labourers. When he lost patience with fellow oligarchs, it was because their behaviour traduced the standards he expected his class to conform to: his was a world where rights reflected responsibilties, and duty justified authority. A cavalry officer who sought to transfer into another regiment in order to avoid going on active service was told starkly that: 'he must sail or sell [his commission]'.[15] The social forms were important because they helped define a structure that had to be preserved: FitzRoy Somerset was always Lord FitzRoy, though occasionally he allowed his daughter-in-law to be 'My dearest Lady Douro'.

He opposed reform because he believed that parliament should comprise 'every man noted in the country for his fortune, his talents, his science, his industry, or his influence; the first men of all professions, in all branches of trade and manufacture, connected with our colonies and settlements abroad . . .' It would be better for such a parliament to do its duty than to try to bring it 'to a greater degree under popular influence'.[16] The reform crisis reflected as much a failure of the ruling class to rule decently as the impact of 'infatuated madmen' on public opinion. Wellington ultimately gave way on reform because he feared that the authority of the crown, paramount in his political philosophy, would be tainted by a mass creation of peers. The greatest test of a great general, he always said, was to know when to retreat and to have the courage to do it – that applied as much in parliament as in the Peninsula.

His religious views were shaped by the same process, and were as much political as theological. He told Lord John Russell that George Gleig, 'as most other good clergymen of the Church of England, [was] a zealous Conservative politician . . .'[17] The rise of Methodism in the army concerned him because it was likely to end in Methodist NCOs lecturing wayward officers on their moral responsibility. A gentleman should recognise his own responsibility, and allowing others to point it out could only undermine order. He kept the Bible, the prayer book, Jeremy Taylor's *Holy Living and Dying* and Caesar's *Commentaries* by his bedside, and Gleig observed that they bore the marks that came from frequent use. His courage was the product of a fusion between this belief and his obdurate sense of duty. His staff at Waterloo suffered a casualty rate of 30 per cent, higher than that incurred by the fighting troops. When he said that he felt the finger of God upon him that day, he was reflecting a deep-seated conviction that his survival was determined by more than his famous luck.

His nickname, the Iron Duke, probably coined by *Punch* in

1845 – though Carlyle had termed him 'the cast-metal man' in 1832 – was entirely fitting. He had a quality of inner strength as visible on the retreat from Burgos as on the ride back from the Mint with the mob behind him. One of the consequences of this was that, as Greville maintained, he 'was a good-natured, but not an amiable man; he had no tenderness in his dispositions . . .'[18] Much of this may stem, as his descendent Muriel Wellesley suggested, from that 'lonely little boy' who grew up denied affection. There were moments when the iron cracked, as it did at Badajoz and Waterloo, and, more regularly, in the company of children. But for most of his life Wellington was as stern with himself as he was with others: he is easy to admire, harder, perhaps, to like.

Now that I have followed him from Ireland to India, from the Peninsula to Waterloo, and finally from Walmer Castle to St Paul's Cathedral, I admire him more than I ever have. I know that he would no more welcome my admiration than he would resent my censure: the most I can expect, if I meet him on the other side of a celestial hill, will be two conjoined fingers raised to a tall hat, and perhaps a suggestion that he was right, all along, about the impossibility of writing military history. I admire his courage and his determination, his modesty and his honesty. He was built on a grand scale, and I see little sign of such figures in our own landscape: he was indeed a great man.

REFERENCES

INTRODUCTION

1 Philip Guedalla *The Duke* (London 1940) p. 443.
2 John Wilson Croker *The Croker Papers: The Correspondence and Diaries of John Wilson Croker, Secretary to the Admiralty from 1809 to 1830* (3 vols, London 1885) vol. III p. 28.
3 Elizabeth Longford *Wellington: Pillar of the State* (London 1972) p. 148.
4 Elizabeth Longford *Wellington: Years of the Sword* (London 1969) p. 166.
5 Guedalla op. cit., pp. 221–2.
6 Charles Oman (ed) *Adventures with the Connaught Rangers 1809–1814 by William Grattan Esq late Lieutenant Connaught Rangers* (London 1902) p. 200.
7 Ian Fletcher (ed) *For King and Country: The Letters and Diaries of John Mills, Coldstream Guards, 1811–14* (Staplehurst, Kent 1995) p. 46.
8 Paddy Griffith (ed) *Wellington: Commander* (Chichester 1984) p. 20.
9 Ibid., p. 14.
10 Guedalla op. cit., p. 464.

I   A SOLITARY LIFE

1 Guedalla op. cit., p. 1.
2 T. W. Moody and F. X. Martin (eds) *The Course of Irish History* (Cork 1984) p. 155.
3 R. F. Foster *Modern Ireland 1600–1972* (London 1988) p. 170.
4 Daniel Corkery quoted ibid., p. 195.
5 Guedalla op. cit., p. 5.
6 George Robert *The Life of Arthur Duke of Wellington* (London 1875) p. 4.
7 Ibid., p. 5.
8 Ibid., p. 6.
9 Longford *Sword* op. cit., p. 19.
10 Bellamy Partridge *Sir Billy Howe* (London 1932) p. 6.
11 Frank McLynn *Crime and Punishment in Georgian England* (Oxford 1991) pp. 150–1.
12 Liza Picard *Dr Johnson's London* (London 2000) p. 126.
13 McLynn op. cit., p. 231.
14 See Ian Fletcher *Galloping at Everything: British Cavalry in the Peninsular War and at Waterloo* (London 2000).
15 Literally 'it is monk'. Field-Marshal Sir John French, who commanded the British army in France in 1914–15, was given to similar franglais, translating footman as 'piedhomme'.
16 Longford *Sword* op. cit., p. 21.
17 Ibid., p. 22.
18 Guedalla op. cit., pp. 24–6.
19 Gleig op. cit., p. 9.
20 Guedalla op. cit., p. 28.

21 Longford *Sword* op. cit., p. 22.
22 Guedalla op. cit., p. 29.
23 Ibid., p. 30.
24 Longford *Sword* op. cit., p. 266.
25 Basil Liddell Hart (ed) *The Letters of Private Wheeler 1808–1828* (Adlestrop, Glos 1851) pp. 64, 269.
26 Guedalla op. cit., p. 36.
27 Longford *Sword* op. cit., p. 36.
28 Sir John Fortescue *History of The British Army* (13 vols London 1899–1930) vol. IV part 1 pp. 210–11.
29 William Surtees *Twenty-Five Years in the Rifle Brigade* (London 1973) pp. 16–17.
30 Fortescue vol. IV part 1 pp. 296–7.
31 Philip J. Haythornthwaite *The Armies of Wellington* (London 1998) p. 212.
32 Guedalla op. cit., p. 42.
33 Ibid., p. 43.
34 Ibid., p. 45.
35 Fortescue vol. IV part 1 pp. 320–1.
36 Guedalla op. cit., p. 49.
37 Ibid., p. 50.
38 Thomas Pakenham *The Year of Liberty* (London 1972) p. 17.

II SEPOY GENERAL

1 The best short history of the East India Company is John Keay *The Honourable Company* (London 1991).
2 Roger Hudson (ed) *Memoirs of a Georgian Rake: William Hickey* (London 1995) p. xiv.
3 Dennis Kinkaid *British Social Life in India 1608–1937* (London 1973) p. 69.
4 Hudson op. cit., pp. 396–7.
5 Ibid., p. 399.
6 Jac Weller *Wellington in India* (London 1993) p. 30.
7 Ibid., p. 37.
8 Antony Brett-James (ed) *Wellington at War* (London 1961) p. 22.
9 Ibid., p. 25.
10 Ibid., p. 20.
11 Ibid., pp 23–4.
12 Weller op. cit., p. 44.
13 Brett-James op. cit., p. 29.
14 Lord Monson and George Leveson-Gower (ed) *Memoirs of George Elers, Captain in the 12th Regiment of Foot, 1774–1842* (London 1903) p. 100.
15 Weller op. cit., p. 65.
16 Monson and Leveson-Gower op. cit., p. 103.
17 Brett-James op. cit., pp. 32–33.
18 Guedalla op. cit., p. 89.
19 Longford op. cit., *Sword* p. 67.
20 Guedalla op. cit., p. 89.
21 Lieutenant Colonel John Gurwood *Selections from the Dispatches and General Orders of Field Marshal the Duke of Wellington* (London 1841) p. 5.
22 Ibid., p. 4.
23 Guedalla op. cit., p. 100.
24 Gurwood op. cit., p. 6.
25 Ibid., p. 9.
26 Ibid., p. 19.
27 S. G. P. Ward *Wellington* (London 1963) p. 29.
28 Gurwood op. cit., pp. 42–43.
29 Ibid., p. 62.
30 Ibid., p. 69.
31 Anthony S. Bennell (ed) *The Maratha War Papers of Arthur Wellesley* (London 1998) p. 262.
32 Ibid., p. 311.
33 Ibid., p. 227.
34 Weller op. cit., p. 157.
35 Ibid., p. 163.
36 Bennell op. cit., p. 287.
37 Longford *Sword* op. cit., p. 93.
38 Gurwood op. cit., p. 89.
39 Bennell op. cit., pp. 289–90.
40 Gurwood op. cit., p. 90.

41 Bennell op. cit., p. 289.
42 Ibid., p. 290.
43 Gurwood op. cit., p. 96.
44 Ibid., p. 160.
45 Gurwood op. cit., p. 170.
46 Brett-James op. cit., p. 119.
47 Weller op. cit., p. 252.
48 Brett-James op. cit., p. 115.
49 Weller op. cit., p. 251.
50 Ibid.
51 Ibid., p. 262.
52 Ibid.
53 Longford *Sword* op. cit., pp. 101–2.
54 Bennell op. cit., p. 235.
55 Weller op. cit., p. 265.
56 Ibid., p. 266.
57 Gurwood op. cit., p. 124.
58 Ibid., p. 41.

III FALSE STARTS

1 Oliver Warner 'The Meeting of Wellington and Nelson' *History Today* Feb 1968; Guedalla op. cit., pp. 119–20, Longford *Sword* pp. 109–111.
2 Longford *Sword* op. cit., p. 111.
3 Gleig op. cit., p. 48.
4 Longford *Sword* op. cit., p. 121.
5 Brett-James op. cit., p. 124.
6 Gleig op. cit., p. 50
7 Brett-James op. cit., p. 124.
8 Longford *Sword* op. cit., p. 104
9 Christopher Hibbert *Wellington: A Personal History* (London 1997) p. 55.
10 Longford *Sword* op. cit., p. 122.
11 Brett-James op. cit., p. 120.
12 Guedalla op. cit., p. 128.
13 Brett-James op. cit., p. 125.
14 Foster op. cit., p. 290.
15 Longford *Sword* op. cit., p. 129.
16 Ibid., p. 131.
17 Hibbert op. cit., p. 58.
18 Longford *Sword* op. cit., p. 132.
19 Brett-James op. cit., p. 127.
20 Ibid., p. 129.
21 Ibid., p. 128.
22 Hibbert op. cit., p. 65.
23 Philip J Haythornthwaite '"That unlucky war": some aspects of the French experience in the Peninsula' in Ian Fletcher (ed) *The Peninsular War* (Staplehurst 1998) p. 31.
24 Ibid., p. 40.
25 Mills, p. 62.
26 Hibbert op. cit., p. 68.
27 Gurwood op. cit., p. 201.
28 Guedalla op. cit., p. 147.
29 Croker I pp. 12–13.
30 Guedalla op. cit., p. 150.
31 Gurwood op. cit., p. 202.
32 Ibid.
33 Croker op. cit., vol. I p. 343.
34 Longford *Sword* op. cit., p. 147.
35 Gurwood op. cit., p. 203.
36 Spelt Vimiero in most British accounts and Vimiera on the colours of regiments which bear it as a battle honour, the village is in fact spelt Vimeiro both in Wellington's dispatches and by its modern inhabitants.
37 Here I rely heavily on Jac Weller *Wellington in the Peninsula* (London 1999) pp. 46–7. For a characteristically common-sense view of drill see Paddy Griffith '"Keep step and they cannot hurt us": The value of drill in the Peninsular War' in Fletcher *Peninsular War* op. cit.
38 Benjamin Harris *The Recollections of Rifleman Harris as told to Henry Curling* (London 1985) p. 50.
39 Fletcher *Galloping* op. cit., p. 86.
40 Harris op. cit., p. 53.
41 Gurwood op. cit., p. 212.
42 Ibid., p. 601.
43 Fletcher *Galloping* op. cit., p. 175.
44 Fortescue op. cit., vol. VI p. 231.

45 Michael Glover *Britannia Sickens* (London 1970) p. 67.

46 The French army of the old regime had only two grades of general officer, marshal of France being technically a dignity of state rather than a military rank. After the revolution these were renamed *général de brigade* and *général de division*. The term *major général* did not designate a rank, but the appointment of chief of staff. There were no exact parallels between the two French general ranks and the more numerous ones in the British army, for a general of division could well command a division, a corps or even an army. As all three British generals involved in the negotiation were of the same rank, lieutenant general, despite their very different seniority, there was no case in protocol for the argument that Kellermann should sign with Wellesley on the grounds that he was an officer of equal rank. The fact that the Convention was drawn up for Wellesley to sign may reflect Kellermann's understanding of his political importance; a desire by Dalrymple and Burrard (for whatever reason) to let Wellesley sign; or it may cast doubt on Wellesley's own version of his involvement. We simply cannot tell which.

47 Gurwood op. cit., p. 215.

48 Ibid., p. 217.

49 Glover op. cit., p. 166.

50 Longford *Sword* op. cit., p. 164.

51 Gurwood op. cit., p. 249.

IV PENINSULA

1 Longford *Sword* op. cit., p. 173.

2 Guedalla op. cit., p. 174. For a discussion of an alternative version see Hibbert p. 81.

3 Wheeler p. 48.

4 Gurwood op. cit., p. 263.

5 Ibid., pp. 266–8; in full in Brett-James op. cit., pp. 154–157.

6 Guedalla op. cit., p. 179.

7 Gurwood op. cit., p. 274.

8 Gleig op. cit., p. 101.

9 Longford *Sword* op. cit., p. 193.

10 Ibid., p. 194.

11 Sergeant Anthony Hamilton *Hamilton's Campaign with Moore and Wellington* (Staplehurst 1998) p. 76.

12 Brett-James op. cit., p. 163.

13 Gurwood p. 277.

14 Ibid., p. 283.

15 Ibid., p. 284.

16 Ibid., p. 290.

17 Longford *Sword* op. cit., pp. 198–9.

18 Ibid., pp. 206–7.

19 Ibid., p. 219.

20 Brett-James op. cit., pp. 172–3. Young Pearse made honourable amends, and was killed at the top of the breach at Ciudad Rodrigo in 1812.

21 Gurwood op. cit., p. 320.

22 Ibid., p. 343.

23 Ibid., p. 389.

24 Ibid., p. 414.

25 Christopher Hibbert (ed) *A Soldier of the Seventy-First* (London 1976) pp. 61–3.

26 Gurwood op. cit., p. 478.

27 Ibid., p. 481.

28 Ibid., p. 479.

29 Longford *Sword* op. cit., p. 256.

30 W.F.P. Napier *History of the War in the Peninsula and the South of France* (6 vols, London 1835–40) vol. III p. 547.

31 Gurwood op. cit., p. 487.

32 Longford *Sword* op. cit., p. 258.

33 Gurwood op. cit., p. 483.

34 Weller *Peninsula* op. cit., pp. 182–3.

35 John Spencer Cooper *Rough Notes of Seven Campaigns* (London 1996) p. 63.

36 Hart p. 64.

37 Fletcher p. 99.

38 Kincaid op. cit., p. 93.

39 Ibid., p. 98.

40 Gurwood op. cit., p. 576.

41 Harry Smith *The Autobiography of Lieutenant General Sir Harry Smith* (2 vols London 1901) vol. I pp. 64–5.

42 Michael Glover (ed) *A Gentleman Volunteer: The Letters of George Hennell from the Peninsular War* (London 1979) p. 14.

43 Richard L. Blanco *Wellington's Surgeon General: Sir James McGrigor* (Durham, North Carolina 1974) p. 125.

44 Antony Brett-James (ed) *Edward Costello: The Peninsular and Waterloo Campaigns* (London 1967) p. 76.

45 Cooper op. cit., p. 84.

46 Oman op. cit., p. 86.

47 Ibid.

48 Hibbert op. cit., p. 118.

49 Fletcher *Galloping* op. cit., p. 169, Gurwood p. 601.

50 Longford *Sword* op. cit., p. 281.

51 Muriel Wellesley *The Man Wellington, Through the eyes of those that knew him* (London 1937) p. 225.

52 Gleig op. cit., p. 479.

53 Sir George Larpent (ed) *The Private Journals of Judge-Advocate Larpent, attached to the head-quarters of Lord Wellington* (London 1854) p. 168.

54 There are many versions of this conversation, which differ in detail but not substance: see, for instance, Guedalla p. 216, Weller *Peninsula* p. 216, and Longford *Sword* p. 285.

55 Gurwood op. cit., p. 615.

56 Weller *Peninsula* op. cit., p. 226.

57 Brett-James op. cit., pp. 240–1.

58 Larpent op. cit., p. 65.

59 Blanco op. cit., p. 131.

60 William Tomkinson *The Diary of a Cavalry Officer* (Staplehurst 1999) p. 210.

61 Ibid.

62 Brett-James op. cit., p. 246.

63 Hart p. 106.

64 Brett-James Hart p. 247.

65 Ibid.

66 Fletcher p. 245.

67 Longford *Sword* op. cit., p. 296.

68 Wellesley op. cit., p. 253.

69 Gurwood op. cit., pp. 645–6.

70 Kincaid op. cit., pp. 97–8.

71 Fletcher p. 264, Costello p. 114.

72 Guedalla op. cit., p. 222.

73 Hibbert p. 111.

74 Ibid.

75 Creevey I p. 280.

76 Roger Norman Buckley (ed) *The Napoleonic War Journal of Captain Thomas Henry Browne* (London 1987) pp. 200–1.

77 G. R. Gleig *The Subaltern* (Edinburgh 1877) pp. 161–2.

78 Buckley op. cit., p. 201.

79 Wellesley op. cit., p. 210.

80 Larpent op. cit., p. 48.

81 Longford *Sword* op. cit., p. 342.

82 John Kincaid *Random Shots from a Rifleman* (London 1835) p. 198

83 Gurwood op. cit., p. 641.

84 Ibid., p. 631.

85 Michael Glover *Wellington's Army* (Newton Abbot, Devon 1977) pp. 137–8.

86 Blanco op. cit., p. 122.

87 Larpent op. cit., p. 96.

88 Hibbert p. 95.

89 John Sweetman *Raglan: From the Peninsula to the Crimea* (London 1993) p. 23.

90 Hibbert p. 96.
91 Longford *Sword* op. cit., pp. 214, 360–1.
92 Larpent op. cit., p. 49.
93 Buckley op. cit., p. 201.
94 Larpent op. cit., p. 52
95 Gurwood op. cit., p. 651.
96 S.A.C. Cassels (ed) *Peninsular Portrait: The Letters of Captain William Bragge* (London 1963) p. 100.
97 Gurwood op. cit., p. 658.
98 Wellesley p. 268.
99 Gurwood op. cit., p. 706.
100 Tomkinson op. cit., p. 253.
101 Buckley op. cit., p. 217.
102 Brett-James p. 292.
103 Guedalla op. cit., p. 232.
104 Longford *Sword* op. cit., p. 330.
105 Gurwood op. cit., pp. 719–20.
106 Nicholas Bentley (ed) *The reminiscences of Captain Gronow* (London 1977) p. 13.
107 Gurwood op. cit., p. 712.
108 Ibid., p. 766.
109 Gleig p. 213.
110 Ibid., p. 217.
111 Gronow p. 15.
112 Longford *Sword* op. cit., pp. 335–6.
113 Ibid., p. 331.
114 Ibid., p. 344.
115 Larpent op. cit., p. 487.

V TWO RESTORATIONS AND A BATTLE

1 Alan Schom *Napoleon Bonaparte* (London 1997) p. 789.
2 Alfred Cobban *A History of Modern France* (3 vols, London 1967), vol. II p. 66.
3 Longford *Sword* op. cit., p. 347.
4 Wellesley op. cit., p. 312.
5 Ibid.
6 Gurwood op. cit., p. 814.
7 Kincaid *Adventures* op. cit., p. 77.
8 Brett-James op. cit., p. 294.
9 Longford *Sword* op. cit., p. 357.
10 Oman op. cit., p. **000**.
11 Wellesley op. cit., p. 310.
12 Guedalla op. cit., p. 248.
13 Ibid., p. 248.
14 Gurwood op. cit., p. 833.
15 Ibid., p. 819.
16 Wellesley op. cit., p. 321.
17 Guedalla op. cit., p. 252.
18 Brett-James op. cit., p. 295.
19 Longford *Sword* op. cit., p. 374.
20 Ibid., p. 375.
21 Brett-James op. cit., p. 296.
22 Longford *Sword* op. cit., pp. 378–9.
23 Wellesley op. cit., p. 336.
24 Ibid., p. 337.
25 Guedalla op. cit., p. 252.
26 Longford *Sword* op. cit., p. 382.
27 Gurwood op. cit., p. 835.
28 Fortescue op. cit., vol. X p. 247.
29 Creevey op. cit., vol. I p. 289.
30 David Miller *Lady De Lancey at Waterloo* (Staplehurst 2000) p. 49.
31 *1815: The Waterloo Campaign: Wellington, His German Allies and the Battles of Ligny and Quatre Bras* (London 1998); *1815: The Waterloo Campaign, Volume 2, The German Victory* (London 1999). See also Peter Hofschröer's useful *The Memoirs of Baron von Müffling: A Prussian Officer in the Napoleonic Wars* (London 1997).
32 John Hussey 'At what time on 15 June 1815 did Wellington Learn of Napoleon's attack on the Prussians?' *War in History* 1999 no. 6.
33 Gurwood op. cit., p. 838.
34 Gurwood op. cit., p. 842.
35 Creevey op. cit., p. 228.
36 Longford *Sword* op. cit., p. 405.
37 Gurwood op. cit., p. 855.
38 Wellesley op. cit., p. 355.
39 Miller op. cit., p. 108.

40 Wellesley op. cit., p. 343.
41 Gurwood op. cit., p. 845.
42 Andrew Roberts *Napoleon and Wellington* (London 2001) p. 159.
43 David G. Chandler *The Campaigns of Napoleon* (London 1967) p. 1092.
44 Longford *Sword* op. cit., pp. 348–9.
45 Brett-James p. 307.
46 Gurwood op. cit., p. 842.
47 Sweetman op. cit., p. 57.
48 Ibid., pp. 57–8.
49 Ian Fletcher *A Desperate Business* (London 2002) p. 33.
50 Jac Weller *Wellington at Waterloo* (London 1967) p. 46.
51 Fletcher *Desperate Business* op. cit., p. 40.
52 Ibid., p. 41.
53 Ibid., p. 51.
54 David Hamilton-Williams *Waterloo: New Perspectives* (London 1993) p. 233.
55 Fletcher *Desperate Business* op. cit., p. 76.
56 Gronow p. 42.
57 Weller *Waterloo* op. cit., p. 93.
58 Hamilton-Williams op. cit., p. 300.
59 Gronow p. 44.
60 Fletcher *Galloping* op. cit., p. 262.
61 John Selby (ed) *Thomas Morris* (London 1967) p. 141.
62 Sweetman op. cit., p. 64.
63 Gronow p. 44.
64 Selby p. 15.
65 Gronow p. 45.
66 Sweetman op. cit., p. 65.
67 Weller *Waterloo* p. 121.
68 Ibid., p. 122.
69 Ibid.
70 Miller op. cit., p. 76.
71 Fletcher *Galloping* p. 273.
72 Kincaid *Adventures* p. 46.
73 Weller *Waterloo* op. cit., p. 152.
74 Wellesley op. cit., p. 367.
75 Weller *Waterloo* op. cit., p. 154.
76 Gurwood op. cit., p. 860.
77 Longford *Sword* op. cit., p. 486.
78 Gurwood p. 865.
79 Brett-James p. 310.
80 Cavalié Mercer *Journal of the Waterloo Campaign* (London 1985) p. 57.
81 Shelley I, p. 102.

VI   PILLAR OF THE STATE

1 Elizabeth Longford *Pillar* op. cit., p. 57.
2 Creevey op. cit., pp. 277–9.
3 Longford *Pillar* op. cit., p. 67.
4 Guedalla pp. 314–5. Longford *Pillar* fn p. 68 points out that the same story is attributed to Lord Uxbridge (then Marquess of Anglesey), the 3rd Marquess of Londonderry, and Theodore Hook. Whoever really said it deserved credit for quick thinking and not a little courage.
5 Hibbert p. 222.
6 Ibid., p. 227.
7 Ibid., p. 231.
8 Longford *Pillar* op. cit., p. 87
9 Guedalla op. cit., p. 318.
10 Ibid., pp. 324–5.
11 Longford *Pillar* op. cit., p. 101.
12 Guedalla op. cit., p. 332.
13 Sweetman op. cit., p. 78.
14 Longford *Pillar* op. cit., p. 114.
15 Sweetman op. cit., p. 79.
16 Christopher Hibbert (ed) *Greville's England* (London 1981) p. 26.
17 Croker p. 121.
18 Hibbert p. 260.
19 Gleig p. 335.
20 Croker p. 124.
21 Longford *Pillar* op. cit., p. 157.
22 Guedalla op. cit., p. 356.
23 Ibid., p. 372.
24 Greville p. 46.
25 Hibbert op. cit., p. 274.
26 Gleig p. 349.

27 Greville p. 48.
28 Ibid., p. 47.
29 Longford *Pillar* op. cit., p. 191.
30 Greville p. 51.
31 Longford *Pillar* op. cit., p. 191.
32 Gronow p. 247.
33 Greville pp. 51–2.
34 Longford *Pillar* op. cit., p. 199.
35 Ibid., p. 201.
36 Ibid.
37 Gurwood op. cit., p. 918.
38 Ibid., p. 927.
39 Cooper op. cit., p. 14.
40 Greville p. 65.
41 Ibid., pp. 76–7.
42 Longford *Pillar* op. cit., p. 224.
43 Guedalla op. cit., p. 391.
44 Greville p. 80.
45 Longford *Pillar* op. cit., p. 245.
46 Ibid., p. 257.
47 Ibid., p. 267.
48 Gleig p. 363.
49 Sweetman p. 99.
50 Greville p. 102.
51 Kenneth O. Morgan (ed) *The Oxford Illustrated History of Britain* (Oxford 1992) p. 441.
52 Guedalla p. 407.
53 Ibid., p. 409.
54 Greville p. 107.
55 Guedalla op. cit., p. 419.
56 Ibid., p. 425.
57 Longford *Pillar* op. cit., p. 313.
58 Guedalla p. 427.
59 Greville p. 139.
60 Sweetman op. cit., p. 116.
61 Ibid., p. 120.
62 Longford *Pillar* op. cit., p. 363.
63 Lady Longford suggests that this may well be apocryphal, but it is worth including 'for its distillation of the Wellingtonian spirit'. (Longford *Pillar* p. 390.)
64 Guedalla op. cit., p. 433.

VII ENVOI

1 Gleig op. cit., p. 457.
2 Longford *Pillar* op. cit., p. 402.
3 Gleig p. 459.
4 Greville p. 239.
5 Guedalla op. cit., p. 462.
6 Ibid.
7 Sweetman op. cit., p. 150.
8 Longford *Pillar* op. cit., p. 400.
9 Greville p. 237–8.
10 Gleig pp. 495–6.
11 Ibid., p. 493.
12 Greville p. 239.
13 Gleig op. cit., p. 483.
14 Longford *Pillar* op. cit., p. 409.
15 Gleig op. cit., p. 492.
16 Ibid., pp. 485–6.
17 Ibid., p. 489.
18 Greville p. 237.

INDEX